A READING
OF THE *ILIAD*

R.M. Frazer
Department of Classical Studies
Tulane University

UNIVERSITY
PRESS OF
AMERICA

Lanham • New York

Copyright © 1993 by
University Press of America®, Inc.
4720 Boston Way
Lanham, Maryland 20706

3 Henrietta Street
London WC2E 8LU England

Library of Congress Cataloging-in-Publication Data

Frazer, R. M. (Richard McIlwaine).
A reading of the Iliad / by R.M. Frazer.
p.   cm.
Includes bibliographical references and index.
1. Homer. Iliad. 2. Epic poetry, Greek—History and criticism.
3. Achilles (Greek mythology) in literature.   4. Trojan War in
literature.   I. Title.
PA4037.F572   1993   883'.01—dc20   93–4812 CIP

ISBN 0–8191–9202–3 (pbk. : alk. paper)

 The paper used in this publication meets the minimum requirements of
American National Standard for Information Sciences—Permanence
of Paper for Printed Library Materials, ANSI Z39.48–1984.

ACKNOWLEDGMENTS

This account of the *Iliad* is of course greatly indebted to other scholars. I think especially of G. S. Kirk, with whom I have enjoyed many good talks about Homer, and also of E. T. Owen, Mark W. Edwards, M. M. Willcock, Wolfgang Schadewaldt, and Tilman Krischer. I have always tried to give appropriate credit. The translations, which aim at accuracy and readability, are my own.

Carroll E. Mace and Joe Park Poe offered perceptive criticisms of my manuscript, and Dennis P. Kehoe helped to convert it into camera-ready copy. I am very grateful to them. My thanks are also due to the following museums for permitting me to reproduce the three illustrations: the British Museum for Illustration 1; the Antikenmuseum Berlin, Staatliche Museen Preussischer Kulturbesitz, for Illustration 2; and the Rijksmuseum van Oudheden, Leiden, for Illustration 3.

TABLE OF CONTENTS

LIST OF ILLUSTRATIONS

INTRODUCTION

It is incumbent upon the author of a new book on Homer to give a good reason for being so daring. In the present work I offer a close account of the contents of the *Iliad* with translations of key passages and comments that seek to illucidate the structure and meaning of the poem. This of course has already been done; one thinks especially of E. T. Owen's excellent *The Story of the Iliad*. But I submit that my presentation is better in certain respects than earlier ones. Every commentary, like every translation, is also an interpretation. The crucial question is which interpretation is truest to the original.

Unlike Owen and many other scholars, I am convinced that a correct appreciation of the *Iliad* depends on understanding (1) that Achilles' wrath is to be distinguished from his vengeance against Hector, and (2) that the poet and his audience are naturally disposed to favor the Achaeans (the Greeks, also called Danaans and Argives). These are controversial matters, for which we shall be arguing later in this Introduction and in many comments on individual passages. The reader must judge.

When age-old problems such as, especially, those bearing on the structure of the poem have had to be faced, I have tried to offer sensible solutions, but for the most part have shied away from controversy and sought simply, with the aid of earlier scholars, to give an accurate picture of what happens in the *Iliad*. Comments will be made on themes, type-scenes, and types of simile, on how the poet foreshadows and prepares for coming events, on how he arranges his scenes in an orderly fashion, on the character of Achilles, on the role of the gods, on the circumstances under which we can imagine that the poem was recited, and on the poet as a moral teacher of his people. A survey of these subjects will be given in this Introduction so that the reader may know what to expect.

Type-Scenes and Parallel Narratives

In the first part of the present century Milman Parry (for his collected essays see Parry 1971) proved that the *Iliad* was composed in accordance with the techniques of oral poetry. It thus consists largely of formulas such as "swift-footed Achilles" and of type-scenes such as the assembly scene, and it strings one thought to another and one scene to another paratactically. Lord 1960.92, who uses the term "theme" instead of "type-scene," well describes how an oral poet—in this case in modern Yugoslavia—creates the elements in a type-scene.

> He knows where he is going. As in the adding of one line to another, so in the adding of one element in a theme to another, the singer can stop and fondly dwell upon any single item without losing a sense of the whole . . . Moreover, he usually signals the end of a theme by a significant or culminating point. The description of an assembly moves inexorably to focus on the chief hero of the song; . . . the larger assembly theme proceeds onward to the decision which will itself lead to further action. The singer's mind is orderly.

Homer uses many different type-scenes, which he expands or contracts according to whether he wants to emphasize or de-emphasize their importance and therefore the importance of the episodes in which they appear. For instance, one of the longest sacrifice scenes in the *Iliad* is that in which Chryses propitiates Apollo in Book 1, and this occurs at the very important point where the wrath of Apollo is giving way to the wrath of Achilles.

Another type-scene is the assembly, for which (following Arend 1933.116) we can list the following elements: the assembly is called; the participants take their seats; the king or leader who called the assembly stands up to speak. Assemblies, in which decisions and programmatic statements are made about coming events, occur at the beginning and end of a day's fighting. The longest, most elaborate assemblies in the *Iliad* are the two called by Achilles. The first, in Book 1, culminates in his announcing his wrath; the second, in Book 19, shows him publicly renouncing his wrath.

The assemblies of the gods are similar to those of men. One thinks especially of the councils of the gods called by Zeus at the beginnings of Books 8 and 20. The first, in which he forbids the gods to take part in the battle during the period of Achilles' wrath, is programmatic for Books 8 through 18; the second, in which he lifts this prohibition, is programmatic for Books 20 through 22.

The arming of the hero, when he is usually inspired by a god with new fighting spirit, is also a type-scene with definite elements in a set order (Arend 1933.92-97; cf. Edwards 1987.72-74). First the hero puts on his greaves, then his breastplate, and finally his helmet; then he takes up one or two spears. At the end of an arming scene we are often told that the hero's armor gleamed brightly, and this portends his success in the coming battle. In the case of Patroclus the omission of this motif apparently portends his death, which is also foreshadowed by the fact that, after putting on Achilles' armor, he is unable to take up Achilles' spear.

The arming of the hero often introduces a series of scenes called the *aristeia*, the great deeds of a hero. Krischer 1971.23-24 (cf. Edwards 1987.79) has described the elements (they might be called type-scenes too) of a normal *aristeia*— no example fully realizes the norm—as follows. First is the arming scene; the gleaming of the armor is usually mentioned. Second are a number of brief encounters in battle ending with the hero and his side putting the enemy to flight. Third is the wounding of the hero and his healing by a god. Fourth is the single combat in which the hero slays his main opponent. Fifth is the battle over the dead body. The first three scenes move forward to the decisive single combat, and then comes the fight over the body.

Often there are two or more instances of the same type-scene with the last of them being the most important, and this produces what I shall call a climactic parallel. For example, a Thetis-Achilles scene—apparently Homer's elaboration on the divine-visitation type-scene—is found both in Book 1, where she agrees to go to Zeus to gain support for his wrath, and in Book 24, where she urges him at the behest of Zeus to give up his vengeance, thus creating a sense of closure and climax. The most striking instances of such parallel narratives consist of type scenes which seem to be the peculiar creations of the poet of the *Iliad*.

Four other examples of climatic parallelism are especially worth noting. First, there are the three meetings of Hector with the women in his life in Book 6, the third of which is the culminating farewell conversation between him and his wife Andromache. Second, there are the similar confrontations (elaborations on the scene in which the hero meets his opponent) of Achilles with Agenor in Book 21 and of Achilles with Hector in Book 22, of which the second is the climactic encounter in Achilles' *aristeia*. Third, there are the similarly complex narratives describing Achilles' two great decisions, first to send Patroclus into battle in Book 16, then to return himself in Book 18. Finally, and most important, there are the parallels between Achilles' wrath over the loss of Briseis and his vengeance against Hector for slaying Patroclus (surely a climactic event, for it entails Achilles' death and the fall of Troy): both begin in grief and are stubbornly carried too far, rejecting all supplications, and both end in pity. On this climactic parallelism the whole structure of the *Iliad* depends.

We shall be emphasizing how one scene is connected with another to create a unified story. Some scholars have seen mirroring or ring composition as the most important method of structuring the narrative. For instance, the similarities between

Books 1 and 24 can be thought of as forming the outermost of a series of
compositional rings (so Whitman 1958.249-84). I agree with Hainsworth
1972.188, however, that climax is a more valid aesthetic principle than mirroring.
The poet is always looking and planning ahead to bring his narrative to a dramatic
conclusion. *Homer's skill as a story teller*

Foreshadowing and Suspense

West 1980.16 has written: "It is a feature of epic composition that the poet
prepares for every important turn of events in advance by means of prophecies,
portents, debates, proposals, decisions of the gods." That is, it is a prominent
feature of epic composition to foretell or foreshadow the future (see Duckworth
1931 and 1933, and also Edwards 1987. 29-41). The term foreshadowing can be
used to cover both clear predictions and more or less vague adumbrations of the
future, and also scenes which, because of their similarity to future scenes,
apparently look forward to them. The programmatic statement is the clearest and
most frequent method of announcing the future. It appears in many other
circumstances besides human and divine assemblies. One thinks, for instance, of
the prophecies of Calchas and Helenus, of the warnings of Polydamas, and of
Zeus' commands delivered by Iris. An example of the vaguer kind of
foreshadowing already mentioned is the gleaming of the hero's armor at the
beginning of his *aristeia*. This is a kind of omen, of which there are many in the
Iliad. Sometimes it is difficult to be sure that a foreshadowing occurs, as in the
similes comparing Hector and Patroclus (12.41ff. and 16. 752ff.) to a lion at bay
whose courage causes its death. I think it very likely that these similes foreshadow
the deaths of these heroes.

Often the poet looks to the future by making a comment in his own voice, as
when he says of Patroclus answering the call of Achilles, "this was the beginning
of evil for him" (11.604). Such comments frequently contain a "not yet" or a
"still." For instance, at 2.419, after Agamemnon has prayed to destroy Troy, we
are told that Zeus is "not yet" granting this; and at 5.662, when Sarpedon is
wounded but not fatally, we are told that Zeus is "still" protecting him from death,
that is, Sarpedon is going to die later. Another important type of foreshadowing
comment is introduced by the word *nepios*, "fool"; a fool is a man of false
expectations. For instance, at 16.46, when Patroclus begs Achilles to send him
into battle, the poet, calling him *mega nepios,* "great fool," says that he is asking
for his own death.

Duckworth 1931.323-24, following the ancient scholia, has distinguished foreshadowing from *prooikonomia,* which we shall usually translate "preparation." The term *prooikonomia* can be thought of as covering passages which later are able to be seen to have prepared us for coming events, though they in themselves do not point to the future, not even vaguely, nor do they describe scenes similar to coming scenes. For instance, in Book 4 Pandarus is said first (89-91) to be among his shield-bearers and then (113-14) to be protected by them when he shoots an arrow at Menelaus. Schol. (=scholia) bT remark that the first mention of shield-bearers is an example of *prooikonomia.* We shall cite many other examples noted in the scholia, and point out others ourselves. Again it is a question of how the poet is planning ahead.

We are rarely left in suspense about where the narrative is headed. The sending out of Patroclus leads to his death, his death to the fight over his body, the fight over his body to Achilles' learning about it, Achilles' learning about it to his giving up his wrath, and his giving up his wrath to his vengeance against Hector. Episode after episode ends with new goal after new goal in view. But often, within the framework of an expected event, the unexpected happens. This adds a feeling of real life and rouses suspense. Unexpected retardations are a regular feature of epic composition. For instance, we know that on the great day of battle Hector is going to be successful in breaking through the Achaean wall and firing one of the Achaean ships, but this does not happen all at once in a straight line. There are many retardations.

Homer favors the suspense of anticipation over the suspense of uncertainty. The important events of the future are always foretold, thus preventing the suspense of uncertainty and causing the unexpected merely to increase our anticipation of the expected. Why has the poet followed this method? We can give two reasons, which are not mutually exclusive. First, as Duckworth 1931.337, following the scholia, notes, the purpose of foreshadowing may be "to give to the Homeric audience a pleasing anticipation of a fulfillment that is desired rather than to leave any uncertainty concerning the outcome of the future action." This fits in with the view of the scholia (with which I largely agree) that the poet is sometimes eager to soothe the pro-Achaean feelings of his audience. Thus during the period of Achilles' wrath when the Achaeans are being defeated we are several times assured that Troy is destined to fall (outside the action of the *Iliad*). Second, and more important, foreshadowing seems to be a technique of early Greek *oral* epic poetry. Later literate epic poets, such as Apollonius of Rhodes and Virgil, use it much less frequently than Homer (Duckworth 1933.116-22). The oral poet apparently felt constrained by his method of composition constantly to anticipate himself and point out the direction in which he was guiding his narrative. This should become clearer after the discussion in the next section on the cataloguing style.

The Cataloguing Style

Krischer 1971 has argued persuasively that Homer often creates his narratives in a cataloguing style, that is, as a list of scenes methodically arranged. We are first given a general view of what is to come, say two different but connected actions, and then there follows in an orderly way detailed descriptions of each.

The *Iliad* contains many catalogues. The most famous is the Achaean Catalogue in Book 2. Other examples are Agamemnon's Review of the Troops at the end of Book 4, the Shield of Achilles in Book 18, and the contests at the funeral games in Book 23. In some of these catalogues it is clear that the poet has not simply added one item to another as he went along but planned the whole analytically beforehand, for he gives his audience at the beginning a general prospect of what to expect. For instance, he begins the description of the Shield by saying that Hephaestus put on it the earth, the sky, and the sea, thus leading us to expect a picture of the world, which he then proceeds to describe. Also, the longest section of the Shield, which is devoted to the cities of peace and of war, is preceded by another general prospect, the statement that Hephaestus created two cities. Similarly, the Review of the Troops is introduced by a general description, with sample speeches, of how Agamemnon blames and praises his men, before we are given a catalogue of his specific encounters with certain leaders in which he makes speeches blaming or praising them.

After citing the above passages as examples of the cataloguing style, Krischer 1971.132-33 goes on to discuss how the poet uses this method in *aristeia* and in narratives created in accordance with Zielinski's law. Zielinski 1902 (cf. Whitman and Scodel 1981) observed that Homer describes simultaneous events consecutively and as if they happened consecutively. A good example occurs in Book 15 when Zeus, on the top of Mount Ida, awakes to discover that he has been beguiled by Hera. He sends her to Olympus to summon Iris and Apollo to him, for, as he tells her, thus informing us of his purpose beforehand (the general prospect), he will have Iris order Poseidon off the battlefield, and Apollo heal Hector and exhort him to battle. When Hera has obeyed and the two divinities have appeared before him, Zeus first sends Iris to Poseidon (the first item or strand in the catalogue). She goes off, meets with Poseidon, and persuades him to withdraw. Then we return to Zeus, who now gives Apollo his orders (the second strand), with the remark that Poseidon has returned to the sea; thus the Iris strand of the narrative is thought of as already completed. Apollo accordingly goes off and heals Hector and exhorts him to battle. It seems likely that the poet, on a realistic level, considered the Apollo and Iris strands to be contemporaneous but that he described them consecutively and as if they happened consecutively because thus he was able to construct his narrative in an orderly way by taking one event at a time to its conclusion. By cataloguing events and keeping them separate it was easy for him to remember what he had already said and what he still wanted to say.

Zielinski explained his law on the supposition that the poet is always describing events as if he were seeing them. Thus, since it is impossible to see more than one scene at a time, we are given a succession of scenes. Somewhat similarly, Fränkel 1931 suggested that the poet lacked an abstract idea of time. Krischer, however, rightly rejects both of these explanations. Homer was not concerned with time as such. Rather, knowing he wanted to described two or more parallel happenings, he handled them consecutively so as not to confuse himself or his audience. Accordingly, Zielinski's law is simply another example of the cataloguing style and was probably, like the description of battles in terms of *aristeiai*, a traditional technique of early Greek oral poetry.

Sometimes it is clear without any announcement beforehand that two events are parallel happenings. This is the case, for instance, with the Achaean and Trojan assemblies at the end of the first day of battle. On a realistic level they occur at the same time, at the end of the day, but they are described consecutively. First, at the end of Book 8, comes the Trojan assembly which ends with the picture of the Trojans lighting their watchfires. Then, at the beginning of Book 9, comes the Achaean assembly in which Nestor mentions the Trojan watchfires, as if the Trojan assembly were already completed (which for the audience of course is true, however false it may be when we analyze it realistically).

We have noted above that the *aristeia* of a hero is constructed according to a set sequence of scenes. This in itself gives the poet a system for cataloguing the description of long battles. Moreover, usually the hero's chief opponent in his *aristeia* has already had his own *aristeia*; for instance, Hector, Achilles' opponent, has earlier slain Patroclus, and Patroclus has earlier slain Sarpedon. There is clearly a classifying system at work here, but we must beware of taking it too far. Krischer 1971.80 suggests that the poet uses the *aristeiai* to rank the heroes as follows: first Achilles, second Hector, third Patroclus, fourth Sarpedon, and fifth Ajax. It is hard, however, to believe that Hector is really a match for Ajax or even Patroclus whom he has a great deal of help in slaying.

The cataloguing style enabled the audience to follow the story. They knew what to expect, often from the beginning. Catalogues like the Shield begin with a prospect of the ensuing narrative. At the beginning of a hero's *aristeia*, his armor typically gleams portending his victory. The programmatic statements at the beginning of parallel actions give us an outline of what is to come. Thus foreshadowing and the suspense of anticipation are features of the cataloguing style.

A Story in Three Parts

Jebb 1886.5-6 made the following comment on the overall structure of the *Iliad*: "As a help to the memory, the story of the *Iliad* may be divided into three parts. The first ends with Book IX, when the Greeks sue to Achilles, and are repulsed. The second ends with Book XVIII, the last in which he remains aloof from the war." Thus the second part begins with Book 10, the night adventure in which the Trojan spy Dolon is slain, and ends with the Shield in Book 18. Book 10 and the Shield are points at which scholars who support a threefold division of the *Iliad* tend to disagree.

Sheppard 1922.82-83, 182 offers much the same scheme as Jebb, but he speaks of movements instead of parts and has the first movement end with what he calls the interlude of Book 10, which he sees as comparable to the Shield as the interlude at the end of the second movement. Owen 1946.106-7 again has the same three parts as Jebb; although, like Sheppard, he treats Book 10 and the Shield as interludes, he would, with Jebb, put Book 10 at the beginning of the second day's recitation. Wade-Gery 1952.14-16 agrees with the threefold division, but suggests that the second performance, which he would begin with Book 10, should end at 18.353; thus the dialogue between Zeus and Hera and the description of the Shield are put at the beginning of the last performance. Taplin 1992.25 and 201-2 has the same scheme except that he rejects Book 10 as non-Homeric. Whitman 1958.346, in agreement with Sheppard and Jebb, puts the Shield at the end of the second day's recitation, and apparently follows Wade-Gery and Jebb in putting Book 10 at its beginning. For Schadewaldt 1959.485 the first day's recitation ends with Book 9, and Book 10 is treated as a later addition; the second day's recitation ends with Book 18, "very peacefully with the description of the Shield." He makes the following sensitive remark: "When a day of recitation came to an end, it had also become evening in the poem. When they began again the next morning, the sun was also rising in the poem."

Following Sheppard, we shall divide the *Iliad* into three Parts, the first ending with Book 10, the second with Book 18. Among the above scholars only Wade-Gery and Taplin, who note that the dividing of our text into twenty-four books probably occurred long after Homer, recommend that the break between Parts 2 and 3 be put within Book 18; they would have Part 3 begin at 18.354 with the dialogue between Zeus and Hera and the description of the Shield. Assuming, however, that the poem was recited during the day, it seems much better to begin Part 3 with Book 19 (line 1) at the beginning of a new day; Hephaestus makes the shield during the previous night. Moreover, the dialogue between Zeus and Hera, in which Zeus apparently acquiesces in the fall of Troy and so in the death of Hector, a main event of Part 3, is paralleled by the dialogue they have in Book 8 at the end of the second day of battle, in which Zeus predicts the main events of Part 2. Taplin 1992.292 rightly says that, in line 3 of Book 19, the Greek word *he,* "she," which refers to Thetis, "signals the continuity" with the end of Book 18 where there is the unforgettable picture of Thetis coming through the night with the new armor for Achilles, but this is a continuity which, in my opinion, we can imagine being easily maintained during an over-night break between these books.

Scholars have debated since antiquity whether Book 10 is a later addition to the *Iliad,* for it is the one book which might be omitted without being noticed. But once it was added, it seems likely that the break between the first two recitations came after it, for it tells an adventure that takes place on the same night as the embassy in Book 9, and surely Shadewaldt is right in thinking sunset a better time than sunrise for reciting such poetry.

Was the *Iliad* composed for a special occasion? Kirk 1962.280-81 (so also Wade-Gery 1952.69), who is understandably skeptical about our ability to determine the setting for the earliest production, suggests that the poet may have created the occasion. The fame of the *Iliad* may have attracted an audience and made them willing to listen to it patiently through long hours of recitation.

A related question is whether the *Iliad* was performed during the day or night. There is no way of being certain, but with most scholars, against Thornton 1984.29-31 (so also Notopoulos 1964.15-16 and Taplin 1992.29-30), I prefer the day. I like (admittedly a subjective argument) having the recitations coincide in time with the fact that day begins and night ends each of our three main parts. Xenophon (*Symposium* 3.6) supports performance during the day in the fifth century B.C., for he has someone say, at the end of the Great Panathenaea, that he has been listening to the rhapsodes (that is, reciters of epic poetry) "almost every day" (*oligou an hekasten hemeran*). Also, it seems worth remarking that three successive nights of listening to the *Iliad* (are there really any clear, well-documented modern parallels?) would no doubt have required a drastic change in the sleeping habits of the audience. The fact that Odysseus tells his adventures to the Phaeacians after supper at night and that modern oral poets often sing their songs under similar circumstances is no evidence for when the *Iliad* was performed.

The argument most frequently brought against our threefold division is that the resulting parts are very unequal. Part 1 consists of ten books, Part 2 of eight books, Part 3 of six books. The audience had much more listening to do on the first day than on the second, and on the second than on the third. But might not the great poet who had created the occasion also have created the terms on which he used it? He may have liked the dramatic acceleration: the slow beginning of the long exposition of the first day, the lengthy but well directed battle of the second day, and the relatively swift *aristeia* of Achilles ending in the ransoming of Hector's body on the third day. Moreover, it is possible to imagine that the second and third days were filled out with other entertainments. We simply do not know.

The *Iliad* can be recited in three days (see Thornton 1984.47). If we figure about eleven lines a minute (so Davison 1965.24; Notopoulos 1964.12 figured about ten lines a minute), it takes about nine and a half hours to recite Part 1, less than nine hours to recite Part 2, and less than six hours to recite Part 3. But could Homer have done it all? I think it likely that there was a team of singers led and instructed by him, and that he created the *Iliad* with this audience of fellow poets especially in mind, and often with their help.

The inequality in our division is no doubt a reason why some scholars have put Book 10 at the beginning of Part 2, and the Shield at the beginning of Part 3. It is clearly the main reason for the alternative division proposed by Davison 1965.23-25 and Thornton 1984.46-63. They suggest that the *Iliad* was composed in six four-book groups, two of which were recited at each of three successive recitations, first Books 1-8, then Books 9-16, finally Books 17-24. This is mathematically very neat, but one wonders how an audience liked having the complementary night assemblies of Books 8 and 9 split between the first and second recitations, or ending the second recitation with the death of Patroclus. The fact that four-book divisions work well for the *Odyssey* is no reason for thinking they were used for the *Iliad*.

The division we have adopted offers a much better presentation of the story of the *Iliad*. It is strikingly dramatic for Part 1 to end with Achilles' refusal to return to battle (followed by the interlude of Book 10) and for Part 2 to end with his decision to give up his wrath and return to battle (followed by the interlude of the Shield); the *Iliad* after all is a poem about Achilles. Moreover, in our comments and summaries we shall try to point out similarities in structure between the three Parts: the fact, for instance, that in each an expected goal is delayed by a long retardation. But admittedly this is an aesthetic and therefore subjective matter. Again the reader must be the judge.

The Character of Achilles

Homer has often been praised for his lifelike characters. On the Trojan side there is Hector, the foremost warrior and main defender of Troy, a man who loves his wife and son; Paris, by contrast, though a good enough fighter, would rather enjoy his power to charm women than look after the best interests of his people. On the Achaean side there are Agamemnon, the king and commander-in-chief, a good soldier but a somewhat nasty person, cruel and bullying; Diomedes, a great fighter, young and impetuous (a stand-in, as it were, for Achilles during his absence in Part 1); Nestor, the garrulous old man, an embodiment of wisdom; the big Ajax, a great defensive fighter, a man of few words; Odysseus, brave but practical. There are many others, of course, whose mere names, such as Priam, Hecuba, Andromache, Helen, Menelaus, and Patroclus, immediately call to mind vividly drawn characters. But none of them is nearly so complex as Achilles.

Many people find Achilles to be a very unsympathetic character. It is easy to caricature him as a petulant youth given to fits of anger who runs weeping to his mother for comfort whenever he is disappointed. But the Greeks in the main thought otherwise. The great medieval commentator Eustathius put it well when, on *Odyssey* 11.505, he said that the poet is "altogether a lover of Achilles" (*panu philachilleus*). We might compare Achilles with Antigone or Socrates, who, in their readiness to die in pursuit of their goals, are very much in his mold.

Achilles, the greatest of the Achaeans, towers above all the other characters of the *Iliad* (see King 1987.2-3). He is the handsomest, swiftest, and strongest; his beautiful and powerful youth (only Diomedes and Antilochus are so young) is like that of the gods. But, though the son of the goddess Thetis, he is not himself a god; he is a mortal who can be fatally wounded. Certainly Homer, if he knew it (as he well may have done; see Janko 1992.409), rejected the story that Thetis by dipping the baby Achilles in the river Styx made him invulnerable except in the place on his heel where she held him. Achilles is the "most swift-doomed/short-lived of all men," *okumoros peri panton* (1.417, 505; 18.95, 458). These words are used only of him and only by Thetis. As King 1987.5 says, Achilles' knowledge that he is destined to die young at Troy and Thetis' "tender, mournful, and immortal motherhood accentuate the shortness of his life."

He is not a god, and not a beast either in spite of the fact that he rages like a lion and is blamed for descending to the level of a brute in his vengeance against Hector. But King 1987.28 rightly speaks of the bestial in him as well as the divine. Apparently the poet by showing his nearness to both wanted to define what it means to be human.

Achilles was given (9.412-16) a choice between a long but inglorious life if he remained at home and a short but glorious life if he went to fight at Troy. Being the man he was, he of course chose to win honor and glory, and thus we can understand his deep hurt and anger at being dishonored by Agamemnon. This dishonor threatened to invalidate his choice of lives, the whole meaning of his life. His choice presupposed the horrible reality of death, to which his soul in the Underworld, at *Odyssey* 11.489-91, refers: I would rather live in dishonor than be king of the dead. Since he had to die, he preferred a short life with honor to a long one without it.

We are sometimes made aware of a gentle side to his nature. He is naturally kind and polite, and always obeys the gods. When a god gives him advice, as Athena does in Book 1 or Thetis in Book 24, he promptly obeys. He shows concern for the feelings of the heralds when in Book 1 they come at Agamemnon's command to take Briseis from him; and in Book 9 he hospitably receives the envoys from Agamemnon. His reception of Priam in Book 24 shows him in a conflict of emotions as he tries to check his grief and anger over the slaying of Patroclus: he has deep sympathy for the old king but insists, even to the point of threatening to kill him, that he accept his hospitality before being given the body of Hector. Moreover, we are told that the centaur Chiron had taught Achilles to play the lyre, which he does in Book 9, and to practice the art of medicine, which he in turn taught Patroclus. Finally, we should mention Achilles' love for Briseis and Patroclus and the Achaeans in general. Briseis is more than a prize of war and a symbol of honor; he loves her like a wife. Patroclus, his charioteer, a somewhat older man (cf. 11.787), is like another self, his dearest friend; he represents his gentler side during the period of his wrath and moves him by tearful exhortation and, finally, by his death to pity the Achaeans. Achilles' concern for the Achaeans is shown in Book 1 when he calls the assembly to find out the cause of the plague. Although he later blames them for siding with Agamemnon, the death of Patroclus causes him to return to the action to be their leader and protector.

Nagy 1979.69-83 has argued for the derivation, proposed by Palmer 1963.79, of the name Achilles from *Achi-laos, which he interprets to mean "he whose army (*laos*) has grief (*achos*)." This makes sense when we think of how Achilles gives grief to his own people by withdrawing from battle and later (outside the *Iliad*) by being killed himself. An alternative interpretation would translate "he who gives grief to the enemy's army," that is, for instance, by his slaughter of the Trojans during his *aristeia*.

Homer, however, emphasizes another connection between Achilles and *achos*. As again Nagy 1979.79-81 points out, the poet uses this word to describe Achilles as a man of griefs. At 18.429-61, when Thetis is summarizing the action of the *Iliad* in Parts 1 and 2, she says that Achilles was born to *achos*, first because of his grief (or grievance) against Agamemnon and then because of his grief at the death of Patroclus. Both griefs result in angers, the first in the wrath, the second in the vengeance. Achilles is angry during most of the *Iliad*, and he is pictured as a young man easily given to anger, but we should not dismiss him as a continuously angry man. We must distinguish his two angers as having arisen out of two very different griefs, and understand that grief often gives rise to anger. One is naturally angered at being dishonored or at having one's best friend killed. Often of course in the *Iliad* the deaths of their comrades spur men to avenge them.

Homer clearly distinguishes the wrath from the vengeance. They are caused by different griefs; the first, in contrast to the second, is especially supported by Zeus; and they end in different kinds of pity: the first in pity for one's own people, the second in pity for one's enemy. Nevertheless, this summary of differences also makes clear the similarities between the wrath and the vengeance. *Menis*, *menithmos,* "wrath," and *menio*, "to be wrathful," are used only of the first god-supported anger, but *cholos*, "anger," and *choloumai,* "to be angry," are used of both. And *eleos*, "pity," and *eleeo, oikteiro*, "to pity," are used of both pities.

Thus the vengeance (described in Part 3) creates a climactic parallelism with the wrath (described in Parts 1 and 2). This, as we have already said, is the most overarching structure of the poem. Although the vengeance, unlike the wrath, is not especially supported by Zeus, it brings Achilles into the fulfillment of his chosen destiny and makes him an instrument in the destruction of Troy, to which Zeus has agreed. Moreover, Achilles' grief over the death of Patroclus is a more powerful emotion than his sorrow at the loss of Briseis; and the pity for his enemy, with which the vengeance ends, is a loftier and more difficult emotion to attain than the pity for his fellow Achaeans.

The Teacher of the Greeks

Plutarch in his treatise *How a Young Man Should Listen to Poems* frequently cites passages from the *Iliad* that show Homer as a moral teacher. He concentrates on the heroes, whom he sees as models created by the poet to teach his fellow countrymen how to live. Achilles, for instance, a young man who is tested in his relations with friends and enemies and gods, has much to teach the later young men of Greece. The gods, however, are often unworthy of imitation until the stories about them have been allegorized.

For Plutarch there is no conflict between Homer's being a moral teacher and his having pro-Achaean sympathies. In fact, one of the ways Homer teaches is by comparing the Achaeans with the Trojans to the disadvantage of the latter. For instance, many of the Trojans are captured alive, but none of the Achaeans; and sometimes Trojans—Adrestus, the sons of Antimachus, Tros, Lycaon, and Hector—beg for mercy, but never the Achaeans, for "it is a trait of barbarian peoples to make supplication and to fall at the enemy's feet in combat, but of Greeks to conquer or die fighting" (Babbitt 1969.159). Other evidence Plutarch might have used has been noted by modern scholars; for instance, that of the five major *aristeiai* in the *Iliad* four are by Achaeans (Achilles, Patroclus, Diomedes, and Agamemnon), only one by a Trojan (Hector). The same attitude is found in the scholia. For instance, in schol. bT on 7.89-90,192, 226-27, 284, and 289 Ajax is praised as a level-headed warrior while Hector is blamed for being tyrannical and boastful. And in schol. bT on 10.14-16 there is the sweeping generalization *aei philellen ho poietes,* "the poet is always a philhellene."

Among modern scholars who are in general agreement with Plutarch and the scholia, though not without criticism of their excesses, are Lattimore, van der Valk, and Griffin. Lattimore 1951.31 writes as follows: ". . . the *Iliad* was composed for a Hellenic audience, of the upper class, among which many claimed to trace their ancestry back to the heroes of the Trojan War. The pro-Hellenic bias is plain, though not crude, though tempered by a considerate sympathy for the Trojans; and the pro-Hellenic bias involves the reputation of the Achaean heroes."

Van der Valk 1953.5-26 has pointed out that Hector, though favorably viewed in his relations with his family, comes off badly in his encounters with the Achaean heroes; and that when the story requires the defeat of the Achaeans, the poet has Zeus, at 15.561 and 599-602, assure his audience that this will be only temporary. Moreover, Paris, and not Hector, is pictured as the typical Trojan. Toward the beginning of the poem, in Book 3, his vainglorious, cowardly, voluptuous character is emphasized to show his responsibility in the crime of carrying off Helen.

Griffin 1980.3-6 notes that when the two armies clash for the first time in the poem, at the beginning of Book 3, Paris, dressed in a panther skin, challenges the Achaeans to fight but that, "beautiful as a god," he leaps back in fear when Menelaus comes to meet him. He is thus a typical Trojan like the Trojan ally Nastes earlier (2.872) and Euphorbus later (17.51). This picture of Paris and the contrast between how the Trojans and Achaeans advance against each other at the beginning of Book 3 show us that the Trojans are "gorgeous, frivolous, noisy," the Achaeans "serious and grim." Paris must be shamed by Hector into the duel with Menelaus, and later Hector himself, though he has boasted of his readiness to fight Achilles, will flee when he sees him approaching. "This pattern," Griffin 1980.5 concludes, "is vital to the *Iliad*, it is no mere Greek chauvinism. The Achaeans win the war because their discipline is better, as we are told explicitly; their silence and obedience to their commanders go with this. The Trojans lose because they are the sort of people they are—glamorous, reckless, frivolous, undisciplined. And the archetypal Trojan is Paris."

This view of Homer and the *Iliad* is rejected by Kakridis 1971.54-67 (=1956.61-32 revised; cf. de Jonge 1987.8-12 and Taplin 1992.110-15). He suggests, in criticism of van der Valk, that the poet is motivated by artistic reasons rather than nationalistic sympathies when he delays the defeat of the Achaeans during the great day of battle. It is unnecessary, however, to see a conflict between these two motivations. Moreover, Kakridis does not adequately explain why the *Iliad* does at times favor the Achaeans; for instance, why the ratio of Achaeans to Trojans slain in battle is 53 to 189. He believes that Homer was influenced by earlier poetry about the Trojan War, which, so far as we can tell, dealt almost exclusively with Achaean victories. In other words, pre-Homeric poetry was pro-Achaean. But Homer, according to Kakridis, with his story of a defeat of the Achaeans due to the wrath of Achilles departed radically from this tradition. This may well be true, as I like to think, but it is hard to accept that the poet has retained the pro-Achaean elements in the *Iliad* against his own better inclinations.

It is certainly one of the great glories of the *Iliad* that it asks us to look at the Trojan War with sympathy for both sides, "with a compassion for the common fate of man" (Kakridis 1971.64). One thinks of the many similes which raise us above the battle and ask us to view it in the broad perspective of human suffering. (Even here, however, preference is shown for the Achaeans in that they are compared to strong animals like lions rather than weak ones like deer much more frequently than the Trojans.) One also thinks of the death of Hector and the ransoming of his body by his old father—moving scenes of sorrow. Homer can be magnificently impartial, but it is not necessary to see this impartiality as being in conflict with his sympathy for his own people His sympathy for mankind can be thought of as rising out of his sympathy for his own people. "I am a Greek," he might have said, "and therefore nothing human is foreign to me."

Plutarch is very conscious of the poet's impartiality, and often asks the young man who is studying the *Iliad* to learn from the faults of Achaean as well as Trojan heroes, especially Achilles. He is thus being true to the *Iliad* which makes us feel the most severe disapproval of Achilles, whom we can believe to be the poet's favorite character.

In the first sentence of the *Iliad* (the proem) Homer describes the wrath of Achilles, which brings countless Achaeans to death, as *oulomenen,* "accursed"; and, at 1.223, he introduces Achilles' final angry speech to Agamemnon by saying that it was spoken "with baneful words." Later, at 15. 598, he tells us that Zeus, when about to bring about the defeat of the Achaeans at the ships, was fulfilling the *exaision aren,* "unreasonable prayer," of Thetis to support the wrath. (I think it unlikely that, as de Jonge 1987.139 suggests, the poet is here giving, not his own opinion, but only that of Zeus.) Moreover, Achilles' rejection of the embassy in Book 9 and his refusal to return to battle in Book 16, where he admits that Zeus has fulfilled his promise, must have dismayed the Greek audience. They must have been greatly relieved and delighted when he cursed his wrath in Book 18, saying that it was wrong from the beginning, and chose to return and fight for his own people.

This feeling of elation probably lasted for some time, but with increasing misgivings. The capture, at 21.26-32, of twelve Trojan youths to be sacrificed on Patroclus' pyre seems horrible; and the poet comments on their sacrifice, at 23.176, that Achilles "devised bad deeds in his mind." Moreover, Achilles' relentless pursuit of the Trojans, in which no suppliant is spared, seems non-human— godlike perhaps, but also brutal.

With the slaying of Hector Achilles attains his goal, and the audience must have cheered him, although the poet makes us feel great sympathy for the dying Hector. But then Achilles goes too far by dishonoring and mutilating the dead body. Homer introduces the mistreatment of Hector's body by saying that Achilles was "devising unseemly deeds" (22.395=23.24). This may refer only to the ugly way in which the body is treated, but it seems likely to be also a criticism of Achilles. At any rate, it is hard not to agree with the gods, at 24.22-76, when they show their displeasure and decide that he must give up the body for proper burial. We can thus believe that the Greek audience must have been increasingly displeased with Achilles' vengeance and so were greatly relieved when he rose above it in pity for Priam. For all their nationalism, they wanted that sublime view of what it means to be a human being which Homer finally gives them.

Gods and Men

The gods of the *Iliad* are feared, worshiped with prayer and sacrifice, and asked for omens, but they are also pictured fighting with each other, being in undignified, laughable situations, and encouraging humans in immoral acts. This unflattering picture has been explained in several ways. Later Greeks, long before Plutarch, resorted to allegory. Modern scholars have emphasize that the carefree and unaging blessed immortals are being viewed as foils to poor human beings who are subject to old age and death and beset by numerous cares. Moreover, the gods have a knowledge of the future—they know what will be the result of their actions—whereas we, who are ruled by deceptive expectations, can only hope (*elpomai*). Man never is but always to be blessed.

There is also the fact that the gods in general and Zeus in particular are often equated with the amoral power of fate (*moira*). This equation is vividly expressed by Achilles at 24.525-33 when he tells Priam about the jars of Zeus. The gods have spun (*epeklosanto*, connected with the noun *Klotho*, "Spinster," one of the Moirai) for wretched mortals to live in grief while they are free from care; for Zeus has two jars in his storeroom, one of good things, the other of bad things, from which he apportions to humans at birth: to some he gives a mixture, to others only from the jar of evils, to no one only from the jar of goods, and so no one has an all-blessed life like that of the gods.

Often Zeus' actions can be seen as an expression of fate. When he weighs the fates of two heroes or of the two armies in his scales, he is showing what he knows and sometimes has told us beforehand is fated to happen. Although he allows Sarpedon to die, Hera implies that he might go against fate and make him immortal. Zeus never goes against fate, but usually represents it. One feels that he is very much in charge of what happens on earth. Throughout the *Iliad* he is in control of the plot, which he announces in his predictions and commands step by step. It is his will that the Trojans should be victorious during the period of Achilles' wrath (Part 1), and without his backing this could not have happened (Part 2); and it his will that Troy should not fall before its fated time and that therefore Achilles should not take it on the day of his *aristeia* (Part 3).

The conference Zeus has with Hera and Athena at the beginning of Book 4 shows a sublime unconcern with questions of right and wrong. Zeus tells Hera that she may destroy Troy, one of his favorite cities (which she hates, probably because of the Judgment of Paris though Homer never says so), but that she must not oppose him when he wants to destroy one of her favorite cities; and she answers that he may destroy Argos, Sparta, and Mycenae in return. Then he orders Athena to go down to the battlefield and see to it that the Trojans attack the Achaeans and so break the treaty they have just solemnly sworn to uphold. Athena obeys and successfully urges Pandarus to wound Menelaus by shooting him with an arrow. How can we explain these immoral, or at least amoral, divine actions? Only, I think, by considering the gods as representatives of what is fated. Troy did fall, and the cities of Argos, Sparta, and Mycenae were destroyed. These were therefore fated happenings, like the death of a hero, for the poet and his audience. Since Troy was fated to fall, the war had to be continued and therefore the treaty had to be broken. We should note, however, that Homer is capable of having it both ways; the religion of the *Iliad*, like many religions, has its inconsistencies. The breach of the truce is wrong, and Paris' later refusal to honor it is a reaffirmation of his original crime in carrying off Helen and offers moral justification for the destruction of Troy. Moreover, Athena's role in the treachery of Pandarus does not lessen his guilt, for he was already predisposed so to act.

We should think of the gods in terms of their powers. Each of them has a certain sphere of influence and honor. Zeus has the greatest power, for he is king of the gods and father of gods and men. The word "father" here means paterfamilias, not begetter; it is a synonym for king. Zeus presides over the world of the gods. In Book 5 he tells Aphrodite that she as a goddess of love has had no business trying to act like a goddess of war. In Book 15 he has Poseidon ordered off the battlefield in spite of the fact that Poseidon can claim a right to be on the earth as well as in the sea.

Zeus' governance of men is somewhat different. Human kingship is a reflection of his, and he supports the rights of human kings. Kings on earth resemble him and are often called Zeus-born or Zeus-nurtured; some, like Sarpedon, are actually his sons. Of even greater importance, however, is the fact that Zeus and the other gods require humans to worship them and to obey certain moral principles in their relations with each other. Zeus sends omens, forbids men to swear falsely or to commit adultery, and commands them to spare suppliants. The Trojans put themselves in the wrong as perjurers by breaking the truce in Book 4, Paris is guilty of adultery for carrying off Helen from the house of Menelaus where he had been received as a guest (Zeus is the god of guest-friendship), and the theme of supplication is a leitmotif of the *Iliad* (see Thornton 1984). We think of the priest of Apollo who supplicates the Achaeans to give him back his daughter in Book 1, of the Trojans on the battlefield who plead for their lives or at least for a proper burial, and of the series of supplications of Achilles, by the embassy in Part 1, by Patroclus in Part 2, and by Priam in Part 3.

The morality of the *Iliad* is centered on the cry of the suppliant for pity: reverence the gods and have pity. We are asked to raise our consciousness of human suffering. This makes a contrast but is not inconsistent with the moral theme of the *Odyssey* expressed in the saying, "Evil deeds do not succeed" (*Odyssey* 8.329).

Burkert 1955.76 has pointed out that pity is not only the motivating force in the supplications of humans by humans but also the spark that for brief moments creates a link between the easy-living gods and human need. In Book 8 Hera, seeing the Achaeans being defeated, pities them (*idous' eleese*, 350), and she and Athena start in their chariot to come onto the battlefield but are turned back by the command of Zeus. In Book 13 Poseidon, who is keeping no blind lookout (*alaoskopien*, 10), pities (*eleaire*, 15) the Achaeans being defeated and comes in his chariot to their aid. In Book 15 Zeus, when he awakes from his beguilement by Hera, sees Poseidon leading the Achaeans in a successful counterattack and Hector lying wounded on the ground; seeing Hector he pities him (*idon eleese*, 12) and has Hera summon Apollo and Iris in order that he may have them go onto the battlefield to remedy the situation. In Book 16 Zeus, seeing Sarpedon and Patroclus about to fight, has pity (*idon eleese*, 431), for he knows that now Sarpedon, his son, is destined to die; he wants to save him and sheds tears of blood but is persuaded by Hera not to go against fate but, instead, to send Sleep and Death to carry the dead body to its native land for proper burial. In Book 17 Zeus, seeing the immortal horses of Achilles standing immobile and weeping for their dead charioteer Patroclus, pities them (*idon eleese,* 441) and gives them the spirit—Hector will not be permitted to catch them—to race over the battlefield at full speed in spite of their grief. In Book 19 Zeus, seeing Achilles refusing to eat because of his grief and weeping over Patroclus while Agamemnon and other leaders of the Achaeans grieve with him, has pity (*idon eleese*, 340) and sends Athena to instill ambrosia and nectar into his chest to prevent him from being hungry. In Book 24 all the gods except Hera, Poseidon, and Athena, seeing the dead Hector being mistreated by Achilles, pity him (*eleaireskon . . . eisoroontes*, 23), and Zeus finally decides that Priam should ransom the body; then, when Zeus sees Priam with the ransom

coming onto the plain to go to Achilles, he pities the old man (idon eleese, 332) and
sends Hermes to be his guide. (The verb *olophuromai*, "to bewail," "to pity," is
sometimes used like *eleairo* and *eleeo* in the above examples; cf. 8.245 and
22.169.) Pitying, naturally and so formulaically, goes with seeing a pitiable sight.
We are reminded of how in the Bible God is called upon to behold the plight of his
worshipers and not turn his face away.

The involvement of the Olympians with humans threatens their peaceful,
carefree life as deities. They suffer and rejoice because of their attachment to men,
ephemeral creatures who are destined to wither and die like the leaves. As if in
response to this danger, the immortals often show a cold indifference to human
suffering. They look at the battle like uninvolved spectators or turn their shining
eyes to happier scenes (Griffin 1980.178-204 has some good remarks on the divine
audience of the *Iliad*). Their indifference can be thought of as an expression of the
gulf between them and men and fits with the picture of them as foils to poor
mortals.

The intervention of the gods in the affairs of men is sometimes difficult for us
to understand. We have already said that Pandarus is not absolved from
responsibility by the fact that Athena urges him to break the truce. He is both god-
and self-motivated and so gives us an example of what Lesky has explained as
double motivation. Lesky 1966.72 notes among other examples two very
important ones concerned with Achilles. When Achilles puts up his sword in Book
1, he does it both on the advice of Athena and in his own right; and when he returns
the body of Hector to Priam in Book 24, he acts both in obedience to the gods and
as the winner of "his last and greatest victory, victory over his own passionate
heart."

But there are times when this psychological explanation is insufficient because
the gods make a physical difference. In Book 23 Athena actually (a miracle) returns
his whip to Diomedes in order that he may win the chariot race. Willcock 1970 has
persuasively explained that Athena favors winners and that Diomedes is to be
placed among those Achaean mortals, like Achilles and Odysseus, who are natural
winners. Thus her aid to Diomedes simply adds to the glory he was going to win
on his own.

A more troublesome instance of her intervention occurs in Book 22 where she
helps Achilles slay Hector. She dupes Hector into making a stand and then, when
the two men have thrown their spears without harming each other, returns his spear
to Achilles, leaving Hector with only his sword. Surely Achilles, who is certainly
the much stronger man, does not need this aid. It makes us feel sorry for Hector.

The glory that the presence of Athena confers on Achilles is a cold, cruel, and frightening thing. She is there because Achilles, a natural winner, is one of her favorites, yes, but also as a supporter of the Achaean cause and as an embodiment of fate. She is one of those deities (Hera and Poseidon are the most important others) who will see to it that Troy falls as it is destined to do, and this means that Hector, the defender of Troy, must die.

There are also gods who favor the Trojans. In Book 3 Aphrodite intervenes to save Paris, swooping him off the battlefield, when he is about to be slain by Menelaus, into his bedroom with Helen. In Book 16 Apollo, during the single combat between Patroclus and Hector, knocks Patroclus silly, disarming him completely, after which the foppish young Euphorbus and then Hector finish him off. We feel sorry for Patroclus, and here it seems very doubtful that Hector is the natural winner. Apollo, a pro-Trojan god, has favored Hector because he is the leader of the Trojans and has come against Patroclus as an embodiment of fate, for, as Zeus has told us, now Patroclus is destined to die.

Although some gods are pro-Achaean and some pro-Trojan, both peoples have the same Olympian religion. For instance, both pray to Athena, Apollo, and Zeus. Moreover, Zeus, who feels pity for both Achilles and Hector and who can make all the other gods act according to his will, is impartial. The fact of a common religion underlines the common humanity of Trojans and Achaeans.

The same can be said with regard to the various peoples who go to make up the Achaean side. They come from all over Greece, as the Achaean Catalogue at the end of Book 2 shows, and no doubt in actual, historical fact had slightly different cults—for instance, the worship of Athena tended to dominate in Athens, that of Hera in Argos—but the *Iliad* pictures them all with the same religion. The *Iliad* is a Panhellenic poem, and its Olympian religion is Panhellenic and universal.

Similes: Types and Sequences

The similes can be studied from many different points of view. We shall concentrate here and in our later comments on simile sequences and types of similes used in battle scenes. Moulton 1977 has made a valuable study of simile sequences, how pairs or series of similes are used to articulate the narrative. An example of a simile pair occurs in Book 11 where Hector first (297-98) enters the battle like a stormwind stirring up the sea and then (305-8) wreaks havoc among the Achaeans like Zephyrus driving together the clouds of Notus in a deep stormwind, causing the waves to rise and roll with scattering foam. The second simile is longer, more detailed, and intensifies the action of the first one. In the list below of simile types occurring in battle scenes we shall point out several other examples of simile sequences.

There are five times as many similes in the battle scenes of the *Iliad* as in other parts of the poem. A reason often given for this is that the battle scenes are especially in need of the relief and variety that similes offer. Moreover, the everyday life pictured in the similes makes a nice contrast with the fighting; this explains why the *Odyssey* has fewer similes than the *Iliad*: its world is too much like the one that they depict. But, as Krischer 1971 has pointed out, similes are connected especially with *aristeiai* and not with just any fighting. Following him, we can classify the *aristeia* similes into nine types according to the different features of the narrative they describe, and note that some of these types are also applied to the army as a whole.

1. The arming of the hero and army, and the marshaling of the troops; the gleaming of the armor. A simile often foreshadows the victory of the hero by comparing the brightness of his armor with fire, lightning, the shining of a star. This gleaming is absent when Patroclus and Hector put on Achilles' armor, for they are destined to die. A sequence of four similes of this type are used of Achilles. When he appears without any armor at the trench, Athena causes a fiery golden cloud to shine around his head like that arising from a city on fire (18.207-13); when Priam sees him advancing, he is like Sirius, the brightest star (22.26); when he comes against Hector, his armor shines like a great fire or the rising sun (22.134-35); and when he is about to kill Hector, the point of his spear shines like the evening star (20.317). As Krischer 1971.38 says, "The great victory is thus announced each time a new stage is reached: before the beginning of the *aristeia*, before the beginning of the encounter with Hector, before the decisive spear-cast." This series of similes shows that the theme of gleaming occurs not only under type 1 but at other points in our classification as well. At 19. 357-58 the armor of the Achaeans being marshaled under the command of Achilles is said to have the brightness of thickly falling snow.

2. The advance into battle. The image of a wounded lion is used of Diomedes at 5.136-42 and of Achilles at 20.164-73; the two similes, however, are quite different. At 11.297-98 (which, as we have seen, is paired with 11.305-8, a type 3 simile) Hector is compared to a stormwind, at 15.263-68 to a proud stallion; the latter simile is also used of Paris at 6.506-11. At 12.299-306 Sarpedon advances against the Achaean wall like a lion against a sheepfold. At 13.298-300 Idomeneus, in his brief *aristeia*, is compared to Ares. Associated with this group of similes are those describing the whole army advancing to attack. These are

especially frequent in Books 2 through 4, that is, in the march-out to the first battle in the *Iliad*, where they sometimes contrast the Achaeans with the Trojans. The noise of the advancing army is like that of birds, a storm, bleating sheep; their ranks are like waves rolling over the sea; they are like a coming cloud, a swarm of wasps.

3. The attack. The hero is like a force of nature, a stormwind on the sea, a river in flood, or a wild animal. Of the five major *aristeiai* only that of Patroclus lacks this element, whereas that of Hector has it four times because of frequent retardations of his advance: he attacks like a stormwind causing the sea to foam (11.305-8, making a pair with 11.297-98, a type 2 simile), like a wild boar or a lion (12.41-48), like a boulder that rolling down a hill comes to a halt on the plain (13.137-42), like a wave falling into a ship (15.624-28).

4. Flight and pursuit. The pursuer is like a lion, a dog, a falcon; the pursued like cattle, deer, hares, smaller birds. The pictures of the wind driving the clouds, and of locusts fleeing a fire, also occur. In Patroclus' *aristeia* in Book 16 there is a series of these similes, called by Moulton 1977.33-36 a dispersed sequence. In lines 278-83, when Patroclus has first driven the Trojans back from the ship of Protesilaus, it is as if Zeus has driven the clouds away (seen from the Achaean point of view). In lines 364-65, when the Trojans flee in disorder over the trench, it is as if Zeus has sent a storm into the blue sky (seen from the Trojan point of view). In lines 384-92, when the Trojan horses groan as they flee, it is as if the earth were burdened under a storm sent by Zeus to punish men for their injustice. Notice the role of Zeus in all three similes and the fact that in the third the storm, which is coming on in the second, lets go its water. From whose point of view is the third simile composed? Perhaps (so Krischer), as in the second, that of the Trojans. But perhaps the poet is only addressing his audience. At any rate, we are being told that Zeus, now that he has fulfilled his promise to Thetis, will punish the Trojans. Similes of this type also appear outside of *aristeiai*. At 8.338-40 Hector, like a hunting dog pursuing a lion or boar but on guard against its turning round, chases the Achaeans into the safety of their camp at the end of the second day of battle. At 17.755-57, immediately before the scene shifts to Achilles at the beginning of Book 18, the Achaeans flee before Hector and Aeneas like starlings or cranes before a hawk, crying in fear of death, which they see coming on, though still at some distance, for the Ajaxes are protecting their retreat. Both these similes emphasize climactic points in the narrative. Notice also that the first, by showing how Hector fears a sudden Achaean counterattack, puts the retreat of the Achaeans in a favorable light, and that the situation in which the second appears, though desperate, is not a complete rout of the Achaeans. In Book 22 there is a series of

similes (compare Moulton 1977.83-84) describing Achilles' pursuit of Hector; this is a major turning point in the poem. In lines 139-42 Achilles is like a falcon chasing a dove; in lines 162-64 he and Hector are compared to two race horses; in lines 189-92 Achilles is like a dog chasing a fawn; and in lines 199-200 they are compared to the pursuer and the pursued in a dream: the pursuer is unable to catch the pursued (seen from Achilles' point of view), and the pursued is unable to escape the pursuer (seen from Hector's point of view).

5. The victor and his victim. The hero is compared to a beast of prey, his opponent to a helpless animal. At 15.690-92 Hector springs upon the defenders of Protesilaus' ship (his victim) like an eagle diving upon a flock of birds. At 21.22-24 Achilles drives the Trojans into the Scamander, killing them, like a dolphin attacking smaller fish. In 22.308-10 Hector rushes upon Achilles like an eagle against a lamb or a hare. This is the only instance in which such a simile does not describe a victor—a pathetic touch, no doubt. We admire Hector's bravery, but Achilles, who as victor is not given a simile of this type (would it seem too trite?), kills him with that spear whose point shines like the evening star, the most beautiful of all the stars in heaven (317-18). There is one place, 16.352-55, where this type of simile is used of the whole army, that of the victorious Achaeans: they fall upon the Trojans like wolves killing lambs and kids.

6. Even or indecisive battle. These similes often appear in battles over a dead body and often introduce a break in the narrative; they are used to describe both individual heroes and the armies in general. In Book 4, at the beginning of the first day of battle, the armies rush together like two raging rivers (452-56) and like wolves fighting each other (471). In Book 16, in Patroclus' *aristeia*, there are the even battles over the bodies of Sarpedon and Cebriones. Patroclus and Hector, as they clash over Sarpedon, are compared (428-29) to two shrieking vultures fighting on a high rock; the noise of the general battle is (633-34) like that of woodsmen cutting down oaks in the mountains, and the men of both armies (641-43) swarm over the body like flies around a milk pail in spring. During the battle over Cebriones, Patroclus and Hector are said (756-58) to fight like hungry lions over a slain deer, and the two armies are compared (765-79) to two howling winds struggling with each other in a mountain hollow, causing the trees to crash. Book 17 tells of the battle over Patroclus' body, which is the longest and most important such battle in the *Iliad*; in lines 737-39 the fighting is compared to a roaring, city-destroying fire. In Book 12 the object of contention is the Achaean wall, and a series of similes belonging to this group is used to describe it (compare Moulton 1977.64-67). First, Asius' attack on the left ends in an even battle with a simile

(156) in which the rocks thrown by both sides are compared to snowflakes. Second, Hector's attack in the center ends in the same way, an even battle with another snow simile (278-86). Third, Sarpedon's attack near the center ends in even battle with the comparison (421-23) of two farmers fighting over the boundary line between their properties. Finally, before Hector breaks through the central gate of the wall, the even battle along the whole front is made vivid by the image of a woman weighing wool in a balance (433-35).

7. Resistance. During the second, great day of battle, in Books 11-18 (Part 2), similes of resistance are used of the Achaeans. The wild boar, which unlike the lion typically fights only when attacked, is a favorite image. At 11.414-18 the encircled Odysseus resists like a wild boar come from its lair to face the hunters and dogs. In Book 12 the two Lapiths resist Asius like mountain oaks against a storm (132-34) and a wild boar against hunters and dogs (145-50), and Asius compares them to wasps or bees protecting their young from hunters (167-70). At 13.471-75 Idomeneus is like a wild boar as he awaits Aeneas' attack. At 15.618-21 the Achaeans withstand the Trojans like a rock in the surf. At 17.747-51 the Ajaxes protect the Achaean withdrawal like a hill that causes streams to change their course. During the *aristeia* of Achilles, in Books 19-24 (Part 3), similes of this type are used of the two Trojans Agenor and Hector. At 21.573-78 Agenor prepares to withstand Achilles like a panther come from its lair to attack the hunters and dogs, and at 22.93-95 Hector prepares to withstand Achilles like a snake circling its hole to protect it against an oncoming man; but in the event both Agenor and Hector flee.

8. Retreat. At 3.33-35 Paris withdraws in fear at the sight of Menelaus like a man who has seen a snake; this is a prelude to their duel. At 5.597 Diomedes withdraws with a shudder before Ares like a traveler stopped by a mighty river. He has been told by Athena not to fight with any deity but Aphrodite; later Athena comes and helps him defeat Ares. During the great day of battle (Part 2), when Zeus is giving the victory to Hector, the Achaeans are frequently forced to withdraw. At 15.586-88 Antilochus retreats before Hector and the Trojans like a wild animal who, having killed a dog or a shepherd, goes off before other men arrive. At 17.109-12 Menelaus, who is withdrawing before Hector to call for Ajax's help in protecting Patroclus' body, is compared to a lion that, turning again and again, is driven from a fold by shepherds and their dogs. At 17.657-65 Menelaus, when at the urging of Ajax he is going to find Antilochus to tell him to try to gain the help of Achilles in protecting Patroclus' body, is compared to a lion that, having broken into a fold, fights all night before withdrawing exhausted. The

same simile, at 11.548-55, is the first of a pair used of Ajax when he is forced by Zeus to withdraw; the second, at 11.558-62, compares Ajax to an ass which, cudgelled by weaker boys, finally, after he is satisfied with eating, leaves a field. As Krischer 1971.70 remarks, "Ajax must withdraw because Zeus wills it, not because the Trojans are stronger." Similes of retreat are used predominantly of Achaeans, as those of flight are of Trojans.

9. The warrior falls. He is compared to a tree being felled, a sacrificial animal being slaughtered, an animal falling into the mouth of a lion, and once, at 8.306-7, as having his head sink like a flower heavy with dew. This type of simile occurs at several different places in the *aristeia,* and in fact wherever there is fighting. Of the more than fifteen examples listed by Krischer only two describe Achaeans: at 5.554-60 two young Achaeans are overcome by Aeneas like young lions killed by men protecting their steading, and they fall like lofty fir trees; at 16.823-28 Patroclus falls to Hector like a wild boar overcome by a lion when they are fighting over a spring.

Two other groups of similes that seem especially worth mentioning are those concerned with the journeying of a god and those describing emotions or states of mind. Similes are used to make vivid the emotions of grief, anger, and pity, and the mental state of indecisiveness (compare type 6 similes above on even battle). Gods are usually said to come swiftly like a bird or a shooting star; many other comparisons serve this purpose.

Moulton 1977.88-116 has also shown how similes are used to characterize the heroes, especially Achilles. Achilles receives more and speaks more similes than any other character in the *Iliad.* He is compared to fire, a lion, and a deity, and describes himself as a mother bird to the Achaeans (9.23-25) and as a mother to Patroclus (16.7-90). The image of him as fire predominates during his *aristeia* (Part 3).

The simile is one of the most important devices of composition, but, as we have seen, there are many others that are also very useful in describing a scene and suggesting how we should feel about it. In our account of the *Iliad* when we mention the presence of a device, we are not simply enumerating phenomena but rather, it is hoped, focusing the attention of the reader on how the poet wants us to view his narrative. Homer is a protean creator, and no one passage of his poem can be equated exactly with another. Our purpose is always to summon the reader to a closer reading of the text. There is no better interpreter of Homer than Homer.

PART 1

THE EXPOSITION OF THE PLOT

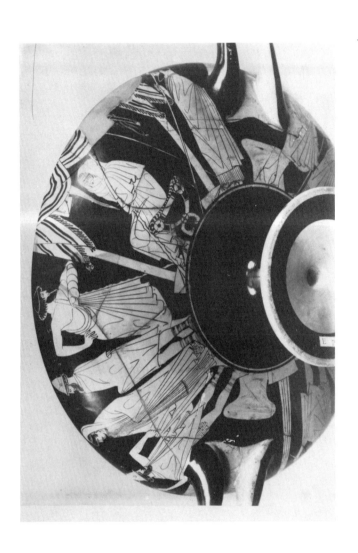

1. Briseis Being Led from the Grieving Achilles—from a red-figure vase of around 480 B.C., British Museum, E 76. She is in the charge of the heralds Talthybius and Eurybates (compare *Il.* 1.320-21). Achilles sits in his hut, on each side of which is a sympathetic figure, one of whom is probably Patroclus.

BOOK 1: THE BEGINNING OF THE WRATH

Proem, 1-7

Sing, goddess, of the wrath of Peleus' son Achilles,
which, accursed, sent countless woes upon the Achaeans
and hurled many mighty souls of heroes down
to Hades and made their bodies to be a prey of dogs
and a feast of birds—so the will of Zeus was fulfilled—
from the time that those two first stood apart in strife,
Atreus' son, the king, and godlike Achilles.

This is the proem of the *Iliad*. The wrath which it announces is often said to cover not only Achilles' anger against Agamemnon (the son of Atreus) but also his vengeance against Hector. The proem, however, makes clear that the wrath is to be distinguished from the vengeance by saying that it caused countless numbers of Achilles' own people, the Achaeans (Greeks), to perish (this is not true of the vengeance) and that it was accomplished in accordance with the will of Zeus (something not emphasized as true of the vengeance). The poet by describing it as *oulomenen*,"accursed," in line 2 expresses the horror of his pro-Achaean audience. Achilles' wrath is directed against his own people; his vengeance, though growing out of his wrath, determines him to give it up and, being reconciled with his own people, to direct his energies against the enemy. The main structure of the *Iliad* is based on these two movements. (See Introduction 2-3, 13, 15-17.) At first sight it may seem strange that the proem refers only to the first movement, but we can compare the proem of the *Odyssey* which mentions only the homeward journey of Odysseus and says nothing about his revenge on the suitors. The word for Achilles' wrath, the first word of the *Iliad*, is *menis*; it is never used of the vengeance but elsewhere refers to the wrath of a god, like that of Apollo later in this book.

The effectiveness of Achilles' wrath will be dependent on the backing given it by Zeus. This is the plan of Zeus, alluded to in line 5, in accordance with which many Achaeans will perish (so Bassett 1922.53-54). In the present book we shall be told how Thetis, Achilles' mother, gains from Zeus the promise to support her son's wrath by making the Trojans victorious. This plan should not be confused, as is often done (for instance, by Schadewaldt 1938.42 and 111) with Zeus' predictions of future events at important junctures in the poem, especially in Books 8 and 15. Of course Achilles' wrath will lead to Patroclus' death and other future events, and Zeus as the great deity (sometimes equated with Fate) can, in a general sense, be said to will them. Moreover, it is true that the poet uses Zeus to stage-manage the events of the *Iliad*. Nevertheless, Zeus is also a special character in the poem who puts into effect against other divinities his special plan of supporting Achilles' wrath. Without Zeus' backing, as we shall see, Achilles' withdrawal would not have been enough in itself to tilt the balance of battle in favor of the Trojans. At the beginning of the vengeance, in Book 20, we shall find that Zeus has another special plan, to prevent Achilles from taking Troy. This second plan can be thought of as paralleling the first one as the vengeance does the wrath.

Prelude, 8-52

A prelude (so Schadewaldt 1943. 144) follows immediately. This can be divided into two parts (Krischer 1971.136-40), the first of which can be described as an epic regression, the second as an epic progression. In the first (8-12) the poet tells us that Apollo caused Agamemnon and Achilles to quarrel by sending a plague upon the Achaeans to punish Agamemnon for dishonoring his priest Chryses. The much longer and fuller second part (12-52) consists of a dramatic retelling of the same events in chronological order: Chryses came to the Achaean camp to ransom his daughter Chryseis, but Agamemnon harshly rejected his plea; then the old priest, going off by the seashore, prayed to Apollo for vengeance.

> So he prayed, and Phoebus Apollo heard him
> and came from the peaks of Olympus angry at heart,
> with his bow on his shoulders and his well-covered quiver.
> The arrows clanged on his shoulders as he in his anger
> moved into action and came like the coming of night.
> Sitting apart from the ships he let go an arrow.
> Terrible to hear was the noise of the silver bow's twanging.
> First he attacked the mules and the flashing-swift dogs,
> and then the men, his sharp, piercing arrows striking
> them down; a rash of funeral pyres always was burning.   (43-52)

This is a typical scene of divine visitation, but untypically it does not end with Apollo's return to Olympus (so Edwards 1980.11). The reason is clear: Apollo's withdrawal now would leave us with the impression that the plague is over whereas it continues unabated during the Achaean assembly and until he is propitiated in line 457. We shall see that the point at which Apollo gives up his wrath coincides with that at which Achilles' wrath begins to become effective, when he gives up Briseis to the heralds of Agamemnon and prays to Thetis to win the support of Zeus. This is the key turning point in Book 1.

The Assembly. Achilles' Conflict with Agamemnon, 53-303

When the plague has lasted nine days, Hera inspires Achilles to call an assembly of the Achaeans, for she loves them especially and is determined for them to destroy Troy. No doubt the poet causes her to work through Achilles because he is to be the main character in the *Iliad*. Moreover, it was apparently the custom for the convoker of an assembly to speak first and, if he was not the commander-in-chief, to begin by addressing the commander-in-chief. We are thus being prepared for the conflict between Achilles and Agamemnon.

Achilles opens the assembly with the following speech:

> Son of Atreus, now I think we'll be driven away
> and forced to return home again, if indeed we escape death,
> if we aren't slain by this plague as well as our warring.
> But come and lets us inquire of some prophet or priest
> or some interpreter of dreams, for dreams are from Zeus,
> the reason for Phoebus Apollo's being so angry,
> whether he finds some fault with our prayers or our sacrifices,
> so that by means of the savor of lambs and of goats
> we may persuade him to drive this destruction away.   (59-67)

Achilles is concerned for the welfare of the army; we can imagine that this was his usual attitude before his wrath. It is noteworthy that he does not suggest that Apollo's wrath may be due to Agamemnon's dishonoring Chryses. Perhaps he is being diplomatic. Frequently, however, a person in Homer suggests several wrong answers to his question, with the result that when the right answer is given it is felt with special force.

Instead of Agamemnon, whom Achilles has addressed, the prophet Calchas, apparently taking his cue from Achilles' mention of a prophet, replies. He will explain the wrath of Apollo if Achilles will swear to protect him, for he fears the anger of one "who greatly rules over all the Argives and whom the Achaeans obey" (78-79), that is—as no one can help understanding—Agamemnon. Then Achilles, who now is certainly not being diplomatic, swears by Apollo to protect him even if "you mean Agamemnon" (90). And so Calchas says that Apollo "does not find fault because of some unfulfilled vow or some omitted sacrifice but because Agamemnon has dishonored the priest" (93-94), and that the god will continue to send the plague until they give Chryseis back to her father and send a propitiatory sacrifice to Chryse (the hometown of Chryses and Chryseis and the site of a shrine of Apollo). We have thus moved gradually but inevitably to Calchas' naming of Agamemnon as the responsible party.

Now Agamemnon, being deeply angered, speaks (106-20). He blames Calchas for always opposing him. Nevertheless, in order to save the army, he will give up the girl, but they must find him a replacement. It is interesting that Agamemnon ignores Achilles completely, addressing Calchas first, and then, in the final two lines of his speech, the men in general; and this in spite of the fact that Calchas, by gaining the protection of Achilles, spoke almost as his agent.

Agamemnon's speech is the beginning of a set of three altercations in which we see him and Achilles relentlessly move in a crescendo of anger to their fatal breach (so Schadewaldt 1938.144-45). Achilles replies (122-29) by blaming Agamemnon for greediness and asserting that the Achaeans will not be able to repay him for the loss of Chryseis until they have taken Troy.

Then Agamemnon (131-47) accuses Achilles of speaking with the mind of a thief in that he wants to keep his own prize, the girl Briseis, while ordering him to give up his; and he asserts that if a replacement is not found for Chryseis immediately, he will take someone else's girl, either Achilles' or Ajax's or Odysseus'. He thus openly threatens to dishonor Achilles. But this threat is perhaps somewhat lessened by the addition of the other two names, and also by the fact that Agamemnon suggests postponing the consideration of the matter until later. Now they must complete the business for which the assembly was called and propitiate the god by sending a ship with a sacrificial victim and Chryseis under the leadership of a man of good counsel (*aner boulephoros*, 144; used in Book 2 of Agamemnon) such as Odysseus or even Achilles.

Achilles replies (149-71), scowling with anger. He accuses Agamemnon of shamelessness and deceit, and points out that, though fighting Agamemnon's war, he has been doing much more to win it than Agamemnon while getting much less honor (booty like Briseis). Therefore this threat to deprive him of Briseis is intolerable and he will abandon the war and go home.

Agamemnon, answering sarcastically (173-187), commands Achilles to go home by all means and take his Myrmidons with him. He, Agamemnon, will attend to the propitiation of Apollo with the help of those who are faithful to him.

And in order that Achilles and all the other Achaeans may know who is the most superior among them he will deprive Achilles of Briseis.

This is the first speech in the third and final altercation. Achilles is filled with deep anguish (*achos*, 188) as, drawing his sword, he ponders whether to slay Agamemnon. At this point the poet emphasizes the momentousness of the situation by showing how Achilles is religiously motivated: Athena intervenes unexpectedly. She comes from Olympus, sent by Hera who wants to prevent both heroes from harm, and appears only to Achilles. Her intervention occurs between the time he begins to draw his sword (194) and the time when he thrusts it back into its sheath (219-20). Thus for twenty-five lines the scene in the assembly is held in suspense, but the whole episode is "kept severely in place, presumably so as not to detract from the dramatic force of the main argument between the two leaders" (Kirk 1985.75). Athena commands Achilles not to slay Agamemnon but to tell him that he will have to pay for his arrogance many times over. He answers:

> I must needs do, O goddess, what you two say,
> though angered greatly at heart, for thus it is better;
> the gods gladly listen to whoever obeys them.   (216-18)

Achilles is a pious young man who always obeys the gods, even when he finds this very hard to do.

As Athena returns to Olympus, he (225-44), in accordance with her instructions, curses Agamemnon, calling him a drunkard and coward, and predicts that the Achaeans, especially Agamemnon, will miss him when they see Hector slaying large numbers of Achaeans. He swears by the scepter he is holding, which in conclusion he hurls to the ground, that he will not help them.

Agamemnon rages opposite but remains seated. The poet underlines the finality of the breach between the two heroes by having Nestor, the wise old man, make an abortive attempt to reconcile them (254-84). Nestor says that much better men than those now fighting at Troy had listened to him in the past and therefore they should listen to him now. Later in the *Iliad* when he offers advice it is always heeded, but not here.

Agamemnon says that Achilles is trying to take charge as commander-in-chief. And Achilles says that though he will give him Briseis whom, with the consent of the assembly (he blames the whole army), he is taking from him, he had better not try to command him in anything else. Thus the assembly is dissolved. It has been successful in deciding to propitiate Apollo but has failed by giving rise to the wrath of Achilles.

Achilles Gives Up Briseis.   The Thetis-Achilles Scene and the Propitiation of Apollo, 304-492

Achilles returns to his hut with Patroclus (the son of Menoetius), who will have an important, though still silent, role in the coming scene between Achilles and Agamemnon's heralds; and Agamemnon initiates three actions: first, Odysseus is sent with twenty men in a ship to take Chryseis back to her father and to propitiate Apollo; second, the men in the camp are told to purify themselves and offer sacrifice to Apollo; and third, two heralds, Talthybius and Eurybates, are sent to bring Briseis from Achilles. We can imagine these actions as going on simultaneously. But the poet, after he has started the ship on its way, describes the purification of the Achaeans from the effects of the plague and their sacrifice to Apollo, before turning to the sending of the heralds to Achilles. Edwards 1987.182 rightly remarks that this purification would come better after Apollo had called off the plague. The poet, however, seems willing to accept this inconsistency in order to end the narrative with the climactic event of Apollo being propitiated on Chryse, which he will interweave with the Thetis-Achilles scene. Such interweaving of episodes often occurs at important turning points in the story.

When the heralds have arrived at Achilles' hut, he commands Patroclus to hand over Briseis to them, and calls upon them to be witnesses in the future of what they are doing if ever the Achaeans should need him to ward off destruction. Then, going off by himself to the seashore, he prays in tears to his mother, and she comes out of the sea. His tears show the grief that has given rise to his wrath. He addresses her in a long speech (365-412), the greater part of which (366-92) is a summary of events so far in the *Iliad,* many earlier lines being repeated.

Scholars since antiquity have wondered why there is such a summary so close to the beginning of the poem. It seems likely that it is meant to mark the turning point from the wrath of Apollo to that of Achilles. We can compare Thetis' summary to Hephaestus at 18.444-61 at another important turning point in the *Iliad,* and Odysseus' summary to Penelope in *Odyssey* 23.310-41 before the conclusion in the last book of that poem.

Achilles asks Thetis to obtain Zeus' support for his wrath by reminding him of how she had helped him in the past when the other gods led by Hera, Athena, and Poseidon had tried to overthrow him.

> Telling him these things sit before him and take hold of his knees
> to see if he may not be willing to aid the Trojans,
> that they may hem in the Achaeans by the sea at the ships' sterns
> and slay them, giving them all full joy of their king,
> and wide-ruling Agamemnon, the son of Atreus, may recognize
> his insanity in granting no honor to the best of Achaeans.   (407-12)

Thetis promises to do this, but not until an eleven-day interval has passed when Zeus and all the other gods, who yesterday went off to feast with the Aethiopians, return to Olympus; in the meantime Achilles should maintain his wrath and stay out of the fighting.

Thetis' words also have worried scholars since antiquity (for good comments on the problem see Kirk 1985.97). How can the poet speak of all the gods being away from Olympus at a time when we have seen Apollo, Hera, and Athena responding to the events at Troy? Moreover, there will be no battle during the time Thetis tells Achilles not to fight. The poet seems willing to tolerate these inconsistencies. Why is this so? One important reason, it seems likely, is that he wants to inform us to expect a delay in Thetis' meeting with Zeus in order that he may tell us, as he has earlier announced he will do, the episode of Apollo's being propitiated on Chryse. The sequence of events is as follows: Thetis leaves Achilles in his wrath over the loss of Briseis (429), then Apollo is propitiated on Chryse (430-487), after which we return to Achilles still sitting in wrath (499-92), and then are told that, eleven days having passed, Thetis goes on her mission to Zeus (493ff.). The description of the voyage to Chryse and back lasts through the present night until the morning of the next day and therefore (so Zielinski 1901.438) Thetis' meeting with Zeus cannot occur immediately after her scene with Achilles, for this would necessitate going back to an earlier point in the narrative contrary to epic usage.

Another advantage of this arrangement is that it impresses upon us the wrath of Achilles.

> But he raged on (*menie*) as idly he sat by the swift ships,
> Peleus' noble son, swift-footed Achilles:
> never did he go to the man-ennobling assembly
> nor ever to battle, but ate out his heart with inaction,
> staying behind, though yearning for war cry and battle.   (488-92)

This final picture of him in Book 1, which tells us how he will be until he decides to come back to battle in Book 18, is classified by Edwards 1980.23 as an "Absent But Much Concerned" scene. The lengthy description of the sea-journey to Chryse creates the illusion that he maintains his wrath for a long time. Zielinski 1901.440 (so also Nagler 1974.168) has compared the above picture of Achilles with that at 24.9-21 telling how he maintains his spirit of vengeance even against the dead body of Hector, day after day dragging it around the tomb of Patroclus, until, eleven days having passed (24.31), the gods in council decide that he must relent; iterative past tenses are used in both passages. It is difficult not to believe that the poet was conscious of drawing a parallel between the wrath and the vengeance.

The Thetis-Achilles scene is described by Edwards 1980.17 as "a skillful meshing of three type-scenes": prayer, divine visitation, and supplication. The poet has invented a lively, memorable narrative. Twice again in the *Iliad*, in Books 18 and 24, there will be similar scenes between Thetis and Achilles. By contrast, the narrative of the voyage to Chryse, which is "a cluster of standard type-scenes" (Edwards 1980.23), seems completely conventional. We are told in formulaic language of the ship's arrival at Chryse, the handing over of the girl, the sacrifice, the meal, and entertainment, retiring for the night, and the departure and return voyage. The high moment comes when Chryses prays to Apollo to avert the plague, thanking him for fulfilling his earlier prayer to send it. Chryses' present prayer is a palinode of his earlier one (451-52=37-38); and the favorable response he receives from Apollo is expressed in the same words: "So he prayed, and Phoebus Apollo heard him" (457=43). The propitiation of Apollo is very low key, as if to say that this part of the story is finished. The wrath of Apollo has given way to the wrath of Achilles.

Zeus' Ratification of Achilles' Wrath, 493-611

Immediately after the description of the wrathful Achilles in lines 488-92, we turn to Thetis' mission to Zeus. She has said that after eleven days Zeus and the other gods will return to Olympus, and so we might well expect her to find him in his palace with the other gods; in Book 24 she will be summoned before such a council of the gods. Instead, she finds him on the highest peak of Mount Olympus. But we easily adjust our expectations, realizing that Zeus is the god of mountain peaks, and especially of this mountain peak; and our disappointment will be only temporary, for in the next scene the poet will give us a charming picture of Zeus and the other gods gathered for their evening meal. That Zeus has his meeting with Thetis on a lonely mountain peak adds to the grandeur of his decision to back

Achilles' wrath. Moreover, this secret meeting will also be a reason for Hera to blame Zeus in the next scene and so introduces that friction between them which will be a hallmark of their relationship throughout the *Iliad*.

Thetis asks Zeus to honor Achilles by giving the Trojans the victory. At first he is silent, fearful that his wife may see them and make trouble for him at home. The picture is comical and awesome by turns, but it is the latter aspect that prevails when, ratifying the wrath of Achilles, he nods his head in agreement and causes Mount Olympus to shake.

When their meeting is finished, they go their separate ways, she back into the sea (we can assume she first reports her success to Achilles), he to his palace on Olympus where the gods are convened. Hera immediately blames him for making plans apart from her. He answers that she must not expect to know everything, but promises to tell her first whatever he wishes to divulge. This is a programmatic statement about programmatic statements (so Willcock 1976.167), for later in the *Iliad*, at the end of Book 8 and the beginning of Book 15, he will predict the future to her.

This last episode in Book 1 echoes some of its earlier themes in a light-hearted Olympian tone. The uneventful altercation between Zeus and Hera reminds us of the tragic break between Agamemnon and Achilles. The role of reconciler played there unsuccessfully by Nestor is here played successfully by Hephaestus who causes the gods to laugh with relief. They enjoy their evening meal, after which the Muses sing to the accompaniment of Apollo on his lyre, and then to bed. We are reminded of the voyage to Chryse where the propitiation of Apollo was followed by feasting and retiring for the night. The parallels with these earlier human scenes underline the difference between the carefree, immortal gods and poor human beings.

BOOK 2: THE ACHAEANS DECIDE TO CONTINUE THE WAR

Agamemnon's Dream, 1-47

A Homeric hero was brought up to be a speaker of words and a doer of deeds, and as such was a model for later young men, as Plutarch suggested in *How a Young Man Should Listen to Poems*. (See Introduction, pp. 14-16.) The deeds were primarily those of warfare, the words those spoken in the council of leaders or in the assembly of the people or army. It is the speaker of words or the man of good counsel that is emphasized in the present book, as Neschke 1985 has pointed out. (On the importance of good counsel in the *Iliad* in general see Schofield 1986.) Agamemnon will first tell the council a plan for inspiring the men to battle and then in the assembly try to implement it. Our attention will be focused on Agamemnon as the commander-in-chief of the Achaeans and on his abilities as an organizer and inspirer of his troops. Homer thinks of a great king like Agamemnon as having his power from Zeus, the king of the gods who is able to carry out his plans and is not to be outsmarted.

In order to maintain the morale and backing of his followers a leader must be inspired himself. Accordingly, Zeus, who, while all other gods and men are asleep (1-2), is pondering how he will have the Achaeans continue the war so that he can honor Achilles, inspires Agamemnon by sending him a deceptive dream. The Dream (in the form of the wise old counselor Nestor) tells Agamemnon that now the Achaeans may take Troy, which is false, and that therefore he (in his role as "counselor," *boulephoron andra,* 24) should quickly arm them for battle. Arming entails marshaling the men and exhorting them to battle. The Achaeans are no doubt in need of exhortation, for they are discouraged by their long campaign against Troy and by the plague and Achilles' withdrawal.

> Thus having spoken the Dream departed and left him there
> believing things in his heart which were not to occur,
> for he was thinking that he would take Troy on that day,
> poor fool (*nepios*), who knew not the works that Zeus was devising,
> the pains and groanings that he was still to put
> on Trojans and Danaans struggling in conflicts of battle.   (35-40)

Thus the poet puts us on notice that Agamemnon will not lead the Achaeans to victory now and that, as Kirk 1985.118 notes, the Trojans will not be immediately victorious either.

When Agamemnon awakes, he dresses as befits a counselor, in chiton, cloak, and sandals, and takes his sword and ancestral scepter, the symbol of his kingly right to decide what is best. That he takes a sword is no indication that he is arming for battle, for leaders wore swords as a part of their regular dress; Achilles had his in the assembly in Book 1.

The Council at Nestor's Ship, 48-83

Agamemnon commands heralds to summon the men to assembly while he holds a meeting of the council at Nestor's ship. Devising "a closely thought-out plan" (*pukinen boulen,* 55), he repeats the message of the Dream verbatim (this is the third time we hear it) and then tells the leaders what they must do.

> But come and let us somehow arm the Achaeans.
> I shall test them with words—a customary procedure—
> and give a command to flee in the many-benched ships,
> but you on this side and that restrain me with words.   (72-75)

I take "me" instead of "those fleeing" as object of "restrain"; so schol. bT and Ameis-Hentze against Leaf and Kirk.) Nestor applauds Agamemnon's speech, and repeats the exhortation, "But come and let us somehow arm the Achaeans" (83=72), that is, marshal and exhort them to battle.

Agamemnon's proposal to test the men seems perverse, and the words "a customary procedure" (73) are usually interpreted as an attempt to excuse it. But, as schol. bT and Neschke say, Agamemnon is offering a well thought-out plan. He aims to rouse the spirits of the men by showing his own discouragement, expecting one of the leaders now in the council to speak out against him convincingly. Thus everyone will be inspired to continue the war. We can compare how later in Book 9, when Agamemnon again proposes going home, Diomedes successfully opposes him, saying that this is "a customary procedure." (Another comparable incident is found in Xenophon *Anabasis* 1.3 where Clearchus tests his troops in a similar way.)

The council, which takes place while the heralds are calling the men to assembly, enables us to know what Agamemnon is going to say there and how his fellow counselors are suppposed to react. What we are not told is what Agamemnon does not foresee, that the men will rush for the ships before anyone has a chance to oppose him.

The Assembly, 84-397

The men come to the assembly driven by the spirit of Rumor. Do they hope for an announcement that they are going home? When nine heralds have brought them to order, Agamemnon rises, leaning on his scepter, the importance of which is emphasized—it was made by Hephaestus and came from Zeus through Hermes to Agamemnon's grandfather Pelops—as a symbol of his sovereignty over many islands and all Argos. Agamemnon begins by blaming Zeus.

> Great Zeus, the son of Cronus, bound me with heavy folly (*ate*),
> a cruel god, who promised and nodded his head in agreement
> that I would return home after sacking well-walled Troy,
> but now he has planned an evil deception and commands me
> to return to Argos in ill fame after losing much of my army.
> So this, it seems, is what almighty Zeus had in mind,
> who has already destroyed the fortified tops of many a city
> and still will destroy more, for his is the mightiest sovereignty.   (111-18)

(Later, in Book 19, Agamemnon will blame the power of Ate, that is, Folly, for causing his break with Achilles.) He ends with an exhortation to the men.

> But come and let us all agree to do as I say:
> let us flee in our ships to our dear native land,
> for we shall no longer take wide-wayed Troy.   (139-41)

In Book 9 Agamemnon will make a speech consisting only of these lines: 9.18-28=2.111-18 and 139-41.

His present speech, however, is expanded by a central section (119-38) in which he weighs the reasons for giving up the war. It will be shameful to go home without victory since they far outnumber the Trojans, but the many Trojan allies have kept them from their goal, and their ships are rotting, and their wives and children are waiting for them at home. His words seem calculated to evoke refutation for a number of reasons. First, his complaint against Zeus is premature, as Odysseus will later point out, for Troy is not destined to fall until the tenth year of the war, which time has just arrived. Moreover, the Achaeans outnumber the Trojans and their allies together. And the voyage to Chryse in Book 1 is proof that the ships are still seaworthy. Also, it seems likely that Agamemnon has misjudged his audience in mentioning their loved ones back home, on the assumption that most of them like himself would prefer Trojan captives to their own wives. In any event his speech fails of its purpose.

The assembly consisted of the common foot soldiers and the leaders, including those of Agamemnon's inner circle who had attended the council. Now "everyone in the multitude (*plethus*) who had not attended the council" (143) rushes for the ships. Aristarchus objected to the relative clause here as redundant, for he took *plethus* to mean "commoners" and no commoner took part in the council. But *plethus* can include the leaders (cf. 9.641). So interpreted, we are being told to distinguish in the following scene between two groups of leaders, those not in the council who rush for the ships and those in the council who stay behind in the assembly. The poet is preparing us for the speech of Odysseus to the leaders who run for the ships.

Now Athena intervenes at the behest of Hera who tells her to stop the flight "with gentle words" (164), an expression used of wise kings settling disputes; compare Hesiod, *Theogony* 80-90). She comes to Odysseus (who was a member of the council; cf. 405ff.) and tells him to restrain the men "with gentle words" (180). He is immediately obedient and receives the scepter from Agamemnon, as a symbol that he is acting for him.

Odysseus speaks "with gentle words" (189) to the leaders, reminding them that Agamemnon is their commander whose right to plan their affairs is upheld by Zeus. The following part of his speech has given difficulty.

> You don't know clearly yet what the son of Atreus thinks.
> Now he is testing, soon he will smite the sons of the Achaeans.
> We did not all hear how he spoke in the council.   (192-94)

Many scholars would read line 194 as a question—"Did we not all hear how he spoke in the council?"—which they explain (so Monro quoted with approval by Leaf) by understanding that Odysseus, although he knows that the leaders he is so addressing were not in the council, pretends that they were for rhetorical effect: "But why need I tell you this? Did we not all—we of the council—hear what he said?" This seems overly ingenious, even granting Odysseus' devious personality, and I prefer (with Von der Mühll 1952.41) to take line 194 as a statement that the leaders addressed were not in the council; thus they know, as Odysseus says in line 192, that they are ignorant of Agamemnon's purpose. Either interpretation is only valid if the poet is distinguishing those leaders not in the council from those who were, as we have suggested he did in line 143 at the beginning of the rush for the ships.

Odysseus' speech to the commoners is, by contrast, strongly abusive, and he uses the scepter to drive them back to the assembly. They are of no account in battle or in giving counsel. "The rule of many is no good; one ruler is best, one king to whom Zeus, the son of devious-thinking Cronus, has given the scepter and laws to rule over them." (203-6). In both speeches Odysseus emphasizes the kingship of Agamemnon.

The men return to the assembly, and all take their seats except Thersites, an ugly commoner, who speaks abusively against Agamemnon. "Thersites' arguments are like a parody of those of Achilles in Book 1" (Willcock 1976.20). How will Agamemnon or, as it turns out, Odysseus and Nestor, answer them? Odysseus and Nestor are the chief men of good counsel on the Achaean side in the *Iliad*. Odysseus rebukes Thersites and hits him on the back and shoulders with the scepter, forcing him to sit down in tears. The men laugh in spite of being grieved (*achnumenoi*, 270), realizing that they have been rightly rebuked (so Collins 1987), and say that this is Odysseus' greatest deed as a giver of good counsels (*boulas agathas*, 273) or as a fighter.

Then, as Athena in the form of a herald calls for silence, Odysseus speaks, the scepter still in his hand. He begins by telling Agamemnon that the men are being untrue to their promise not to go home until they have sacked Troy; they are acting like children and widows. Then he asks the soldiers to endure for the little time it will take to see whether Calchas spoke truthfully when at the beginning of the war he predicted the fall of Troy in this, the tenth year. Thus he answers Agamemnon's first reason, given in lines 111-18, for returning home. His speech is greeted with loud applause; and it seems likely that the assembly would have turned out as Agamemnon had wished if only he had spoken earlier.

Then Nestor, endorsing Odysseus' words, blames the men for acting like children and breaking their promises, and tells Agamemnon to continue to guide them with his counsel and let those go to perdition who want to go home before knowing whether Zeus' promise, confirmed by lightning on the right when they set out for Troy, is true. Finally, Nestor suggests that Agamemnon should see to the marshaling of the army in such a way that it will be evident which of the leaders and which of the commoners is shirking. Thus they will know whether their failure to take the city is due to the will of the gods or to their own cowardice and lack of fighting skill. Nestor gives detailed advice (362-68) on how to marshal the men, which will be put into effect as described in the Achaean Catalogue.

Agamemnon praises Nestor as the best speaker among the Achaeans; if only he had ten such counselors Troy would soon fall. But Zeus has given him woes, for he and Achilles have fought over a girl, and he was the first to be angry. If only he and Achilles should agree in counsel (*es ge mian bouleusomen*, 379), evil would soon befall the Trojans. He ends by commanding the men to eat a meal and make ready their horses and equipment for battle, threatening death to anyone he catches staying behind at the ships. In other words, they should get ready to be marshaled as Nestor advised. Agamemnon's reputation as commander-in-chief has survived the assembly, but one has the feeling that without Odysseus and Nestor it would hardly have done so.

The men shout their approval. The noise they make is compared (394-97) to that of waves pounding a headland. This is the last in a series of dispersed similes describing the men in general (so Moulton 1977.38-42). On first coming into the assembly they were like a swarm of bees (87-93); after Agamemnon's first speech they rushed to the ships like waves rolling over the sea and wind blowing over a grainfield (144-49); and in response to Odysseus' rebuke they returned to the assembly roaring like the surf beating upon the beach (207-10). We are impressed by their volatility, their need of a commander-in-chief, a man of good counsel.

Neschke has applied the motifs of the *aristeia,* primarily used of the hero in battle, to Agamemnon in his role as counselor in Book 2. At the beginning of his *aristeia* the hero is usually inspired by a divinity with fighting spirit. So Agamemnon is inspired by the Dream to take charge as the counselor of the Achaeans. Then the hero dresses for battle. So Agamemnon dresses for a meeting of the assembly, taking his scepter. Finally, after some preliminary success, the hero meets with an unexpected reverse, and it takes the intervention of a divinity to reestablish him in his course of victory. So Agamemnon, after his preliminary success in persuading the council to agree to a testing of the men, is faced in the assembly with what amounts to a mutiny of those not at the council, and it is only through the intervention of Athena that the day is saved.

The Council in Agamemnon's Hut, 394-440

The assembly is dissolved. The men then sacrifice and pray to escape death. Contrasted with this pessimistic prayer (as schol. bT note) is Agamemnon's optimistic one. When he has called to his hut the leaders of the council—Nestor, Idomeneus, the two Ajaxes, Diomedes, and Odysseus; Menelaus comes on his own (405ff.)—he sacrifices for their meal an ox to Zeus with a prayer for victory.

> Most glorious and great Zeus, black-clouded, dwelling on high,
> grant that the sun not set and the evening come on
> before I have made of the palace of Priam a smouldering
> ruin and destroyed the gates of the enemy with fire
> and torn the chiton of Hector around his chest,
> ripping it trough with my bronze sword, and may his companions
> lying around him take the dirt in their teeth.   (412-18)

This prayer shows that Agamemnon is still inspired with the false hope given him by the Dream. He is destined to be disappointed, as the poet immediately informs us.

> Thus he spoke, but Zeus was not yet fulfilling this,
> but took his sacrifices while increasing his ceaseless labor.   (419-20)

This comment, like that after the Dream departed, sets the record straight. Zeus is "not yet" going to fulfill the prayer of Agamemnon (or his promise to Thetis); instead, he is going to stir up battle for the Achaeans and Trojans. Leaf I.81 rightly remarks that by receiving the sacrifice while at the same time rejecting the prayer Zeus "is deliberately deceiving Agamemnon"; he is reinforcing his earlier deception through the Dream.

After the sacrifice and prayer, and after the leaders have had a hearty meal, Nestor urges them to delay no longer: Agamemnon should order heralds to gather the army, and they, the leaders, should quickly rouse in the men the spirit of warfare. This Agamemnon does, and the leaders set about exhorting the men, marshaling them in their contingents.

Catalogue of Achaean Contingents, 441-785

Athena helps in the marshaling by going among the men with the aegis and inspiring them with fighting spirit, thus continuing her role as promoter of the Achaean offensive which she has had in this book since her intervention to prevent them from returning home.

> And strength she put into them,
> into each heart, to war and fight without ceasing.
> And immediately war became sweeter to them than
> to return in their hollow ships to their dear native land.   (451-54)

This assurance to the audience seems especially important after the testing of the troops. Now the Achaeans no longer want to go home.

The poet calls upon the Muses to help him in the difficult task of listing the forces. This is the longest catalogue in the *Iliad,* but we are given no scheme to follow it (as we are for the Shield; see Introduction, p. 6). On analysis, however, it is clear that the poet has proceeded as follows: first the cities of Boeotia are listed in a circle clockwise; then those of the Peloponnese are listed in the same way; then the islands and mainland of northwest Greece; then the islands of Crete and those northward along the southern coast of Asia Minor; finally, the cities of Thessaly, taken for the most part counterclockwise (see Kirk 1985.183-84). We have in this geographical survey of the Greek world the earliest expression of the Panhellenic spirit and a strong indication that the *Iliad* was composed for a general, not a local, Greek audience.

Since the Achaean Catalogue gives the number of ships brought by each contingent, it is probably based on an earlier list describing the armada that set sail for Troy at the beginning of the war. But it has been adapted to its present position in the *Iliad,* for in in several places (543-44, 553-55, 577-80, 588-90) we are made aware that the leaders are marshaling their men, and the entry on Achilles and his Myrmidons show them acting in accordance with his wrath.

> Now for all those who dwelled in Pelasgian Argos,
> those who lived in Alos or Alope or Thrachis,
> those who held Phthia and Hellas of the beautiful women
> and went by the name of Myrmidons, Hellenes, Achaeans,
> their fifty ships were under Achilles' command.
> But they were not thinking of grievous war,
> for no one was there to lead them against the enemy.
> Swift-footed, noble Achilles sat at the ships
> angered (*choomenos*) over a girl, the lovely Briseis,
> whom he had taken from Lyrnessos after much fighting,
> after sacking Lyrnessos and the walls of Thebe
> and defeating the spearmen Mynes and Epistrophos,
> the sons of king Euenos, son of Selepos.
> He sat grieving (*acheon*), but soon he was going to rise up.   (681-94)

The poet intends "to emphasize still further Achilles' withdrawal from active participation on behalf of the Achaeans, and to remind the audience yet again (after all the detail about other contingents which must, to an extent at least, have been distracting) of the great quarrel that is to determine future events" (Kirk 1985.229). The picture of Achilles here reminds us of that at 1.488-92 when we last saw him. We will not see him again until Book 9. The Myrmidons will not return to battle until Book 16 when Patroclus leads them out; Achilles himself will not rise up until Book 18. He will continue to sit beside his ships, that is, remain idle, out of the action, nursing his grief and wrath.

The Achaean Catalogue ends by informing us that the best horses are the mares of Eumelus—they will lose the chariot race at 23.375-76 through no fault of their own—and that the best hero will be the big Ajax, the great defensive fighter, as long as Achilles maintains his wrath (*ophra' Achileus menien,* 769). Notice how the poet thinks of the wrath as ending when Achilles reenters the fighting.

The Achaean Catalogue is both introduced and concluded by a series of similes. The earlier series (455-83) describes the men being marshaled and advancing to battle: the gleam of their armor is like the brightness of a forest fire; their advance onto the plain like the landing of flocks of noisy birds in a meadow (simile type 2); and Agamemnon is compared to Zeus, Ares, and Poseidon, and to a bull who stands out among the rest of the herd, for Zeus is giving him glory. The later series (780-85; a pair of type 2 similes) again describes the advance of the Achaeans: it is as if the whole earth were possessed by fire; the noise made by the earth under their feet is like that of Typhoeus (Typhon) being struck by the thunderbolts of Zeus. We should think of the roaring of a volcano, to which the myth of Typhoeus alludes. The only other mythological simile in the *Iliad*, that of the cranes migrating south to fight the pygmies, will occur at the beginning of the next book, after the Trojan Catalogue and thus in a parallel position, to describe the advance of the Trojans.

Catalogue of the Trojan Contingents, 786-877

At the end of the Achaean Catalogue the Achaeans are advancing and we therefore expect an imminent clash of the two armies, but first the Trojans must marshal their forces. We thus have two simultaneous actions described as if they happened consecutively (Zielinski's law; see Introduction, pp. 6-7). The poet lessens our sense of incongruity by emphasizing the swiftness of the Trojan reaction (so Krischer 1971.113). Iris, sent by Zeus, comes on her swift wings in the form of a Trojan lookout and tells the Trojans assembled at the palace of Priam to marshal their men and allies immediately, each in his individual language group.

Hector is swift to obey. Book 2 ends with a list of the Trojan forces, which is much shorter than the Achaean one.

Both catalogues have been much studied for any light they might shed on early Greece and the poetry behind the *Iliad*. The important thing for us is the fact that the poet uses them to describe the beginning of the first day of battle in the poem. We are given a survey of the two armies and the dramatis personae in preparation for the coming drama. Moreover, these long lists have a slowing effect suitable to the beginning of the action. The *Iliad* begins very slowly.

BOOK 3: THE DUEL BETWEEN PARIS AND MENELAUS

An Unexpected Truce, 1-120

Two similes (type 2) synchronize the descriptions of the advancing armies. The cacophonous noise of the advancing Trojans (they speak different languages) is compared to that of cranes flying south to war against the pygmies, whereas the Achaeans advance silently; the dust raised by the feet of both armies is like a mist in the mountains, "so very swiftly they crossed the plain" (14; the same words were used at 2.785 to conclude the Typhoeus simile describing only the advancing Achaeans).

Battle is joined (cf. 3.132-33), but our attention is concentrated on Paris who challenges any of the enemy to single combat. He is wearing a leopard-skin and has a bow, a sword, and two spears; being an archer he needs no armor (so Edwards 1987.72). Menelaus sees him with the joy of a hungry lion finding a recently slain deer or goat; he wants to take vengeance on him for carrying off Helen. But Paris jumps back into the safety of the Trojan lines like a man suddenly seeing a snake (simile type 8: retreat). This abortive encounter, in which Menelaus appears as the better man whose cause is just, foreshadows their abortive duel.

Hector rebukes Paris, saying that though he is the handsomest of men he is a deceiver who should never have been born, a plague to the Trojans for having gone overseas and abducted the wife of another, whom now he is afraid to fight.

> You wouldn't withstand Menelaus dear to the war-god
> and learn what he's like whose beautiful wife you have.
> Of no help your lyre then and Aphrodite's gifts,
> your hair and good looks, when you'd be mated with dust.
> As for the Trojans they are terrible cowards
> for not having stoned you to death for all your crimes.   (52-57)

Hector does not foresee that Aprhodite will come to Paris' rescue when at the end of the duel he is mingling in the dust.

Paris answers that there should be a truce and that he and Menelaus should fight for Helen and her possessions. This will end the war, for they should swear to abide by the decision of the duel.

> The man who is victor, he who comes off the winner,
> shall rightly carry off Helen and all her property.
> The rest shall abide by the terms to which they have sworn:

Trojans shall dwell in rich Troyland, Achaeans return
to horse-breeding Argos and Achaea of the beautiful women.   (73-75)

These are the conditions of the treaty, which we know cannot be kept since the war must continue.

Then Hector (76-78) goes out between the two armies and, holding a spear by the middle (apparently to show that he wants a truce), has the Trojans sit down. Agamemnon in response has the Achaeans stop shooting and listen. Hector repeats Paris' proposal. Menelaus accepts it, and specifies what both sides need to bring for the swearing ceremony.

Bring two lambs, one white and the other black,
for Gaea and Helios; we'll being a third for Zeus.
And summon great Priam to cut the oaths himself;
I fear that his sons, for they are arrogant and faithless,
might transgress and destroy the oaths of Zeus.
Always the minds of younger men are fluttering,
but when an old man, who looks to the past and the future,
is present, it turns out best for both parties concerned.   (103-10)

As Edwards 1987.191 remarks, Menelaus' demand that Priam participate stresses the importance of the oath-sacrifice, in preparation for its later violation; and it also readies us for his appearance in the following episode with Helen, the Viewing, in which he will play a more prominent role than in the oath-sacrifice.

Both sides respond to Menelaus' speech by gladly taking off their armor. And Hector sends two heralds to Troy to bring the lambs and summon Priam; Agamemnon sends a herald to the Achaean camp to bring a lamb. The preparations for the duel are under way

The Viewing from the Walls, 121-244

But now Homer introduces the episode of the Viewing (which takes place while the heralds are coming to Troy) by having Iris summon Helen to the walls to see the duel. The summoning motif is used in this book to change scenes: first the summoning of Helen by Iris to introduce the Viewing; then the summoning of Priam onto the battlefield by Idaeus to introduce the oath-sacrifice and duel; and finally the summoning of Helen to Paris' bedroom by Aphrodite.

Iris takes the form of Laodice, one of Helen's friends, a daughter of Priam and daughter-in-law of the Trojan counselor Antenor. She finds Helen with her

women in Paris' palace weaving pictures of the present conflict which she has
caused. Helen's self-reproach will be the keynote of her character. Iris says:

> Come along, dear bride, that you may see the wonderful works
> of the horse-taming Trojans and the bronze-chitoned Achaeans.
> Earlier they were joining together in much-tearful warfare,
> being full of desire for baneful battle,
> but now they are sitting in silence—the battle has ceased—
> resting on their shields, their long spears grounded beside them.
> Now Paris and Menelaus dear to the war-god
> contending with long spears will fight a duel over you,
> and you'll be called the dear wife of him who is victor.   (130-38)

Helen is filled with desire for her husband, homeland, and parents. She goes to the
walls veiled and attended by two of her women, feeling homesick.

There she finds Priam with Antenor and other elderly Trojan counselors, who
remark on how understandable it is that a war should be fought for so beautiful a
woman, but even so would have her go home and leave them in peace. Then Priam
asks her to identify the Achaean leaders as if he were seeing them for the first time,
at the beginning of hostilities. This on a realistic level is hard to believe, but Homer
frequently brings earlier events into his story, such as, it seems likely, the duel
between Menelaus and Paris to end the fighting; this seems better suited to the first
year of the war than the last. Later material, like the death of Achilles and the fall of
Troy, is used in a similar way.

Helen first identifies Agamemnon: "a good king (a man of good counsel, as
he has shown himself to be in Book 2) and a mighty spearman," and the brother-in-
law of her shameful self. The men she mentions are all in some way connected
with herself. Then, when she has named Odysseus, Antenor remarks that before
the war Odysseus and Menelaus had come to Troy on a mission concerning her (to
obtain her release by peaceful means), and he praises these envoys, but especially
Odysseus, for their abilities as public speakers. (Edwards 1987.193 suggests that
Antenor's comment "prepares the way for the choice of Odysseus as an envoy in
Book 9.") Then Helen identifies Ajax, whom she connects with herself by adding
that Idomeneus, who is standing nearby, had often been entertained by Menelaus in
their home. Finally she asks why her brothers Castor and Polydeuces are not to be
seen—a question which draws from the poet the comment:

Thus she spoke, but the life-giving earth was covering them
back in Lacedaemon, there in their dear native land.   (243-44)

Thus the Viewing ends on a note of tragic irony in sympathy with the self-reproachful and nostalgic Helen.

How can we explain the unexpected introduction of the Viewing? Edwards 1987.191 compares other scenes of "summoning of a woman by a goddess in a sexual context": Athena calling Nausicaa in *Odyssey* 6.13ff., Athena calling Penelope in *Odyssey* 18.187ff., and Aphrodite calling Helen later in the present book. Kakridis 1971.31-39 points to similarities with the common story of two men fighting to decide who shall marry a woman: the woman is often present to watch the duel. So in Sophocles, *Women of Trachis* 497ff. (See Thompson 1955-58. H.331: "Suitor contests: bride offered as prize.") But in other examples of this motif the woman appears in order that the duelists may see her as the prize for which they are fighting, whereas in Homer, as Kakridis notes, this is not so. Moreover, in the Viewing nothing at all is said about the duel; our attention is concentrated on the personality of Helen.

The chief reason for the Viewing is to put before us the characters involved, Priam, the Achaean heroes whom Helen identifies, and especially Helen herself. We have just been introduced to Menelaus and Paris and told that they are going to fight a duel for her. Thus the poet has made us want to see her. Moreover, the Viewing is necessary to the later scene in which Helen will ridicule Paris for having been defeated by her husband.

The Oath-Sacrifice and Duel, 245-382

In lines 245-48 we find the Trojan heralds in Troy with the lambs for the sacrifice and also some wine; and the herald Idaeus with a mixing-bowl and cups has joined them. This passage thus creates with the earlier one describing the sending of the heralds a ring composition around the Viewing, and at the same time introduces the episode of the oath-sacrifice and duel. Idaeus, like Iris earlier, is an unexpected addition and, as Iris summoned Helen, so he summons Priam to swear the oaths in preparation for the duel. This parallelism is further emphasized by the fact that lines 251 and 253 of his speech are identical with lines 131 and 136 of her speech, and lines 254-55 of his speech are very similar to lines 137-38 of hers.

His announcement of the duel is clearly news to Priam (Helen has said nothing about it), for Priam shudders in response, apparently fearing that Paris will be killed. But he commands his chariot to be readied, and he and Antenor ride

through the Scaean Gate onto the plain. These lines (259-63) create a transition to
the oath-sacrifice.

The poet gives almost as much space to the oath-sacrifice as he does to the
duel. Agamemnon, who makes the sacrifice, prays to Zeus as follows:

> Zeus Father, ruling from Ida, most glorious and greatest,
> and Helios who sees all things and hears all things,
> and Rivers and Gaea and those down below who punish
> men who have died if any have perjured themselves,
> you be our witnesses and keep our oaths faithful.
> If Paris should slay Menelaus and come off the winner,
> let him have Helen and let him have all her possessions,
> and we shall return to our homes in our seafaring ships.
> But should blond Menelaus slay Paris and win,
> the Trojans must give back Helen and all her possessions.
> And they must pay to the Argives adequate recompense
> such that men of the future will ever remember.
> If Priam and the sons of Priam refuse
> to grant me this due when Paris has fallen defeated,
> I shall remain here and shall continue to fight
> for requital until I have brought this war to an end.   (276-91)

This is the first we have heard of the Trojans' having to pay adequate recompense
in addition to returning Helen and her property. Then a libation is poured and the
participants say:

> Most glorious and greatest Zeus and you other immortals,
> may that side which is first to break these oaths
> have, like this wine, their and their children's brains
> poured on the earth, and their wives subjected to others.   (298-301)

This is what is going to happen to the Trojans after the fall of Troy, but not
immediately, as the poet emphasizes:

> Thus they spoke, but Zeus was not yet fulfilling this.   (302)

We should compare the "not yet" comment at 2.419. The fall of Troy is going to
be delayed because of Zeus' promise to Thetis.

At the conclusion of the ceremonies Priam says that he cannot bear to watch Paris fight, and so he and Antenor return to Troy. These lines, 303-313, create a ring composition around the oath-sacrifice with lines 259-63 describing the coming of Priam and Antenor.

Then Hector and Odysseus measure off the ground for the duel, and Hector shakes lots to see which man will have the first throw. As this is being done, both sides pray to Zeus that the one who has caused the war will die. This certainly means Paris; but the lots give Paris the right of first throw and so an advantage. Then the two men arm themselves, Paris, taking the breastplate of his brother Lycaon. He usually, as we have seen, fights as an archer and so does not have armor of his own. Is it not likely that thus he will be less adept than Menelaus at hand-to-hand fighting? As the duel proceeds, however, Paris is always, providentially it seems (as in his winning of the right to throw first), escaping from the naturally superior Menelaus. He cannot be slain now, for the tradition put his death much later.

Paris' throw hits the shield of Menelaus without penetrating it. Then Menelaus, praying for vengeance to Zeus (as the protector of guest-friendship which Paris violated in abducting Helen), pierces the shield and even the chiton of Paris, but, almost miraculously, misses Paris himself. Then Menelaus tries his sword, but this shatters on Paris' helmet; Menelaus blames Zeus, calling him the most baneful of gods. Then he seizes Paris' helmet to drag him toward the Achaean army, but Aphrodite intervenes and, causing the helmet-strap to break, carries Paris off to his bedroom in a cloud of invisibility. Menelaus hurls the helmet among the Achaeans and lunges among the Trojans in a vain search for his opponent.

Gods several times rescue their favorites in the *Iliad*. For instance, at 5.311-12 Aphrodite will rescue Aeneas when he is about to be slain by Diomedes. So here (373-74) we are told: "And now Menelaus would have dragged him off and won unspeakable glory, if the daughter of Zeus, Aphrodite, had not taken quick notice." The poet has constructed the duel to end in the climax of a divine rescue.

Helen and Paris at Home While Menelaus Searches for Paris on the Battlefield, 383-461

The motif of the divine rescue makes a nice transition to the immediately following motif of the divine summons, Aphrodite being the divinity involved in both. Now she calls Helen back to the palace, to Paris' bedroom. Appearing to her

in the form of an old serving woman, a worker in wool who had come with her
from Lacedaemon, she says:

> Come along, Paris is calling you to return to the house.
> He is in the bedroom sitting on the beautiful bed,
> radiant in handsomeness and clothing. You wouldn't think
> he had come from fighting a man but that he was off
> to a dance or had just sat down having come from a dance.   (390-94)

Aphrodite's speech begins with the same two words as Iris' earlier speech to
Helen, "Come along," but the similarities between the scenes consist more in their
overall forms. Kirk 1985.321 speaks of "a repetition of the divine-summons
motif." Both divinities come in human disguises, Iris as Laodice, the daughter of
Priam and daughter-in-law of Antenor, Aphrodite as an old serving maid. In each
case the disguise is especially suited to the circumstances. Laodice is a young
married woman like Helen, and her father and father-in-law are Helen's
interlocutors in the Viewing. Here Aphrodite's disguise as an old woman suits that
of a go-between in a love affair, like the nurse in *Romeo and Juliet*.

Helen sees through Aphrodite's disguise and rebukes her insultingly. Now,
she says, Aphrodite wants to make her someone else's wife since Menelaus has
defeated Paris and will take her home. Thus she assumes that Menelaus has won
the duel. But Aphrodite forces her to go to Paris.

Helen treats Paris with scorn, telling him she wishes Menelaus had killed him
and urging him to challenge Menelaus to another duel. He claims that Menelaus
won with the aid of Athena, and that he will defeat Menelaus in the future, for he
has gods who favor him. But now he leads her to bed, saying that he finds her
more attractive than when they first made love (nine years ago after he had abducted
her). As Edwards 1987.196 notes, we have here "a reenactment of the original
seduction"—another example of how Homer adapts to the *Iliad* material from earlier
in the story of the Trojan War

This scene in the bedroom is in breach of the treaty and impresses upon us
that Paris has no intention of fulfilling it.

> And so these two lay in the beautiful bed,
> but Menelaus was going through the throng like a wild beast
> searching to find the divinely handsome Paris.   (448-50)

The juxtaposition of the two scenes seems laughable. Book 3 ends with the Trojans showing their hatred of Paris and with Agamemnon claiming victory for Menelaus to the applause of the Achaeans. None of the Trojans and none of their allies would have hidden Paris, so hated was he by all. Agamemnon demands that the Trojans return Helen and her possessions and pay the adequate recompense as required by the oath-sacrifice.

Many scholars think that Paris cannot be considered a loser in terms of the oath-sacrifice, for the slaying of the loser is stipulated by Agamemnon as a condition at 281-84 (so Kirk 1985.330). But on both sides, and by Zeus at the beginning of the next book, it is assumed that Paris has lost; and the Trojans never claim the inconclusiveness of the duel as a reason for invalidating the terms of the oath-sacrifice. Whenever the question arises (cf. 4.13, 7.49-52), it is always assumed that Paris was defeated by Menelaus and that therefore the Trojans should return Helen and her possessions and pay the indemnity. The war should now be over.

BOOK 4: THE TREACHERY OF PANDARUS

Zeus Restarts the War, 1-84

We switch somewhat abruptly to the gods on Olympus. It is as if the poet had said that the war would have been over if a god had not intervened. The gods are drinking, toasting each other as they look down at Troy, and Zeus teasingly chides Hera and Athena for not having helped Menelaus. He goes on to say:

> The victory belongs to Menelaus dear to the war-god.
> So let us consider what will result of these deeds,
> whether we shall stir up harsh war and dire battle again
> or make a peace of friendship between the two sides.
> If the latter course is dear and agreeable to all,
> King Priam's city may continue to be inhabited
> and Menelaus may carry home Argive Helen.   (13-19)

Hera answers that Zeus is completely disregarding all her trouble in assembling the Achaeans. Whereupon, though much against his will, he grants her permission to destroy Troy. Then she, having promised that he may destroy her three favorite cities in return, suggests that he send Athena to cause the Trojans to break the truce. Zeus agrees. We are reminded of how Hera sent Athena in Books 1 and 2 to prevent the Achaeans from going home.

Athena comes from Olympus like a shooting star—a portent to the men on both sides who say:

> Either there shall be harsh war and dire battle again
> or a peace of friendship is being made between the two sides,
> whichever Zeus, the steward of war, decrees.   (82-84)

These words—the first two lines echo lines 15-16 of Zeus' speech—bring to an end this first scene, which is important programmatically, for it motivates the breaking of the truce and reaffirms the eventual fall of Troy.

Zeus, as the steward of war (84), usually presides over the beginning of a day's battle. Thus at councils of the gods at the beginnings of the second and fourth days of battle (in Books 8 and 19) he will give programmatic views of coming events, and will start the third day of battle (in Book 11) by sending Eris (Strife) onto the battlefield. We have already seen him start the first day of battle by sending the false Dream to Agamemnon in Book 2; but now, because of the truce, he must restart it. Thus the present scene is really not so unexpected.

The Breaking of the Truce, 85-219

The two armies are still arranged as in Book 3. Athena, in the form of the Trojan Laodocus, finds Pandarus standing

> at rest, and around him the strong ranks of his shield-bearers
> who had followed him from the streams of the Aesepos.   (90-91)

She persuades him to try to kill Menelaus; thus he will win the favor of the Trojans, especially Paris. Schol. bT note that the mention of shield-bearers in lines 90-91 is an example of *prooikonomia* (preparation) for lines 113-15 , for while Pandarus strings his bow

> his goodly companions cover him with their shields
> lest the warlike Achaeans should attack him before
> he has hit Menelaus, Atreus' warlike son.   (113-15)

Pandarus' shoots his arrow, which passes through the three pieces of Menelaus' armor and hits him in the thigh, but without wounding him fatally, for Athena protects him. Two similes emphasize the moment of suspense when Menelaus' life hangs in the balance.

The scene ends with a passage in which Agamemnon, characteristically, shows his concern for his brother and how easily discouraged he is himself. He despairs of their expedition, affirming however that Troy will eventually fall (to some other force) because of this breach of the truce (164-68). Menelaus rebukes him: such talk will demoralize the army, and his wound is not fatal. Then, Agamemnon having summoned the physician Machaon, we are given a detailed description of the treatment of Menelaus, which corresponds to that of his wounding, thus creating a satisfying ring composition.

Agamemnon's Review of the Troops, 220-445

> While they were treating Menelaus good at the war cry,
> the ranks of the Trojan shield-bearers advanced to attack,
> and the Achaeans rearmed and rekindled their courage.   (220-22)

It seems that the Trojans are quicker to respond than the Achaeans, but the poet is emphasizing the rearming of the Achaeans as an introduction to the Review.

Next we are told:

> You wouldn't have seen godlike Agamemnon dozing
> or cowering back or being unwilling to fight
> but greatly hastening into the glory of battle.   (223-25)

He has his charioteer follow him with his chariot as he marshals the men on foot. At first the language seems to suggest that he is about to engage in battle, but then we realize that he is going to review the troops.

The Review reminds us of the Achaean Catalogue in Book 2, for there is a repetition of the same general pattern (so Edwards 1987.198). But now the marshaling of the army will lead to a sustained conflict between the two sides. We feel the climactic effect, first of the reaffirmation of the guilt of the Trojans and now of the renewal of the war.

Agamemnon is shown going among his men and exhorting them to battle. We begin with two general speeches (compare the speeches of Odysseus at 2.188-206) that typify how he will speak to individual leaders. (See Introduction, pp. 6-8, on the cataloguing style.) To those who are already hastening to battle he says that Troy is destined to fall because the Trojans have perjured themselves.

> Argives, now don't relax in your valor at all,
> for Zeus Father doesn't give aid to those who are perjurers.
> These who have been the first to destroy the oaths
> shall have their tender flesh devoured by vultures,
> and we, when we have taken their city, shall carry
> their dear wives and baby children away in our ships.   (234-39)

But to those who are holding back he says that they should be ashamed of themselves for being so listless.

> Argives, you boasters, you disgraces, where is your shame?
> Why do you stand at rest, gazing like fawns
> who being wearied with the chase across a great plain
> stand at rest and lack any spirit to put up a fight;
> so you are standing at rest, gazing, not fighting.
> Are you waiting for the Trojans to come to us here,

> to our well-sterned ships drawn up on the shore of the gray sea,
> to test if Zeus will hold his protecting hand over you?   (242-49)

These typical speeches introduce five encounters in which Agamemnon speaks in encouragement or rebuke.

The first is with Idomeneus, a reliable middle-aged leader, and his comrade Meriones, who are already exhorting their men. Agamemnon can do nothing but praise them, and Idomeneus urges him to go and exhort others,

> since the Trojans have poured out
> the oaths; now there awaits them a future of suffering
> and death since they were the first to destroy the oaths.   (269-71)

Idomeneus also, like Agamemnon, is certain that Troy will fall.

The second encounter is with the two Ajaxes, whose men, compared in lines 274-82 to a cloud moving over the sea (simile type 2), are already following them to battle. Again Agamemnon can only praise them. If only all the Achaeans had such a spirit,

> then King Priam's city would soon fall to the ground,
> being captured and destroyed by the might of our hands.   (291-92)

The third encounter is with Nestor, who is marshaling his men in the best possible battle order, telling them that

> thus the men of former times sacked cities and walls,
> having in their breasts such a will and spirit for battle.   (308-9)

Again an allusion to the sack of Troy, and again there is no occasion for Agamemnon to complain. He only wishes, as does Nestor, that Nestor were still young enough to fight.

It is not until the last two encounters that Agamemnon feels justified in delivering a rebuke. Coming to Odysseus and Menestheus, who have been waiting for other contingents to move out, he blames them for their listlessness, their "standing at rest" (340; compare Agamemnon's second typical speech, 242-49). But Odysseus protests that Agamemnon is wronging them and that he will prove his valor among the forefighters once hostilities have been begun. Accordingly, Agamemnon apologizes for his hard words.

Finally, he comes to Diomedes and Sthenelus whom he finds "standing at ease" (365, 366). He begins his rebuke to Diomedes as follows:

> Ah me, son of fiery-hearted, horse-taming Tydeus,
> why do you shrink back, why gaze down the causeways of battle?   (371-72)

Addressing him as an older man speaking to a much younger and much less experienced one, he goes on to say that Diomedes is no match for his father Tydeus.

Diomedes receives this rebuke in silence, but Sthenelus, Diomedes' charioteer and the older of the two, answers that Agamemnon knows that he is lying. Sthenelus and Diomedes are better than their fathers, for they succeeded in capturing Thebes whereas their fathers had failed to do this. Whereupon Diomedes rebukes Sthenelus, saying that Agamemnon is not to be blamed for exhorting the army,

> for glory will attend upon him if the Achaeans
> defeat the Trojans and capture sacred Ilium,
> but great grief will be his if the Achaeans are defeated.   (415-17)

Here again, at the end of the Review, we have the theme of the fall of Troy. Diomedes has been described as having an old man's head on a young man's shoulders. The poet seems to have drawn his character to contrast with that of Achilles.

Agamemnon makes no reply. The Review ends with the picture of Diomedes leaping from his chariot to move into action.

> Thus speaking he leaped armed to the ground from his chariot;
> the bronze rang terribly on the breast of this king moving
> to war; even a stout-hearted man would have feared him.   (420-21)

These words remind us of how Agamemnon left his chariot to enter the battle—and exhort the troops—at the beginning of the Review.

The importance of the Diomedes entry is signaled by its coming last, in the climactic position, and by its being longer and more complex than the earlier entries. The first encounter consists of 20 lines, the second of 18 lines, the third of 32 lines, and the fourth of 36 lines, whereas this fifth and last about Diomedes consists of 56 lines. In the other entries Agamemnon addresses and is addressed whereas in the last things are more complex: he rebukes Diomedes, who is defended by Sthenelus, and then Diomedes rebukes Sthenelus. Moreover, in the other entries there is no real conflict. In the first three Agamemnon can find no fault, and even in his encounter with Odysseus must finally admit that his rebuke was unwarranted. The Diomedes entry, however, ends in unresolved conflict, and therefore we remember it especially. It prepares us for his *aristeia* in Book 5. He will be the great hero of the first day of battle, and twice later, in Books 9 and 14, will remind Agamemnon of how he wrongly rebuked him.

At the end of the Review a series of similes (422-46) introduces the clash of the armies. We are reminded of the similes which introduced and concluded the Achaean Catalogue in Book 2, and of those at the end of the Trojan Catalogue at the beginning of Book 3. The present series ends with the picture of Ares driving on the Trojans, and Athena driving on the Achaeans, with the demons of Deimos (Terror), Phobos (Rout), and especially Eris (Strife) presiding over all.

The Resumption of Hostilities, 446-544

> When into one place they had come to clash in battle,
> they hurled their shields, hurled their spears and men
> bronze-armored against each other; their shields with bossed nobs
> met each against each, and great was the uproar arising.
> There was the groaning of those being slain, the boasting
> of those who were slaying, and the earth was running with blood.
> As when full rivers in winter streaming down mountains
> hurl heavy waters to mix in a valley below,
> issuing from great springs into a hollow ravine,
> with noise that a shepherd far off in the mountains can hear,
> so was the shouting and conflict of these joining battle.   (446-56)

Lines 446-51 occur again at 8.60-65, where they describe the first phase of even fighting. The simile in lines 452-56 belongs to our type 6: even or indecisive battle. It is followed by a detailed description in which the slayings alternate in chain-reaction fashion (so Fenik 1968.10) in three phases. The first and second phases each contain a simile (type 9: the warrior falls) describing a fallen Trojan warrior. The second ends with the Achaeans gaining the advantage, but in the third phase Apollo and Athena see to it that the conflict is renewed.

Phase one (457-72) begins with Nestor's son Antilochus killing Echepolus, who falls like a tower (462; simile type 9). Then Agenor kills Elephenor while he is trying to strip Echepolus of his armor. We leave this phase with Achaeans and Trojans fighting like wolves (471; simile type 6) over the body of Echepolus. A situation of even battle often arises in the fighting over a dead body.

Then, in phase two (473-507) Ajax kills Simoesius who falls like a poplar (482-87; simile type 9); and Antiphus, missing Ajax, hits Leucus, Odysseus' companion. Odysseus, seeking vengeance, hurls his spear and hits Democoon. The Trojans withdraw some distance. The Achaeans recover the dead and drive forward. Although they have the advantage, they have not routed the enemy.

Finally, in phase three (507-38), Apollo from Troy, seeing the withdrawal of the Trojans, exhorts them not to yield: the Achaeans are not invulnerable,

> nor is Achilles, the son of lovely-haired Thetis fighting,
> but is nursing his soul-paining wrath (*cholos*) at the ships. (512-13)

(When Achilles reenters the battle in Book 19, it will be as if the Achaeans are invulnerable.) In answer Athena exhorts the Achaeans, with the result that the conflict is reestablished. We might compare the activity of Apollo and Athena here with their roles in Book 7 in bringing this day of battle to an end. Now the Trojan ally Peirous of Thrace kills the Achaean Diores, leader of the Epeans, and the Achaean Thoas kills Peirous. The deaths of Diores and Peirous are very similar, balanced deaths.

> Thus they lay in the dust beside one another,
> the leader of the Thracians, the leader of the bronze-clad Epeans,
> and many others were killed while fighting over them. (536-38)

In a concluding, summarizing passage (539-44) we are told that if a man had been conducted safely through the battle by Athena he would not have been able to find any fault with it,

> for many of the Trojans and the Achaeans were on that day
> stretched face down in the dust beside one another. (543-44)

The last line here echoes line 536 about Peirous and Diores, and the whole passage, whether by Homer or a later singer (see Kirk 1985.398-99), makes a nice summary of the even battle before the *aristeia* of Diomedes.

BOOK 5: THE *ARISTEIA* OF DIOMEDES

Athena Inspires the Hero to Wound Aphrodite, 1-448

Book 5, the first book of the *Iliad* wholly dedicated to the description of battle, is, as battles tend to be, somewhat confusing. The gods play an important part, and it becomes clear that Zeus cannot fulfill his promise to Thetis so long as they are active (so Erbse 1961.185). The narrative can be divided into three phases (note the woundings). The first ends with Diomedes wounding Aphrodite, the third—a climactic parallel—with him wounding Ares. In the second the Trojans, led by Ares, who is exhorted to action by Apollo, temporarily gain the advantage, though the Trojan ally Sarpedon is wounded by Tlepolemus. There are many foreshadowings. Diomedes' *aristeia,* especially his defeat of Aeneas and the pro-Trojan gods, foreshadows Achilles' *aristeia* in Part 3. Ares' leading the Trojans in a counterattack foreshadows Apollo's doing this in Part 2, and the wounding of Sarpedon foreshadows his death in Part 2. In the third phase Hera and Athena enter the action with Zeus' blessing, which foreshadows their abortive attempt to do this against his will in Book 8.

Book 5 contains two other significant woundings, those of Diomedes and Aeneas. In an *aristeia* we expect the hero to be wounded, but Diomedes' wound, somewhat unexpectedly, is left unhealed. And we expect the hero to slay his main opponent and then fight for possession of the body, but Diomedes' main opponent is the god Ares whom he can only wound and who speedily returns to Olympus. His main human opponents are Pandarus and Aeneas who attack him in the chariot of Aeneas. Having slain the first, he can only wound the second, for Aeneas is destined to survive the fall of Troy. Apollo spirits Aeneas away, leaving behind an image of him to be fought over.

We begin with Athena causing a fire to blaze from Diomedes' helmet and shield. This is the glow of the hero's armor at the beginning of his *aristeia*; it usually occurs when the hero is arming, but Diomedes has been armed since the Review in the last book. He first encounters two sons of a priest of Hephaestus; he is on foot, they in their chariot. He slays one of them, but Hephaestus saves the other. Diomedes gives their horses and chariot to his companions to drive to the ships. This little episode apparently foreshadows his encounter with Pandarus and Aeneas.

The spirits of the Trojans are shaken, and Athena prevails upon the pro-Trojan Ares to retire to the sidelines.

> Ares, O Ares, you plague, blood-stained, wall-battering,
> shouldn't we leave the fighting to the Trojans and Achaeans,
> to see to which side Zeus Father will grant the victory?
> Let us retire and avoid the wrath of Zeus.   (31-34)

Thus she prevails upon Ares to be seated on the banks of the Scamander; and this prepares us (*prooikonomia*; see Reinhardt 1961.141) for Aphrodite's later finding him here. Athena's reason, that they should avoid the wrath of Zeus, seems an ad hoc invention, for Zeus does not forbid the gods to take part in the battle until Book 8.

Now the Trojans are routed, and Diomedes wreaks havoc among them until Pandarus wounds him with an arrow in the right shoulder. This is the first of two encounters between these two. Pandarus boasts that he has slain Diomedes. Diomedes, after Sthenelus has extracted the arrow, prays to Athena to be able to kill Pandarus.

> Grant that I slay him, that he come within range of my spear,
> who struck me first and boasted, not thinking that I
> would live to see the bright light of the sun any longer.   (117-20)

In answer Athena comes and says:

> Now be bold, Diomedes, to fight the Trojans,
> for I have put in your breast your father's strength,
> the fearless strength of the shield-wielding horseman Tydeus;
> and also I've taken from your eyes the mist that was there,
> enabling you clearly to distinguish gods from men.
> So should a god now come to test your strength,
> don't fight with him, not with any immortal
> except Aphrodite, the daughter of Zeus. If she should
> enter the battle, give her a stab with your sharp bronze.   (124-32)

This is a programmatic speech. Diomedes will be able to recognize the gods but should fight with none of them except Aphrodite. Athena says nothing about the killing of Pandarus. Instead, she puts before us the wounding of Aphrodite as the goal of the first phase of Diomedes' *aristeia*.

When Athena has left him, Diomedes reenters the battle with renewed vigor. His strength is that of a wounded and therefore fiercer lion (136-42, simile type 2).

Why has Athena not healed him? Probably, I think, because the poet wants to use the wounding later to draw a parallel between the first and third phases of Diomedes' *aristeia*; another example of *prooikonomia*.

Now Diomedes kills four pairs of the enemy fleeing on their chariots, and this causes Aeneas to seek the help of Pandarus. By means of Aeneas the poet will combine the killing of Pandarus with the wounding of Aphrodite (so Owen 1946.51). Aeneas asks Pandarus to use his bow to put an end to Diomedes' slaughter. Pandarus replies that his bow has failed twice, first (in the last book) against Menelaus and now already (in this book) against Diomedes; he ought to have brought his horses and chariot and be fighting as a spearman. Then Aeneas asks him to mount his chariot either as fighter or charioteer, and Pandarus chooses to be the fighter since he knows that no one can handle horses so well as their master.

Sthenelus alerts Diomedes to the approach of Pandarus and Aeneas, and advises retreat in their chariot. But Diomedes refuses. His strength, in spite of his wound, is still sound. If Athena grants him victory, Sthenelus should get control of Aeneas' wonderful horses, descended from the breed given by Zeus to Tros.

Pandarus hurls his spear, which passes through Diomedes' shield, but no further; again he vainly boasts of victory. Then Diomedes, helped by Athena, kills him with a spear cast through the mouth. Aeneas leaps from his chariot to protect Pandarus' body, but Diomedes crushes his hip-socket with a large stone and would have killed him if Aphrodite—and then Apollo—had not intervened.

> And Aphrodite put her white arms around her dear son
> and hid him protectively in a fold of her gleaming gown
> to ward off the missiles, lest one of the swift-horsed Danaans
> slay him, hitting him in the breast with a bronze spear.   (314-17)

At this point (319-29) Sthenelus gains possession of Aeneas' horses. (Diomedes will rescue Nestor with these horses in Book 8 and win the chariot race with them in Book 23.) When we return to the battle, Diomedes is attacking Aphrodite. He wounds her in the wrist, his spear passing through the fold of the gown in which she has wrapped Aeneas, and causes her to drop him; her immortal blood (ichor) flows. But Apollo intervenes on behalf of Aeneas—a climactic parallel to Aphrodite's intervention (compare lines 314-17 above).

> And Phoebus Apollo saved him in his arms

in a dark cloud, lest one of the swift-horsed Danaans
slay him, hitting him in the breast with a bronze spear.   (344-46)

Then we return to Aphrodite (347-430). Taken from the battle by Iris, she
finds Ares on the sidelines with his spear and chariot. She gets permission to use
his chariot, in which she goes off to heaven, Iris acting as her charioteer. Thus
Ares is left with his spear, which he will later use, but without his horses and
chariot, which he will not need when he is wounded, for he will shoot up to heaven
by himself; another example of *prooikonomia* in connection with Ares.

In heaven Aphrodite is consoled by her mother Dione, who tells her of other
gods wounded by mortals and that Diomedes had better remember his human
limitations. Then she heals her. Athena is amused, as is Zeus, who with a smile
tells her that hers are the works of marriage and that she should leave the works of
war to Athena and Ares.

When we return to the battlefield, Diomedes is trying to kill Aeneas in spite of
Apollo's protection. Three times Apollo drives him back and then, as he attacks the
fourth time, cries out in a terrible voice for him to remember the difference between
gods and men (440-42)—an admonition that reinforces for us Dione's words about
human limitations. Diomedes had better yield; and so he does, thus preparing us
for the retreat of the Achaeans in the next section. The present episode is rounded
off with a brief description of how Apollo takes Aeneas to his temple in Troy,
where Leto and Artemis heal him.

The Trojans Drive the Achaeans Back, 449-710

Apollo also creates an image of Aeneas for the Achaeans and Trojans to fight
over (in order to reestablish a situation of even battle) and, having returned to the
battlefield, exhorts Ares.

Ares, O Ares, you plague, blood-stained, wall-battering,
will you not now enter the battle and ward off this man,
Tydeus' son, who would fight now even with Zeus Father?
First he wounded Aphrodite in the wrist at close quarters
and then like a demon attacked even me myself.   (455-59)

We are reminded of Athena's earlier exhortation of Ares. A situation of even battle
is often restored by the leaders of the retreating or fleeing army making speeches of
exhortation, and this is what happens here. Ares responds to Apollo by taking the

form of the Trojan ally Acamas and exhorting the sons of Priam to save the body of Aeneas.

Then Sarpedon, the leader of the Lycians, exhorts Hector. Sarpedon, who is a type of the noble hero in the *Iliad*, has a relationship to Hector somewhat like that of Achilles to Agamemnon. He complains that he, though only an ally of the Trojans, is doing more to help the cause for which he is fighting than those who are directly involved.

Hector responds by rallying his forces, who turn and make a stand, and thus a situation of even battle is restored. Ares is helping the Trojans, covering the field in darkness; his presence and the absence of Athena signal that the Trojans are about to be favored. In the confusion and darkness Aeneas, his wound now healed, returns; no more is said about his image. The Achaeans at first stand fast. Agamemnon exhorts them.

> Friends, be men, have a heart of valiant resistance,
> don't act shamefully in the mighty encounters of battle.
> When men avoid shame there are more that survive than are slain,
> fleeing they lose all glory and strength to resist.   (529-32)

Ajax will repeat these lines (with a minor variation in the first) at 15.561-64, where Zeus is giving the Trojans the victory in fulfillment of his promise to Thetis.

There follows a chain-reaction battle, fought on even terms (533-89). Agamemnon kills a companion of Aeneas. Aeneas kills two Achaeans. Menelaus, urged on by Ares, who hopes that he will be killed, goes after Aeneas. But Antilochus comes to Menelaus' aid, and, Aeneas having withdrawn, they kill two Trojans. (Pylaemenes, who is slain by Menelaus here, at 5.576-79, reappears at 13.658; see our comment there.)

Then Hector, with the help of Ares and Enyo, the goddess of war, attacks Menelaus and Antilochus. Ares, wielding his huge spear, is now actually leading the Trojans. They are going on the offensive. Diomedes calls for a retreat.

> Friends, to think how we marveled that noble Hector
> is such a spearman and such a courageous warrior.
> But always a god is beside him to ward off destruction,
> as Ares disguised as a mortal is doing now.
> So let us retreat, but always facing the Trojans,
> let us not stand and try to contend with the gods.   (601-6)

Diomedes recognizes Ares and reminds the Achaeans of the truth, just impressed upon him by Apollo, that mortals cannot contend with gods.

The Achaeans begin to retreat (607-26). Hector slays two of them. Then the big Ajax slays a Trojan, but is unable to strip him of his armor, for he is forced to withdraw before the oncoming Trojans. His withdrawal can be thought of as symbolizing the retreat of the whole Achaean army, as later in Books 11 (544-74) and 15 (esp. 643-746).

Then comes the single combat between Sarpedon and Tlepolemus. Sarpedon is a son, Tlepolemus a grandson, of Zeus. Throwing their spears simultaneously, Sarpedon kills Tlepolemus, Tlepolemus wounds Sarpedon in the thigh. The poet emphasizes that Sarpedon is not destined to die at this moment, for Zeus, his father, is "still" protecting him (662) . While he is being carried off, Odysseus attacks and slays several of the Lycians. But Hector comes to the rescue and fills the Achaeans with fear. Sarpedon urges him to save his body, wrongly thinking that he is going to die, for he is carried to safety behind the lines, where the spear is extracted and the North Wind revives his spirit.

In this second phase of the battle the Trojans have gained the upper hand. Diomedes has called for an orderly retreat. Ares and Hector are pushing the Achaeans back.

> Now who was the first and who was the last one slain
> by Hector, the son of Priam, and brazen Ares?
> Godlike Teuthras and then the horseman Orestes,
> the Aetolian spearman Trechus, Oenomaus,
> Oenops' son Helenus and bright-belted Oresbius,
> who lived in Hyle and took great care of his wealth,
> close by Lake Cephisis where the other
> Boeotians live, the owners of very rich farmlands.   (703-10)

These are minor Achaeans about whom we know only that they are slain here. Their names seem invented for the present passage, and it seems unlikely that their deaths would have aroused deep emotions in the Greek audience. Nevertheless, this catalogue impresses upon us the seriousness of the Achaean withdrawal.

Athena Inspires the Hero to Wound Ares, 711-909

The sight of Hector and Ares driving back the Achaeans stirs Hera on Olympus. She tells Athena that they should put an end to Ares' activity in order to keep their promise to Menelaus that he will sack Troy. This reason seems an ad hoc invention, but it fits with the theme, connected with Menelaus since Book 3, that Troy is destined to fall. Athena is eager to comply.

She dresses in her battle outfit in the palace of Zeus. Hera, who acts as charioteer, gets ready the horses and chariot with the help of Hebe. The Hours open the gates of Olympus, and the goddesses ride out. But before descending to the battlefield they consult Zeus, whom they find seated on the topmost peak of Olympus (where he was when Thetis consulted him at the end of Book 1). Zeus grants them permission to drive Ares from the battlefield. The wounding of Ares is thus set as the goal of the third phase of Diomedes' *aristeia*.

Having arrived in the Troad, the goddesses leave their horses and chariot, walking like pigeons. The detail seems charming and humorous. We have left behind the seriousness of the Sarpedon episode. They go to where the best Achaeans are gathered around Diomedes. Taking the form of Stentor, Hera exhorts them, shouting with the voice of fifty men. Such exhortations, as we have seen, typically introduce a change in the battle. Have a sense of shame, she says, reminding them that the Trojans did not dare to come outside the gates of Troy when Achilles was fighting.

In the meanwhile Athena is encouraging Diomedes whom she finds cooling his wound. She blames him for being worse than his father Tydeus, who had once bravely disobeyed her when she had forbidden him to fight. There is a clear parallel with her earlier inspiration of Diomedes: now as then she comes to him when he is nursing his wound, and now as then she exhorts him by reminding him of his father. Diomedes responds that he can see through her disguise (apparently she has taken the form of some hero), and insists that he has been right to avoid Ares in obedience to her earlier command. The goddess is pleased with his reply (compare the good-humored exchange between her and her favorite Odysseus at the beginning of *Odyssey* 13). But now she will help him to attack Ares.

The tone of the scene in which Ares is wounded is humorous. Athena acts as Diomedes' charioteer. The axle creaks beneath her weight, and she puts on a cap of invisibility to escape Ares' notice. They find him, like a mortal hero, stripping the armor off a man he has just killed. He hurls his spear at Diomedes, but Athena deflects it. Diomedes hurls his spear, and Athena directs it into the belly of Ares, who howls with the voice of nine or ten thousand men joining in battle. (Later, in Book 21, Ares will remind Athena of how she wounded him here.)

He goes off to heaven, like Aphrodite earlier, but whereas she got there on his chariot, he shoots up like a whirlwind. Having arrived in Olympus, he complains to Zeus. Zeus is amused, as he was by the wounding of Aphrodite. Ares, he says, is his most hated child, for he takes after his mother Hera. Still, he orders him to be to healed, and, this being done, and Hebe having given him a bath, Ares is restored to his former glory, as was Aphrodite.

Now Athena and Hera return to heaven. They have accomplished their mission by driving Ares from the battlefield, which now is left to the human participants.

BOOK 6: HECTOR IN TROY

Helenus' Advice to Hector, 1-236

The *aristeia* of Diomedes continues. It will cause Hector to go into Troy to get his mother Hecuba to pray to Athena to end it. At first the battle being left to the human participants rages indecisively, but then the Achaeans gain the advantage. Even without Achilles and with no gods intervening, they are stronger than the Trojans. The big Ajax is the first to break through the Trojan front by killing Acamas, the man whose form Ares took in the last book.

Then Diomedes kills a pair, and Euryalus, who is also from Argos like Diomedes, kills two pairs. The killing of pairs (fighters with their charioteers) means that the Trojans are fleeing on their chariots (so Willcock 1978.241). Then seven other Achaeans each slay a Trojan.

This catalogue of Achaean successes ends with the description of Menelaus' encounter with Adrestus. Adrestus, thrown to the ground by his fleeing horses, begs Menelaus to take him captive. This is the first battlefield supplication, all of which are made by Trojans or their allies to Achaeans. Menelaus is about to yield when Agamemnon rushes up shouting.

> O my dear one, Menelaus, why do you now so
> care for these men? Did the Trojans treat you so well
> when visiting you? Let no one escape steep destruction,
> the force of our hands, not even the baby whom
> the mother still has in the womb, let everyone perish
> in Troy, vanish without any burial or tomb.   (55-60)

Lines 56-57 allude to Paris' abduction of Helen, which was a breach of guest-friendship with Menelaus. The poet comments that Agamemnon was persuading "just things" (62), that is, the Achaeans have justice on their side because of the Trojan espousal of Paris' wrongdoing. So Menelaus pushes Adrestus away, and Agamemnon kills him.

We return to the rout of the Trojans. Nestor is urging the Achaeans not to interrupt their pursuit to strip the dead. Then the Trojans would have been chased back into Troy if Helenus, the Trojan prophet, had not given timely advice to Aeneas and Hector. (Aeneas apparently is left in command when Hector goes to Troy.)

> Aeneas and Hector, since it rests upon you especially

to command the Trojans and Lycians, for you are the best
in every action, both in fighting and planning,
call on our army to make a stand here at our gates,
going among them, before they run to their wives' arms,
fleeing, collapsing, and giving delight to the enemy.
When you have got all our ranks in straight battle order,
we will fight with the Danaans, holding our places,
though very hard pressed, for so necessity forces us.
Then, Hector, enter the city and ask our mother,
your mother and mine, to gather the old women together
on the citadel at the temple of bright-eyed Athena,
and when she has opened the doors of the sacred room
and chosen that gown she deems most lovely and large
and dearest to her of those she has in the palace,
to put it on the knees of beautiful-haired Athena,
and vow to sacrifice twelve heifers in front of her temple,
yearlings, ungoaded, praying that the goddess have pity (*eleese*)
on Troy and the wives and infant babes of the Trojans,
and hold off Tydeus' son from holy Troy,
that wild spearman, that strong deviser of rout,
whom now I consider the strongest of the Achaeans,
for never so frightening was even Achilles, the leader
they say was born of a goddess, but this one rages
exceedingly and no one is able to equal his strength.   (77-101)

This programmatic speech divides the coming narrative into two strands: first the
reestablishment of even battle, which will last during Hector's visit in Troy; then
Hector's meeting with Hecuba. Moreover, it sets the pattern for Hector's later
programmatic speeches to Hecuba, to Paris and Helen, and to Andromache. Each
of these speeches will divide the coming narrative into two simultaneous actions
which will be told as if they happened consecutively. Thus Book 6 as a whole is
constructed in accordance with Zielinski's law. See Krischer 1971.108-9.

Now Hector, leaping from his chariot (on which we can imagine that he was
retreating) rallies the Trojans, who turn round and make a stand. The Achaeans
yield, thinking that a god has intervened (108); we are thus prepared for Diomedes'
asking in the next scene whether Glaucus is a god. Hector tells the Trojans that he
is going into Troy to get "the old men of good counsel and our wives" (113-14) to

pray for them. (Perhaps he mentions the old men, about whom nothing more will be said, only because they along with the women typically stayed at home in time of war.) Hector goes off, with his body shield hanging against his back and bouncing against his neck and ankles (117-18). We have the impression that he will return as soon as possible.

While he is on his way, the encounter between Diomedes and Glaucus occurs. Diomedes asks whether Glaucus is a god or a man; if a god, he will not fight him; if a man, he will kill him. Diomedes apparently no longer has the ability, given him by Athena in Book 5, to distinguish gods from men. Glaucus answers that he is a man, and gives an account of his genealogy, with an emphasis on his grandfather Bellerophon. Diomedes realizes that they are hereditary friends, for his grandfather Oeneus had been the guest-friend of Bellerophon: these had exchanged gifts, Oeneus getting a gold cup, Bellerophon a beautiful belt (probably the less valuable gift). Accordingly, Diomedes and Glaucus decide not to fight with each other, and exchange shields as a sign of their friendship. Glaucus gives his gold shield for Diomedes' bronze one, and the poet remarks that Zeus must have deprived him of his wits.

Donlan 1989.1-15 (cf. Traill 1989.301-5) has suggested that Glaucus is being shown in a submissive role. Diomedes, by telling him about the gifts exchanged by their grandfathers, has indicated the pattern of submission he expects him to follow. Thus in this last episode in his *aristeia* Diomedes is victorious by means of his wits; and we, having left the battlefield on a note of amusement, should feel less urgency about it during the coming scenes in Troy.

Hector's Three Meetings, 237-529

Book 6, as Griffin1980.31 says, "repeats the same pattern three times, in a crescendo of emotional power: the woman attempts to hold back the fighting man, to keep him in her own world of comfort and safety." Each scene is longer than the preceding one: that with Hecuba 43 lines (242-85), that with Helen and Paris 57 lines (312-68), that with Andromache and Astyanax 124 lines (369-493). There are a number of similarities between these scenes. For instance, as we have already mentioned, each ends with a programmatic speech by Hector dividing the coming narrative into two strands.

When we return to Hector after the Diomedes-Glaucus episode, we pass into a very different world. We are about to see Helen again, and Hecuba and Andromache for the first time; these are the most important women (as distinct from goddesses) in the *Iliad*. Hector is entering Troy.

> When Hector came to the Scaean Gate and the oak tree,
> the wives and daughters of the Trojans ran up on all sides
> to ask him about their sons and brothers and friends
> and husbands, and he responded by urging them each
> to pray to the gods, and loaded many with sorrow.   (237-41)

This general passage prepares us for the catalogue of Hector's specific meetings with the three women in his life: first his mother, then his sister-in-law, and finally his wife (so Schadewaldt 1959.212).

The scene with Hecuba begins with a sentence (242-52) made long by a parenthesis describing the palace compound. We learn that the many sons and daughters of Priam have rooms in his palace. Thus (an example of *prooikonomia)* it will be easy for Hector to visit Paris and his own family.

Hector finds Hecuba leading one of her daughters, Laodice (whose form Iris took at 3.124), apparently to Priam's house. The presence of this daughter, a silent character, shows Hecuba's love for her children. We are about to hear the mother of Hector. She takes him by the hand, a sign of affection. Assuming he has come to pray to the gods to end the Achaean offensive, she offers to bring him wine to pour as a libation with his prayer, and suggests that he should take some himself. But Hector refuses: wine is not what he needs now, for he must return as soon as possible to the battlefield. And, in accordance with Helenus' advice, he urges her to try to propitiate Athena, ending his speech as follows:

> But you proceed to the temple of warlike Athena
> while I go on to Paris. I'll summon him forth,
> if only he'll listen to me. How I wish that the earth
> would swallow him, for he's a huge plague, a curse from the gods
> for Trojans and great-hearted Priam and Priam's sons.
> If only he'd die and I saw him descending to Hades,
> you can be sure that my heart would forget to mourn.   (279-85)

Hector's speech is programmatic, like Helenus' earlier one. The action will be divided into Hecuba's attempt to win Athena's favor and Hector's visit with Paris (and Helen, whom we left at home with Paris at the end of Book 3). And we learn the purpose of his visit with Paris: to summon him to battle.

While Hector is going to Paris' house, Hecuba gathers together the old women and, having chosen a most beautiful gown (one brought by Paris from

Sidon to Troy), goes with them to the temple of Athena. There the priestess offers the gown to the goddess and vows a sacrifice of twelve heifers in return for the death of Diomedes (more than Hector, following Helenus, told Hecuba to ask for). But Athena refuses; and again we are reminded that Troy is destined to fall.

When the description of this service is complete (in reality it must coincide, at least in part, with Hector's visit with Paris and Helen), we return to Hector, who has arrived at the house of Paris, which Paris has built himself with the help of the best carpenters in Troy (313-17).

> Hector, dear to Zeus, entered, and in his hand
> he held his spear, eleven cubits long, at whose end
> flashed a bronze point, around which was a ferrule of gold.
> He found Paris in his bedroom fingering his very beautiful
> armor, his shield and his cuirass, and handling his bent bow;
> and Argive Helen was there with her maids around her
> telling them how to do their excellent work.   (318-24)

This passage, like the one in which we were introduced to Hecuba attending upon her daughter, gives us a thumbnail sketch of the characters we are about to see in action.

Hector exhorts Paris, saying that it is wrong for him to be nursing his anger (*cholos*, 326). Paris replies:

> Hector, since you rebuke me as I deserve,
> pay attention and listen to what I now say.
> Anger (*cholos*) and indignation at the Trojans aren't why
> I sit here so much as my wish to give way to my grief (*achos*).   (333-36)

Hector assumes, perhaps mainly for the purpose of his rebuke, that Paris has withdrawn (like Achilles and, as we shall see in Book 9, Meleager) because of his anger, but Paris attributes his withdrawal to his grief which (unlike that of Achilles and Meleager) has not made him angry. He is like the men in Book 2 (cf. line 270) who felt rightly rebuked for having rushed for the ships, and Helen in Book 3 who was full of self-censure (so Collins 1987). We can imagine that Paris feels anguish over his defeat by Menelaus and also over the fact that his abduction of Helen has caused his own people such trouble, in spite of the fact that he is unwilling to give her up in return for peace. The poet has painted him, like Helen, in a not altogether unsympathetic light. He has made him, as Alexander Pope (1967.VII.345-46) noted, a man of fine tastes and accomplishments. Paris is a connoisseur of beautiful clothing (having brought from Sidon the gown offered to Athena), beautiful houses, beautiful armor (as lines 321-24 show), and beautiful women. Paris ends his speech by saying that he will now return to battle; he has already been persuaded by Helen to do this. Victory, he adds, is always changing sides. Hector should either wait until he has put on his armor or go ahead and he will catch up with him.

At this point Helen insists that Hector should stay, but he answers that he must return to the battlefield as soon as possible. She should spur on Paris, and Paris should catch up with him while he is still within the city.

> For I am going off now to my house to see
> those of my household and my dear wife and baby son.
> I don't know if I shall come and see them again
> or die by will of the gods at the hands of the Achaeans.   (365-68)

Thus, just as he told Hecuba of his intention to visit Paris to summon him to battle, so now he tells Helen and Paris of his intention to visit his family because he may never see them again (a thought that will inform his conversation with Andromache). Again his speech is programmatic and divides the coming action into two strands. First we will be told of his visit with his family and then of Paris' catching up with him.

When Hector reaches his house, he learns that Andromache, with a nurse carrying their infant son, has gone to the walls to look for him on the battlefield. Fearing for his safety, she has run off "like a maenad," that is, a crazed worshiper of Dionysus. Thus we are immediately given a characterization of her, as we were of Hecuba and of Paris and Helen: she is the completely loving wife. As Edwards 1987.209-10 remarks, the fact that Hector does not find her at home creates tension, for we expect her to be there weaving. Also, it is more dramatic to have her meet Hector at the city gate when he is about to return to the battlefield; and the poet is preparing Hector to be in the place where Paris will catch up with him.

Hector runs from his home to the Scaean Gate, and Andromache sees him coming.

> When he had gone through the great city to the Scaean Gate,
> through which he was going to go back onto the plain,
> then did his loving wife come running to meet him,

> Andromache—she was the daughter of great-hearted Eetion,
> who had his dwelling in the area beneath wooded Placus,
> in Thebes under Placus, and was king of the men of Cilicia,
> having a daughter now married to bronze-helmeted Hector—
> Andromache came to meet him, and with her a maid servant
> holding the happy child in her bosom, an infant,
> Hector's dear son, who looked to him like a bright star.
> Hector called him Scamandrius, but others Astyanax [Lord of the City],
> for Hector alone was the city's protector.   (392-403)

Schadewaldt 1959.215 and Willcock 1978.248 comment that line 393 shows that Hector would have gone directly back to the battlefield if Andromache had not come to meet him. Since, however, he knew that Andromache had gone to the wall to view the battlefield, it is hard not to believe that he hoped to meet her (so Kirk 1990.210). What line 393 does is to underline the fact—immediately before Andromache begs Hector to stay in Troy—that he is not going to stay (so Tsagarakis 1982.10-11).

As Hector smiles at Astyanax, Andromache, taking him by the hand (just as Hecuba had done), accuses him of not pitying (*oud' eleaireis*, 407) herself or his son. She has only him left, for her father and brothers have been slain by Achilles, and her mother, who had been enslaved and freed, is now dead. It is striking how she praises Achilles for the civilized way in which he treated her dead father: he left him his armor and gave him proper burial. This makes a strong contrast with how Achilles will later treat the dead Hector. As Sheppard 1922.58 has remarked: "The poet means Achilles not only to kill Hector, but to drag his body in the dust; and he means it to be tragic that Achilles of all people should thus treat him."

Andromache ends her speech by begging Hector to stay in Troy, to protect the walls at their weakest point. But Hector answers that he is honor-bound to fight, though he knows that Troy is destined to fall.

> For I know this well in my mind and my heart:
> there shall be a day when sacred Ilium shall perish,
> and Priam and the people of Priam of the good ash spear.   (447-49)

Hector goes on to imagine what will happen after he dies, how Andromache, whom he loves more than mother, father, sisters, and brothers, will be enslaved.

Then he turns his attention to his son. Frightened by Hector's helmet, the baby shrinks back crying into the nurse's bosom. Mother and father laugh. Hector removes his helmet and takes up his son. Kissing and rocking him, he prays to Zeus and the other gods that Astyanax will be a greater warrior than himself and so give joy to Andromache. Then he hands the baby to Andromache, who is crying and laughing at the same time, and tells her to go home and attend to her weaving while he goes, as he must, back to the battlefield.

Thus the end of this speech, like the end of his speeches in the other two scenes, announces a division of the action into two strands, first Andromache's return to the house and then his return to the battlefield. Andromache goes off, weeping and turning round to see him as long as she can. Having come to their home, she sets her maid servants to mourning for Hector.

> They lamented for Hector in his own house while he still lived,
> not thinking he'd return again from battle
> and safely escape the strong hands of the Achaeans.   (500-2)

Thus the poet puts Hector in the shadow of death.

Now we are ready for the second strand, Hector's return to the battlefield, which forms a ring composition with his coming into Troy. But we remember that Paris is to catch up with Hector while still in the city. And so the poet passes from the mournful house of Hector back to the house of Paris. When he has put on his armor (it is as if time had stopped since we last saw him), Paris rushes down from the citadel like a beautiful stallion (simile type 2)—one of eight similes used twice in the *Iliad*; it appears again at 15.263-68 for a similar purpose, to describe the return of Hector to battle. He catches up with Hector when Hector, as we last saw him, is leaving the place of his conversation with Andromache in order to return to the battlefield (515-16). There is some pleasant bantering between the two, very different from their earlier conversation. Now Hector agrees that Paris is a good fighter if only he wants to be, and promises that they will be completely reconciled once the Achaeans have been driven away. Hector can be foolishly optimistic.

BOOK 7: THE DUEL BETWEEN HECTOR AND AJAX

Preparation, 1-205

In Book 7 the first day of battle is brought to an end. There are three main episodes, each consisting of two complementary, balancing actions. First, Athena and Apollo, at the same time but from different directions, come onto the battlefield to end the fighting; they decide to do this by having Hector challenge the Achaeans to a duel. Second, there is the almost even duel between Hector and Ajax, the most carefully composed narrative in this book. Finally, as we expect at the end of a day's battle, there are meetings on both sides, related in cataloguing style consecutively though in reality simultaneous (Zielinski's law), and these make very similar plans.

In Book 6 Hector, before leaving the battlefield, exhorted his men and a situation of even battle was established. Now his return with Paris gives new spirit to the Trojans. Each hits a man, as does Glaucus, whose victim is leaping onto his chariot—a sign that he is retreating. The slain Achaeans are minor figures, probably ad hoc inventions for the present list; compare those listed at 5.73-10.

At this point Athena, seeing the Achaeans being slain, descends from Olympus, and Apollo comes from the Trojan citadel to meet her at the oak tree in front of Troy. He makes the following suggestion.

> Now let us put an end to the warfare and battle
> for today; later they will fight until they have reached
> Troy's fated fall since you two goddesses firmly
> are set on bringing about this city's destruction.   (29-32)

(The other goddess is of course Hera.) Troy is destined to fall, but not yet. Athena answers that she too has come to bring the battle to an end. But how can they manage this? Apollo suggests that they have Hector challenge the Achaeans to a duel, and she agrees.

Helenus (compare his role in Book 6) knows what Athena and Apollo intend, apparently by divine inspiration, and advises Hector as follows:

> Have the other Trojans sit down, and all the Achaeans,
> and you yourself challenge the best of the Achaeans
> to fight with you man to man in terrible battle,
> for you will not yet die and meet your end.
> Such a word I've heard from the immortal gods.   (49-53)

Helenus assures Hector that he will "not yet" die, and thus he can feel secure in making his challenge.

Hector reacts in the same way as he did to Paris' agreement to a duel in Book 3 (lines 54-56=3.76-78): he goes out between the two armies, holding his spear by the middle, and has the Trojans sit down. Agamemnon responds, as in Book 3, by having the Achaeans be seated. Athena and Apollo in the form of vultures sit on the oak tree.

Hector reminds the Achaeans of the duel in Book 3 by referring to the oaths taken before it (67-72). Since Zeus did not fulfill those oaths and bring the war to a peaceful conclusion, he must intend that the two sides continue fighting until one of them is victorious. This of course is true: the Trojans will be defeated. But Hector's other possibility will also be realized to the extent of fulfilling Zeus' promise to Thetis.

Hector goes on to challenge the best of the Achaeans to a duel on the following terms: the victor is to take the armor of the vanquished but to return his body for proper burial. He ends his speech, optimistically, by imagining the tomb of the man he will slay.

At first there is no response to Hector's challenge (92-93). This seems hard to believe when we consider the valor of such heroes as Diomedes; but here the poet is probably sacrificing narrative consistency to the desire to create a suspenseful scene (so Owen 1946.75). The hesitancy of the Achaeans increases our impression of the greatness of Hector. Only a first-rate Achaean champion will be able to match him. Who will this be? Finally, Menelaus rises and, while he puts on his armor, rebukes the Achaeans. We immediately fear for his safety, realizing that he is no match for Hector; and we have already seen enough of him as a duelist in Book 3. We are therefore relieved when Agamemnon steps forward and tells him to let someone else be their champion; it is no shame not to be Hector's equal, for even Achilles shudders at the thought of encountering him (certainly a persuasive exaggeration). Menelaus yields.

But still no one else steps forward until Nestor has risen and made a long speech of rebuke (124-60): if only he were young again, he would be eager to fight. Now nine leaders volunteer, and Nestor proceeds to decide among them by lot. While he is shaking the lots in Agamemnon's helmet, the Achaeans pray:

> Zeus Father, may Ajax or Tydeus' son be chosen
> or else the King himself of golden Mycenae.
> So spoke they as the great horseman Nestor was shaking the lots,

and out of the helmet, as they desired, leaped the lot
of Ajax.   179-83)

The name of Ajax is left to the end of the sentence in the striking position of first
word in its line.

What is meant by the fact that the man chosen by lot is the one the Achaeans
wanted? Heubeck 1983.205 comments on *Odyssey* 9.331-35 that it is a good
omen when the four men chosen by lot to help in the blinding of Polyphemus turn
out to be the ones Odysseus preferred. Accordingly, it seems likely that the present
coincidence is a good omen for the Achaean side.

Ajax tells the Achaeans that, while he is arming, they should pray to Zeus, not
silently, as he at first suggests, but openly, for they have nothing to fear. No one
can defeat him. His speech announces two simultaneous actions, the praying of the
Achaeans and his arming.

The Achaeans pray as follows:

Zeus Father, ruling from Ida, most glorious and greatest,
grant to Ajax the victory and glorious honor;
but if Hector is also your favorite and care,
let equal power and glory attend upon both.   (202-5)

It seems somewhat strange that the possibility of Ajax's not being the winner is
considered, but all depends on the will of Zeus. Moreover, this prayer
foreshadows the fact that the duel will end inconclusively—though Ajax will have
the better claim to victory.

The Duel, 206-312

Ajax arms himself and advances, a huge figure resembling Ares going to war.
The Achaeans rejoice and the Trojans fear; Hector fears but is unable to withdraw
since he is the one who has made the challenge (216-18). The poet emphasizes
Ajax's two main pieces of armor, his spear and shield, especially the latter.

And Ajax advanced holding his shield like a wall,
bronze, of seven ox-hides, which Tychius had made,
the very best craftsman in leather, an inhabitant of Hyle.
He had made for Ajax this gleaming shield of seven
superior ox-hides with an outer covering of bronze.
With this in front of him Telamonian Ajax

stood very close to Hector and spoke to him threateningly.   (219-25)

We are being introduced to the main defensive fighter of the Achaeans, and his shield is what most characterizes him, a great body shield extending from his chin to his feet, over which he fights as if over a wall. This is certainly one reason for the poet's describing it in such detail here. But we are also being prepared for the coming duel in which this shield will withstand Hector's attack.

Ajax (226-32) tells Hector that he is about to experience what the best of the Achaeans is like, that is, the best after Achilles who has withdrawn from the fighting because of his wrath; and he offers Hector the advantage of starting. So Hector, opposing Ajax force against force, as he says, hurls his spear, which goes through seven layers of Ajax's shield but is stopped by the eighth. Then Ajax hurls his spear, which goes through Hector's shield (apparently a body shield like Ajax's; compare 6.17-18), breastplate, and chiton, but without wounding him. It is clear that Ajax has had the better of this first exchange. Then, after retrieving their spears, they use them for thrusting. Hector's spearpoint is bent on the outer bronze layer of Ajax's shield whereas Ajax's spear goes through Hector's shield and grazes his neck, drawing blood. Again Ajax has been more effective. Then they go at each other with stones. Hector causes Ajax's shield to ring with his hit whereas Ajax, hurling a much larger stone, strikes Hector's shield and knocks him down. Hector falls on his back, his shield on top of him, and must be helped to his feet by Apollo. Clearly again Ajax has proven himself the better man.

Finally, we are told that they would have continued with their swords if the heralds, Talthybius representing the Achaeans, Idaeus the Trojans, had not intervened. It is the Trojan Idaeus who speaks.

No longer, dear boys, be warring, no longer be fighting.
Both of you are the favorites of cloud-gathering Zeus,
both are fine spearmen; now this is something we all know.
But night is upon us, and yielding to night is a good thing.   (279-82)

Ajax is agreeable if Hector, as the one who has made the challenge, will say this; and Hector does: yes, it is good to obey night. Moreover, they should give each other gifts so that the Achaeans and Trojans may know they have parted "in friendship" (302). So saying, Hector gives a sword with scabbard and baldric to Ajax, and Ajax gives him a belt. Thus the duel is over. The formal, friendly way in which it ends reminds us of the contests at the funeral games of Patroclus in

Book 23 (so Kirk, in Fenik 1978.37-39). Book 7 as a whole has a rather
perfunctory character.

It is the Trojan herald who has asked for an end to the duel, and this "is in
accordance with Homer's Greek patriotism" (Willcock 1978.255). Moreover, Ajax
and Hector are described returning to their respective sides as follows:

> They separated, one of them going to the army of the Achaeans,
> the other to the throng of the Trojans, who were rejoicing
> seeing him alive and coming toward them unharmed
> safe from the might and invincible hands of Ajax;
> amazed at his survival, they led him back to the city.
> Ajax rejoicing in his victory was being led off
> by the well-greaved Achaeans to godlike Agamemnon's hut.   (306-12)

Ajax goes off rejoicing in victory while the Trojans are surprised that Hector has
escaped unharmed. Ajax is clearly the winner. It seems likely that this is also
shown by the gifts they exchange, for the sword Ajax gets seems more valuable
than the belt he gives (so Donlan 1989:14, who compares the gifts exchanged by
Diomedes and Glaucus in Book 6).

Why has the poet chosen to end the first day of battle with this duel? He
probably liked the ring composition it makes with the duel in Book 3. Moreover,
the duel between Hector and Ajax can be thought of as recapitulating the result of
the first day of battle (so Rothe 1910.215): even without Achilles the Achaeans are
superior to the Trojans, and therefore if Achilles is to be honored Zeus must
intervene, as he will do in the next book.

A Truce. The Building of the Achaean Wall and Trench, 313-482

The contrast between the two sides is continued in the last section of Book 7,
which describes their two meetings held simultaneously at the end of this day of
fighting. First, we are told of the council of leaders in Agamemnon's hut. After
they have feasted and honored Ajax, Nestor proposes that on the next day they
should have a truce for burying their dead, and build a wall and dig a trench in
front of it to protect their camp. This proposal, which is programmatic for the rest
of this book, meets with approval.

Meanwhile the Trojans, at the gates of Priam's palace, are deeply disturbed,
in sharp contrast to the Achaeans. Antenor (a Trojan Nestor) rises and proposes
that they should act in accordance with the terms of the treaty made in Book 3.

> Let us give back Argive Helen and her property
> to the sons of Atreus to take home. Now we are fighting
> as men who are oath-breakers, which is the worse course.   (350-52)

Paris answers that he will not return Helen, but only the property he carried off and some additional things.

Then Priam orders them to take their supper and mount guard, as is their custom. On the next day they will send Idaeus to the Achaean camp to report Paris' decision and ask for a truce for burying the dead.

> And let Idaeus propose this, that if they are willing
> we should cease from horrible war until we have burned
> our corpses; later we shall continue to fight until the divine power
> decides between us which shall be given the victory.   (375-78)

We should note that it is the Trojans who propose the truce, as it was the Trojan herald Idaeus who proposed an end to the duel.

At the beginning of the next day Idaeus goes to the Achaean camp to the hut of Agamemnon where the Achaean leaders are assembled. He reports the decision of Paris and asks for the truce, concluding with the same words as Priam (395-97=376-78). At first there is silence, but finally Diomedes speaks up.

> Let no one accept either the possessions of Paris
> or Helen. It is clear to everyone, even a great fool (*nepios*),
> that now the cords of destruction are bound on the Trojans.   (400-2)

This is the same thought, but more strongly put, that Antenor expressed earlier: to fight as perjurers will not turn out to be the better alternative for the Trojans. We are reminded of how Achilles in Book 1, speaking before the heralds who had come to carry off Briseis, called the gods to witness. (Compare also how Telemachus in *Odyssey* 2 calls on Zeus to avenge the wrongdoing of the suitors.)

The Achaeans shout their approval, and Agamemnon tells Idaeus that he has now heard the answer to Paris' proposal. Agamemnon grants a truce for burying the dead and, raising his scepter to all the gods, swears to observe it. So Idaeus returns to the Trojans, who are waiting for him (a balance to the Achaean council), and tells them what has happened. Then (417-32) we are given a brief description of the burying of the dead on the next day.

On the day after this, starting before dawn, the Achaeans build the wall in front of their camp and dig a trench in front of it with stakes on the inner bank (433-41). The gods on Olympus are watching, and Poseidon, a pro-Achaean god, complains to Zeus about it. The Achaeans in their haste have omitted to sacrifice to the gods, and their wall is likely to be more famous than the one he and Apollo built around Troy. Zeus answers that when the war is over Poseidon may destroy the Achaean wall.

> Come now, when it's all over and the long-haired Achaeans
> have returned home in their ships to their native land,
> break up their wall by pouring the vast sea against it
> and cover again the whole long shore in sand
> so that the great wall of the Achaeans may be effaced.   (459-63)

In Book 12, at the beginning of the Trojan attack on the wall, we shall again be reminded that Poseidon is going to destroy it after the fall of Troy. It is as if, both here and in this later passage, the poet wants to say that the Achaean wall belongs with the fulfillment of Zeus' promise to Thetis, which entails a victory of the Trojans at the ships and so a breaching of this wall, and that this episode is a somewhat incongruous part of a larger picture in which the Achaeans will be successful in defeating the Trojans. Moreover, it seems likely that the Greek audience, being made conscious of the neglect of the Achaeans to sacrifice to the gods when building the wall, would fear that it was destined to fail, by will of the gods, as a defense of the Achaean camp. The passage in Book 12 connects the Trojan breaching of the wall with its having been built without proper sacrifice to the immortals.

After the scene in heaven, we are told that it is sunset and that the Achaeans are having supper. Ships from Lemnos sent by the son of Jason have arrived to sell them wine. The mention of Jason reminds us of the earlier adventures of the Argonauts and so puts the story of the Trojan War within the broader scheme of Greek mythological history.

> Far into the night the long-haired Achaeans
> feasted, as did the Trojans in Troy and their allies,
> and far into the night Zeus of the Counsels devised
> evils for them, thundering terribly, and pale fear
> seized them pouring wine from their cups on the ground;

no one dared drink before pouring a libation to Zeus.
Then lying down they took the gift of sleep.   (476-82)

Thus ends Book 7. I agree with Ameis-Hentze and Willcock (against Leaf
and Kirk) that the thunder of Zeus is directed against the Achaeans, for whom he is
preparing defeat on the next day; we also think of the neglect of the Achaeans to
give the gods due sacrifice when building the wall. Twice again in the *Iliad*, at
8.469-83 and 18.356-67, Zeus will make known at the end of one day his
intentions for the next.

The building of the Achaean wall is an important example of *prooikonomia*,
for the Achaeans will use it to defend themselves on the next two days of battle.
And the duel between Hector and Ajax foreshadows their opposition on the great
day of battle when Hector will be wounded by Ajax and will be able to drive him
back only with the help of Zeus.

BOOK 8: THE SECOND DAY OF BATTLE

Zeus Prohibits the Gods from Participating in the Battle, 1-52

The first day of battle has shown that even without Achilles the Achaeans and their gods (Hera and Athena) are stronger than the Trojans and their gods (Aphrodite, Ares, and Apollo) and that therefore if Zeus is to honor Achilles he must intervene in the course of events (so Rothe 1910.219-20). This he does at sunrise on the second day of battle after calling the gods to assembly.

> Hear me, all you gods and all you goddesses
> while I say what the heart in my breast commands me.
> Let not any female divinity nor any male
> try to cross my purpose, but let all
> give way so that I may finish this business most quickly. (5-9)

He ends by threatening to drive back to Olympus or (13) hurl into Tartarus anyone who disobeys him, and flaunts his superior strength by challenging all the other gods to a tug of war: let them, taking hold of one end of a golden cord, try to pull him down from heaven; he, if he seriously (*prophron*, 23) wanted to, would pull up land and sea and, tying the cord around a peak of Olympus, would cause everything to hang in mid-air (and so destroy the whole world). His boastfulness, which seems somewhat comical (compare his teasing speech at the beginning of Book 4), emphasizes his decision that the other gods are not to participate in the battle. This prohibition will remain in effect until the beginning of Book 20.

His words at first meet with silence, but then Athena speaks up.

> O dear father, son of Cronus, highest of rulers,
> we know very well ourselves that your strength is unconquerable,
> but we are filled with pity (*olophurometha*) for the Danaan spearmen
> who shall now perish in fulfillment of an evil fate.
> But we shall stay out of the battle as you command
> and only grant to the Argives our helpful advice
> so that they all may not die because of your anger. (31-37)

Zeus, smiling, replies that he has not spoken in complete seriousness (*thumo prophroni,* 39-40; compare the similar use of the same expression at 22.183-84). This does not mean that he is not completely serious about his prohibition, but that his threat of going against fate and destroying the whole world was an overstatement (so Erbse 1986.288-289). And he apparently permits the other gods to give advice to their favorites, for later in this book Hera will inspire Agamemnon to exhort his men. The word *olophuromai,* "to bewail," "to pity," in Athena's speech describes the emotion with which the gods typically react when they come to the aid of mortals, as Hera and also Zeus, in spite of himself, will do in the coming battle.

The present scene on Olympus will be answered by a corresponding one at the end of this book, after Zeus has given the upper hand to the Trojans. Now, dressed in gold, he rides off in his golden chariot to the top of Mount Ida near Troy, from which he will direct the battle.

The Battle, 53-349

The Achaeans, having eaten quickly, issue from their huts, and the Trojans, being fewer in number, come from their city; a great noise arises. The armies attack each other, and the battle (described in lines 60-65=4.446-51) is evenly fought until midday. Then Zeus weighs the fates of the two sides in his scales, and the Trojans are shown to be the victors. Surely he is not consulting the scales to learn the future; rather he is using them to show what he has already determined will happen.

From now until sunset the fighting can be divided into two phases. In the first (78-244) Diomedes puts the Trojans to flight for a while; his last success is the slaying of Hector's charioteer. Thereafter Zeus gives Hector special strength and with his thunderbolts drives back Diomedes and Nestor, Diomedes' charioteer. Hera tries in vain to get Poseidon to help the Achaeans. Then, when the Achaeans have been pent up behind their wall, Agamemnon, inspired by Hera, exhorts the Achaeans, ending with a prayer to Zeus.

In the second phase (245-488) the Trojans are again forced to retreat for a while, but now Teucer (instead of Diomedes) is the main Achaean hero; his last success (like Diomedes' in phase one) is the slaying of Hector's charioteer. Thereafter Zeus takes control and has the Trojans under the leadership of Hector drive the Achaeans back behind their wall (as in phase one). The Achaeans exhort each other and pray to the gods (compare Agamemnon's exhortation and prayer in phase one). The climactic parallelism created by these two phases impresses upon us the determination of Zeus to implement his will.

At the beginning of the first phase Zeus makes known the decision of his scales by thundering and hurling a lightning bolt among the Achaeans. All of them flee except Nestor who is prevented by a fatally wounded trace horse. While he is trying to get free of this horse, Hector in his chariot is bearing down upon him, and this would have been the end of him if Diomedes had not come to the rescue.

Seeing Odysseus running past, Diomedes calls on him for help in driving back Hector, but Odysseus continues on his way to the ships; thus we are made to feel how desperate the situation of the Achaeans is. Diomedes takes Nestor onto his chariot to be his charioteer. The picture of him and Nestor attacking the whole Trojan army against the will of Zeus while all the other Achaeans are fleeing seems bizarre. Diomedes aims his spear at Hector but, missing him, hits his charioteer. Hector withdraws and finds another charioteer, Archeptolemus (to be killed by Teucer in phase two). In the meantime Diomedes is continuing his attack, and the Trojans would have fled like lambs (131, simile type 4) into their city had not Zeus taken notice and hurled a thunderbolt in front of Diomedes' chariot. That Diomedes and Nestor alone might have driven the Trojans back into Troy seems absurd, but the poet frequently uses such an ultimate threat (the fall of Troy, the destruction of the ships, the death of a hero) to motivate the intervention of a deity.

The horses are frightened by the thunderbolts, and Nestor says:

> Now drive the single-hoofed horses in flight, son of Tydeus.
> Do you not see that the strength of Zeus is not with you?
> For Zeus is bestowing the glory on this man today;
> later he'll give it to us again if only
> he will; no one can alter the mind of Zeus
> no matter how strong he may be; Zeus is much stronger.   (139-44)

Nestor's assessment of the situation is correct. But Diomedes fears that Hector will boast. Nestor answers that, in view of all the Trojans Diomedes has slain, no Trojan would believe such a boast, and he turns the horses in flight to the ships (157). Hector pursues, taunting Diomedes as a weakling, and three times Diomedes is tempted to turn and fight, but each time Zeus thunders from Ida, "giving a sign to the Trojans that the battle has been decided in their favor" (171).

We can give three reasons for the Diomedes-Nestor episode. First, it continues the exploits of Diomedes begun in Book 5; he is the great offensive fighter of the Achaeans in the absence of Achilles. Second, it continues the theme of the natural superiority of the Achaeans; even without the help of the pro-Achaean gods they—in the person of Diomedes—would have been victorious had not Zeus directly intervened. Third, it shows us for the first time the youngest and the oldest of the Achaeans reacting to each other. Diomedes is a great warrior, as Nestor, now too old to fight, had been in his youth; and Diomedes has great wisdom for a young man but not the wisdom of Nestor.

The rout of the Achaeans being complete, Hector tells the Trojans that (as is true) Zeus has granted him the victory, and deduces from this that the Achaean wall and trench will not stand in his way; he will get among the ships and burn them. Then, reminding his four horses of how well Andromache has fed them, he urges them on to try to overtake Diomedes and Nestor (who are driving the divine team Diomedes took from Aeneas in Book 5). If only he could gain possession of the wonderful armor of Diomedes and Nestor, the enemy would flee home in their ships this night.

This speech angers Hera, who shakes in her seat causing Olympus to quake (199). She tries to persuade Poseidon to help the Achaeans, accusing him of having an unpitying heart (*oude nu soi . . . olophuretai . . . thumos*, 201-2), but he refuses, "since Zeus is much stronger" (211; the same words appeared at the end of Nestor's speech to Diomedes,144). Zeus is in control. Meanwhile the Achaeans, having fled to the ships, are hemmed in by Hector, "to whom Zeus has given the victory" (216).

Now Hector would have set fire to the ships had not Hera inspired Agamemnon to exhort his men. Agamemnon does this in tears after going to the midmost ship with a large red cloak to signal his desire to speak. He ends his exhortation with the prayer that Zeus, who is not allowing them to take Troy, may at least save them now. A turning point in battle, we remember, is frequently introduced by an exhortation, and this is sometimes accompanied by a prayer, especially to Zeus as the steward of war. Compare Ajax's exhortation at 17.629-47. It seems likely that Hera is depending on such a prayer to move Zeus to pity.

This is what happens, for the second phase of the present battle begins with Zeus pitying (*olophurato,* 245) the weeping Agamemnon and sending him an eagle that flies over the battlefield and drops a fawn on the altar of Zeus in the Achaean camp—an omen that puts new spirit into the Achaeans. That Zeus sends such an omen at this time is inconsistent with his purpose of bringing about a defeat of the Achaeans, but he is often moved to bemoan a human situation and seems able to be of two minds about the Achaeans, as also about the Trojans whom he pities in defeat. Moreover, the poet wants to create a second phase of battle parallel to the first while at the same time showing Zeus in control.

In lines 253-73 nine counterattacking Achaeans are named, beginning with Diomedes and ending with Teucer.

> Teucer was ninth to advance, stretching his bent bow,
> and stood behind Telamonian Ajax's shield.
> Ajax would shift his shield slightly aside, and Teucer,
> aiming and shooting his arrow into the crowd,
> would hit someone, making him fall and die
> while he, like a child going back to its mother, returned
> again to Ajax who hid him behind his bright shield.   (266-72)

This gives us a general view of Teucer's fighting (he regularly fights with the help of the big Ajax) which is made specific in the following description of some of his exploits.

He kills eight men, but is unable to hit Hector. Aiming at Hector, he hits Priam's son Gorgythion whose dying head droops like a poppy heavy with moisture (306-7, simile type 9). Then, aiming at Hector again, Teucer again hits another, Hector's charioteer Archeptolemus. This causes Hector to go in search of a new charioteer, whom he finds in his brother Cebriones. Leaving his chariot with Cebriones, he attacks Teucer on foot and puts an end to his shooting spree by hitting him with a large rock on the collar bone, causing him to drop his bow and making his arm useless; but Ajax protects Teucer with his shield, and two other men carry him off to the ships.

At this point Zeus gives the Trojans new spirit.

> The Olympian again put strength into the Trojans,
> and they drove the Achaeans straight over the deep trench.
> Hector moved in the vanguard glorying in his strength.
> As when a dog chases after a wild boar or a lion,
> pursuing on swift feet and snapping behind him
> at his flanks and buttocks but watching lest he should turn,
> so Hector kept after the long-haired Achaeans,
> always killing the last one of those in the rout.
> But when they had got through the stakes and the trench
> in flight, though many had died at the hands of the Trojans,
> there by the ships they stopped and stood their ground,
> exhorting each other and praying to all the gods
> urgently, each of them raising his hands to heaven.
> Hector was driving his beautiful horses up
> and down the trench, like a Gorgon or man-slaying Ares.   (335-49)

With this passage we return to the same situation as at the end of the first phase of battle. Pope (1967.VII.417) noted the pro-Achaean sympathy of the poet in the simile (type 4) describing their flight : "he makes them fly like Lions, and as they fly, turn frequently back upon their pursuer; so that it is hard to say if they, or he, be in the greater Danger." Contrast how the fleeing Trojans were compared to lambs in line 131.

Hera and Athena Try to Help the Achaeans.   Zeus Predicts the Future to Hera, 350-488

Now Hera, seeing and pitying the Achaeans (*idous' eleese,* 350), complains about Zeus and Hector to Athena.   Does Athena no longer care about (*kekadesometha,* 353) the dying Achaeans? (Compare how, above in lines 201-2, Hera earlier spoke to Poseidon.) Athena answers that she wishes Hector might die in his own land (as will happen in Book 22) but that Zeus is preventing this, having forgotten how she helped his son Heracles. Zeus, she says, is "carrying out the purposes of Thetis who kissed his knees and took his chin in her hands, begging him to honor city-sacking Achilles" (370-72). Accordingly, so that they can go against Hector, Hera (the charioteer) should get ready their horses while she (the warrior) arms herself for battle.

Hera agrees, and they are about to pass on their chariot out through the gates of Olympus, which the Horae open for them, when Zeus sends Iris to threaten them with his thunderbolt and command them to turn back. He is especially angry at Athena, the disobedience of Hera being less unexpected. Hera immediately advises obedience.

> Alas, O daughter of aegis-bearing Zeus, no longer
> would I allow us to do battle for mortals against Zeus.
> Let one man die and another man live as is destined
> to happen. Let Zeus in accord with those plans of his
> decide for Trojans and Danaans as it seems fitting.   (427-431)

Hera has changed from pity to indifference, as is typical of the gods in their relations with mortals, but her later response to Zeus (lines 464-65 below) will show that she has not spoken here with complete conviction (so Burkert 1955.78).

Having so spoken, she turns back the horses. We are reminded of how Nestor prevailed upon Diomedes to retreat: the older charioteer advises the younger fighter to yield before Zeus, and then turns back the horses (432=157). The Horae (a ring composition with their opening the gates) attend to the horses while the goddesses, being grieved at heart, take their seats among the gods. This abortive attempt of Hera and Athena to interfere in the battle makes a strong contrast with their successful intervention at the end of Book 5 (lines 389-96=5.745-52).

Now Zeus returns to Olympus. Poseidon attends to his horses while he goes and takes his seat on his golden throne among the gods, causing Olympus to reel (443; probably an indication that he sits down in anger; compare how earlier the angry Hera shook in her seat, 199). He sarcastically asks the goddesses why they are so grieved; surely they are not exhausted with slaughtering Trojans. At first they are silent, but finally Hera speaks up in anger.

> O son of Cronus most terrible, what are you saying?
> We know very well ourselves that your strength is exhaustless
> but we are filled with pity (*olophurometha*) for the Danaan spearmen
> who shall now perish in fulfillment of an evil fate.
> But we shall stay out of the battle as you command
> and only grant to the Argives our helpful advice
> so that they all may not die because of your anger.   463-68)

This speech is an almost exact repetition of Athena's earlier response to Zeus (32-37), and shows that Hera still pities the Achaeans in spite of her words to Athena in lines 427-31.

The situation here creates a ring composition and a climatic parallelism with the scene on Olympus at the beginning of this book. The climax comes in the fact that the goddesses have now tested Zeus' determination to maintain his prohibition and been forced to yield. In the earlier scene Zeus answered Athena with a smile; here, however, there are no smiles. He begins his speech to Hera by predicting the course of the next day of battle.

> Tomorrow you shall see the mighty son of Cronus,
> if you so will, cow-eyed queenly Hera,
> destroying even more the great army of the Argive spearmen,
> for powerful Hector shall not cease from battle
> before he rouses by the ships swift-footed Achilles
> on that day when they will fight at the sterns of the ships
> in the fearful narrows over the dead Patroclus,
> for thus it is destined to happen.   (470-77)

He goes on to curse her; for all he cares she may go down to Tartarus. Again we are reminded of the earlier scene on Olympus in which (13) he threatened to throw into Tartarus anyone who disobeyed him. Zeus' prediction gives us an outline of Part 2: Hector will be the victor, Patroclus will be killed, and finally Achilles will return to the action during the battle near the ships over Patroclus' body.

Hera receives Zeus' speech in silence, and the sun sets. The coming of night is unwelcome to the Trojans, but the Achaeans have been praying for it fervently. We remember that they were exhorting each other and praying when last we saw them; this is what they have been doing during the scenes on Olympus. The second day of battle, like the first one, has shown "that, other things being equal, the Achaeans are still more than a match for their opponents, even in the absence of Achilles" (Willcock 1978.268), but other things have not been equal, for Zeus has begun to move to fulfill his promise to Thetis.

The Trojan Assembly, 489-565

There follows the first of several night scenes; this night will last through Book 10. Hector, with his long spear in hand, speaks to the Trojan horsemen on the plain near the ships. Being certain that they will defeat the Achaeans on the next day, he concludes with an extraordinary boast.

> If only I were so certain I'd be
> a god immortal and unaging for ever and ever,
> honored like Athena and Apollo, as I'm certain
> tomorrow shall bring disaster upon the Argives.   (538-41)

Hector will persist in this optimism even after Achilles has returned to the action. Most of his speech, however, is concerned with instructing the horsemen. They must obey night, take their meals, feed their horses, and burn fires on the plain so that the Achaeans will be unable to escape unharmed; and those in the city must be on their guard against a possible sneak attack. Tomorrow he will give them further commands, and he will encounter Diomedes.

The Trojans light the fires, a thousand of them, around which the men and horses eat. Book 8 ends with the beautiful simile comparing the watchfires of the Trojans to the shining of the stars on a clear night. It is thus impressed upon us that the Trojans are now encamped on the plain before the ships. At the end of the first day of battle, in Book 7, they spent the night in Troy. Now, at the end of the second day of battle, they are besieging the Achaean camp.

The defeat of the Achaeans in Book 8 will cause Agamemnon to send the embassy to Achilles in Book 9. Moreover, since we have been informed by Zeus' speech to Hera that Achilles will not return to the action until they are fighting over the body of Patroclus, we know that Achilles will refuse the embassy with tragic consequences to himself (so Owen 1946. 89).

The ancients entitled Book 8 "The Unfinished Battle" from the abruptness with which it is broken off. Many scholars have commented on its sketchiness and have seen it as a foreshadowing of the events of the great day of battle. The defeat of the Achaeans in Book 8 is, as it were, a doublet on a smaller scale of their defeat in Books 11-15. So Schadewaldt 1938.93 and 127, who notes that the unsuccessful attempt to do something in Homer often points to its eventual accomplishment. Thus the thwarted attempt of Hera first to win the aid of Poseidon and then to intervene herself points to her successful intervention with the help of Poseidon in Book 14. And the failure of Hector and the Trojans to cross the trench and breach the wall and fire the ships points to their success in doing these things on the great day of battle.

BOOK 9: THE EMBASSY TO ACHILLES

The Achaean Assembly and Council, 1-181

In the last book Zeus reaffirmed his determination to fulfill his promise to Thetis. In the present book Achilles will reaffirm his determination to stay out of the action. The framework is simple: first, at a meeting of the Achaean council it is decided to send envoys to Achilles to ask him to return to battle; then the mission of these envoys, Odysseus, Ajax, and also Phoenix, is described; finally, there is their report of failure back to the council. What makes this book, like Book 1, one of the most brilliant in the *Iliad* is its speeches. We hear Diomedes, who as a young man perhaps understands Achilles especially well, interacting with Agamemnon and Nestor again; Odysseus, the practical, dependable leader of the embassy (he also led the mission to return Chryseis to her father in Book 1 and acted for Agamemnon to bring the men to order in Book 2); Ajax, blunt and laconic, the main protector of the Achaeans in Achilles' absence; Phoenix, Achilles' old tutor, first introduced here (we should especially listen to him); and finally Achilles in all the anguish of his troubled mind.

Book 9 begins as follows:

> Thus the Trojans held guard, but the Achaeans
> were possessed by the spirit of flight, the companion of cold fear,
> and all the best men were struck with unbearable grief (*penthos*).
> As when two winds stir up the fish-breeding sea,
> Boreas and Zephyrus which blow from the region of Thrace,
> and suddenly arrive and cause the black waves to grow
> to a crest and spew out much seaweed over the coast,
> so was the heart in the breast of the Achaeans in turmoil.   (1-8)

This simile makes a sharp contrast with that comparing the Trojan watchfires to stars in which "the shepherd delights" (8.559). The mood of the Achaeans is one of grief, for which the nouns *penthos* and *achos* are used—*penthos* stressing "mourning," *achos* "anguish"—and the verb *tetiemai*, "to be saddened." Being stricken with great grief (*achos*, 9), Agamemnon has the men called to assembly (this on a realistic level takes place at the same time as the Trojan assembly at the end of the last book; compare Introduction 6-7), and they take their seats in grief (*tetieotes*, 13).

And Agamemnon

> stood up, weeping copiously like a black spring
> which pours forth its dark water down a steep rock;
> so he groaned deeply as he addressed the Argives.   (13-17)

This simile will be repeated at 16.3-4 to describe Patroclus weeping in pity for the Achaeans. Agamemnon—he is naturally inclined to discouragement, a bad trait in a leader—blames Zeus for not fulfilling his promise that they would take Troy, and calls on his men to flee home. This speech repeats what he said in Book 2 (lines 18-28=2.111-18 and 139-41) where he made the same proposal in order to test the troops. Now he is being sincere. The men, probably remembering what happened in Book 2, remain in their seats.

At first there is silence, but then Diomedes opposes Agamemnon, following "the custom, O King, in the assembly" (34; cf. 2.73). He reminds him of how he wrongly rebuked him in the Review at the end of Book 4, and says that Zeus, though he has made Agamemnon a king, has failed to give him stoutheartedness. Go home, he tells him, but the other Achaeans, or at least Sthenelus and himself, will remain until Troy is destroyed, for they have the blessing of Zeus. Diomedes continues to believe in the promise of Zeus.

This speech meets with approval. But Nestor, "implying that an older man might show more tact" (Edwards 1987.217), says that Diomedes, though speaking well, has offered no definite plan of action; and that they must post a guard between the wall and the trench (65-68), and Agamemnon should invite the leaders to a feast in his hut and ask for further advice. The Trojan watchfires are burning nearby. Who can rejoice in them? This night will either destroy or save the Achaeans. Thus the ensuing narrative is divided into, first, a brief account (80-88) of the posting of the guard (which will be mentioned again in Book 10), and then the description (89-181) of the council in Agamemnon's hut.

There, after they have finished eating, Nestor addresses Agamemnon, whom (in order to make him favorably disposed) he praises for his willingness to take good advice. Earlier Agamemnon had not listened to him when he had advised him against depriving Achilles of Briseis. Now they must try to appease Achilles with "soothing gifts and honey-sweet words" (113).

Agamemnon admits that he was wrong to offend Achilles, and is willing to make amends with gifts, which he lists at length (122-57), among them one of his daughters in marriage; and he will swear that he has not had sexual relations with Briseis. But he will make no apology to Achilles. Achilles must submit to the lordship of Agamemnon.

Then Nestor suggests that they appoint an embassy consisting of Phoenix, the big Ajax, Odysseus, and two heralds. This suggestion is approved; and so, after a prayer to Zeus, the embassy sets out.

It seems odd that Phoenix, one of Achilles' people and in fact his surrogate father, has been at the council and, as we soon learn, has eaten with Agamemnon, and now has been made a part of the embassy. But thus we are put on notice of a disaffection with Achilles, which we shall find in Patroclus and the Myrmidons generally (according to Achilles, 16.203-6) and with which we (the Greek audience) can easily sympathize.

The Embassy, 182-668

The envoys go along by the sea from Agamemnon's to Achilles' hut praying for success to Poseidon. We are reminded of the two heralds at 1.327-30 who went along by the sea to bring Briseis from Achilles to Agamemnon. The present mission is like a reversal of this earlier one. We are about to see Achilles again for the first time since Book 1.

A problem much discussed since antiquity is that the embassy is three times (182, 192, and 196) described by a dual instead of a plural verb. The best explanation is probably that Odysseus and Ajax are considered the envoys proper. The heralds are their attendants, and Phoenix has been specially added.

When the envoys reach Achilles' hut, they find him playing his lyre and singing about the *klea andron*, "glorious deeds of men," that is, epic poetry like the *Iliad* about great men of the past who had won glory in battle; and Patroclus is seated opposite him. Achilles is much concerned with glory (*kleos*). We should compare the picture of him looking out at the battle from his place at his ship during the period of his wrath; withdrawal is difficult for him. Now he rises, as does Patroclus, and greets the envoys as his dearest friends. Then he has Patroclus prepare a larger and stronger mixture of wine, and sets a good meal before them. After they have eaten, Ajax nods to Phoenix—probably a signal that they should get down to business, perhaps made to him in deference to his age (and thus also the poet reminds us again of Phoenix's extraordinary presence).

Odysseus, their main spokesman, begins. He thanks Achilles for the meal, but remarks that they have just eaten with Agamemnon too, thus showing that they are table companions to both parties. After reviewing the situation at the end of Book 8, he entreats Achilles to save the Achaeans and reminds him of the advice his father Peleus gave him when he set out for Troy, to keep a check on his anger, "for friendship is better" (256). There follows the list of the gifts and the report of

Agamemnon's promise to swear that he has not had sexual relations with Briseis (264-99=122-57), but Odysseus diplomatically omits the end of Agamemnon's speech in which Achilles is asked to submit to Agamemnon, saying instead:

> But if the son of Atreus is still hateful to you,
> both he and his gifts, take pity (*eleaire*) on all the other
> Achaeans in their distress throughout the army,
> and so be honored like a god with great glory among them.
> Now is your chance to kill Hector; he'd meet you in battle,
> for in his rampaging madness he boasts that no Danaan
> can equal himself of all those come in the ships.   (300-6)

Achilles answers with a flat refusal. He despises deceit and will speak straight out: he will not obey Agamemnon. After risking his life to help Agamemnon and his brother regain Helen, Agamemnon has deprived him of his woman. He dwells on this offense self-pityingly.

> As a bird brings in her mouth to her fledgling chicks
> whatever she catches, and life goes badly for her,
> so I spent many sleepless nights in the open
> and bore many full days of bloody war
> doing battle with men for the prize of their wives.   (323-27)

The tenderness of this simile, in which he thinks of himself before his wrath as a mother bird, is striking.

> Now I shall not be fighting with godlike Hector.
> Tomorrow, after I have sacrificed to all the gods
> and had my ships well loaded and launched in the sea,
> you'll see them there, provided you care to look,
> sailing quite early out on the fish-breeding Hellespont.
> If glorious earth-shaking Poseidon grant me a good sail,
> I should reach Phthia, my rich-soiled homeland, in three days.   (356-63)

He rejects Agamemnon's gifts.

> Not even if ten or twenty times so much he gave
> as he does now, with other things added from elsewhere, . . .

> not even if his gifts were as numerous as the sand and the dust motes,
> not even so would Agamemnon persuade me
> until he's repaid me for all his cruel outrage against me.   (379-87)

(These lines will later be paralleled by Achilles' rejection of Hector's plea for a proper burial; see our comments on 22.349-54.) Achilles asserts that his life is worth more than all the spoils of Troy and all the wealth of Delphi, and refers to his mother's prophecy (410-16; cf.1.352-53) that he must either stay at Troy and die with glory (*kleos*) or return home and live a long life without glory (*kleos*). The other Achaeans should follow his example and return home since Zeus is now protecting Troy (417-20), and the envoys should tell the council to think of a better plan for saving the ships.

> But let Phoenix stay and sleep here with me
> that he may sail with me to our dear home tomorrow,
> if he is willing; I shall not force him to do this.   (427-29)

At first Achilles' answer meets with silence, but finally Phoenix, taking his cue from Achilles' last words, speaks up, weeping. His very long speech can be divided into three parts: his autobiography (434-95), the allegory of the Prayers (496-523), and the example of Meleager (524-605). Of course he will go home with Achilles, whom he addresses as "dear child," if Achilles is really not willing to keep the fire from the ships. But Achilles should listen to him, for his father Peleus sent Phoenix with him to Troy to teach him to be "a speaker of words and a doer of deeds" (443). As a young man, Phoenix at the urging of his mother had lain with his father's concubine, for which his father had cursed him with sterility and put him under house arrest; but he, being greatly angered (therefore he can understand the anger of Achilles; so Plutarch [Babbitt 1969.381-83]), broke down the door and fled to Phthia, where Peleus made him Achilles' tutor. This narrative seems unheroic and half-comic (so Scodel 1982.128-36), calculated to make Achilles' favorably disposed; Phoenix has an old man's tact and charm, like Nestor.

The second part of his speech begins as follows:

> But, Achilles, tame your great spirit. It is wrong to maintain
> a pitiless (*nelees*) heart; the gods themselves are appeased,
> whose glory and honor and power is greater than yours.   (496-98)

These words introduce the allegory of the Prayers. When someone has done some wrong, if he will honor the Prayers, they will beg Zeus to release him from his blind folly (*ate*), and Zeus will oblige them. If, however, the wrongdoer does not honor them, they will have Zeus cast him into even more blindness until he meets with deserved retribution. Accordingly, Achilles should honor the Prayers by accepting the gifts of Agamemnon.

Then comes the warning example of Meleager: "Thus we have heard of the glorious deeds of men (*klea andron*) who were earlier" (524). The Couretes were attacking the walls of Calydon, the city of Meleager's people, the Aetolians. This war had arisen during the hunting of a wild boar, when also Meleager had slain his uncle, his mother's brother. His mother, being angered by this, cursed Meleager, causing him to withdraw from the battle in anger. (In other versions she burns a log connected with Meleager's life by sympathetic magic.) He retired to his room with his wife Cleopatra; and a series of people—first official representatives; then his father, mother, and sisters; and finally his companions—came and begged him to save his people, offering rich rewards. He rejected their pleas, but finally, too late to receive the rewards, his wife prevailed upon him to return.

It seems likely that Homer invented much of the Meleager example—his anger and withdrawal and the embassies to him—to make a significant parallel with the story of the *Iliad* (so Willcock 1964.147-53; but see Kakridis, 1949.19ff., 152ff., and Edwards 1987.226-27). The envoys in the Meleager example can be equated with the envoys to Achilles: the official representatives are like Odysseus; Meleager's family, especially his father, like Phoenix; and Meleager's companions like Ajax. Finally, Meleager's wife Cleopatra can be equated with Patroclus. The names Cleo-patra and Patro-clus consist of the same two elements and so have the same meaning, "glory of the ancestors" (so Eustathius on *Il.* 9.556). Cleopatra and Patroclus show themselves to be the embodiments of the glory of their ancestors by acting in solidarity with their people.

Achilles replies that Zeus will honor him by causing the Achaeans to be defeated, and he blames Phoenix for sympathizing with Agamemnon: friends should support friends. As for Odysseus and Ajax, let them report his answer to the council. But Phoenix should spend the night with him, for they will decide tomorrow whether to return home. Thus Phoenix's speech has had some effect upon him, for now he will consider staying at Troy.

Then Achilles nods to Patroclus to make a bed for Phoenix. Ajax, taking this as a signal that the meeting is over, tells Odysseus that they should leave immediately. Achilles is hard-hearted, like a wild animal, a man with no concern

pitiless

for the friendship of comrades, pitiless (*neles*, 632). Even a man whose brother or son has been murdered will accept payment from the murderer and allow him to remain within the community. But Achilles would rather nurse his anger over a single girl than be gracious to them, his guests, his dearest friends, the representatives of the Achaeans.

Achilles answers that he is unable to give up his wrath, for Agamemnon has treated him like a wandering day-laborer, a man without any civic rights (in contrast to the murderer in Ajax's comparison). He concludes as follows:

> But you two envoys go and report my decision:
> I shall not think again of bloody battle
> until glorious Hector, noble Priam's son,
> arrives at the huts and the ships of my Myrmidons
> killing the Argives and setting my ships on fire.
> But I think that I shall keep Hector away from my hut
> and my black ship, however hot he may be for the fight.   (649-55)

Now Achilles has softened his position even more: he will not return to the action until the fire reaches his huts and ships. Odysseus, Phoenix, and Ajax have all without success begged him to pity the Achaeans. He will not relent until, at the beginning of Book 16, Patroclus, like Cleopatra in the Meleager example, finally moves him to pity.

While Odysseus, Ajax, and the heralds are returning, we are given a brief description (658-68) of Achilles, Patroclus, and Phoenix retiring for the night. Patroclus has a special bed made for Phoenix. Achilles and Patroclus lie beside beautiful women, whom, like Briseis, Achilles has taken captive. The picture is one of normality, as if Achilles were completely satisfied with his decision to reject a reconciliation.

The Report of the Envoys, 669-713

Odysseus reports that Achilles continues to be wrathful and threatens to sail home tomorrow. Lines 684-87 of his speech repeat, in indirect statement, lines 417-20 of Achilles' answer to him. He also tells the council to consult Ajax and the two heralds about what was said, and, repeating the end of Achilles' speech to him (691-87=428-29), says that Phoenix is remaining with Achilles so as to be able to sail with him tomorrow.

Why Odysseus ignores Achilles' responses to Ajax and Phoenix has been a problem since antiquity. The best answer is probably that he considers the reply made to his report of Agamemnon's offer to be Achilles' official response. Moreover, in view of the changeabililty of Achilles' character, he might think it wise for them to expect the worst.

Odysseus' report is met with silence until Diomedes, addressing Agamemnon, says that now they must follow his original plan (Nestor's has failed). They ought never to have sent the embassy; this has only added to Achilles' arrogance.

> He will fight again
> when his spirit or some divinity stirs him.
> Come, let us all agree to do as I say.
> Now we should lie down to sleep, being happily sated
> with good food and drink; this will mean prowess and strength.
> But when bright dawn, rosy-fingered, appears, Agamemnon,
> marshaling the soldiers and horsemen in front of the ships,
> exhort them and take your place in the vanguard to fight.   (702-9)

These words, which are greeted with applause, look forward to Book 11 where at the beginning of the great day of battle Agamemnon will lead out the Achaeans to fight. Now at the end of Book 9, following Diomedes' advice, they lie down to sleep.

BOOK 10: A NIGHT ADVENTURE

Some ancient scholars and a majority of modern ones including unitarians like Schadewaldt consider this book to be a later addition to the *Iliad*. They point out that it is complete in itself and can be omitted without leaving a discernible gap; that it differs in tone from the rest of the *Iliad*, seeming anti-heroic, "a farcical interlude" (Monro 1884.354); and that it contains a number of late forms and late grammatical constructions. But late forms and constructions are found clustered in other parts of the poem (in the Shield, for instance, which according to our scheme ends Part 2 as Book 10 does Part 1); the different tone, including different presentations of similar material, can be explained by the unique subject matter; and granted that Book 10 is a separable interlude, this does not necessarily mean that it was not created by Homer.

In Book 10 the Achaean leaders assemble at the place where the guards are stationed—between the wall and the trench—and take Thrasymedes (Nestor's son) and Meriones, two leaders of the guards, into their counsels. This guard, consisting of seven divisions of a hundred men each, was posted in Book 9, as described in two passages· lines 65-68, where Nestor advised it, and lines 80-88, where the guards assumed their positions. These passages create a balance to Hector's posting of the Trojan guard in Book 8. But perhaps Homer also intended them as a preparation (*prooikonomia*) for Book 10. Or perhaps a later poet used them (or even created them) to connect Book 9 with his addition of Book 10.

On one thing scholars agree, that Book 10 has been tailored to fit its present position in the *Iliad*. It assumes the wrath of Achilles, the building of the wall and trench, and the victory of Hector at the end of the previous day. Moreover, the characterizations of the heroes clearly build on the representations of these men in the earlier books of the *Iliad*.

But why was Book 10 made a part of the *Iliad*? A reason often given is that the success of the Achaean spies helps to explain how the Achaeans, after their defeat in Book 8 and the rejection of their embassy in Book 9, can have the spirit to fight on the next day (so Rothe1910.245-46). But another possible reason is noted by van der Valk 1982.136-37: Book 10 offers a diversion to soothe the pro-Achaean sympathies of the Greek audience. The poet knew that the defeat of the Achaeans, both that already described in Book 8 and that in prospect for the next day of recitation, would displease his Greek audience and therefore added Book 10 which allows the Achaeans to have a marvelous romp at the expense of the Trojans.

Preparations on the Achaean Side, 1-298

We can divide Book 10 into two parallel preparatory sections, the first for the Achaeans (1-298), the second for the Trojans (299-337), in which each side decides to send out a spying mission and in which we find the main links with earlier books; and a third section describing the night adventure proper (338-579). The preparatory section for the Achaeans is much longer than that for the Trojans; it is even longer than the section describing the adventure itself. This seems to show that the poet and his audience have more interest in the Achaeans than in the Trojans.

We begin with the picture of everyone sleeping except Agamemnon. He is praying to Zeus, groaning frequently and shaking with fear as he looks out at the watchfires of the Trojans and hears their flutes and hubbub. His groaning is compared to flashes of lightning sent by Zeus as a portent of some disaster—a deluge or hail storm or snow storm or war.

Having decided to go to Nestor for advice, he dresses in a lion-skin and takes his spear. (The strange clothing suits the unusual adventure about to be told and, since it would not shine at night like regular armor, may be meant as camouflage.) But then the scene shifts to Menelaus who also is fearful and unable to sleep and so dresses himself in a leopard-skin and a bronze helmet and takes his spear—the parallel with Agamemnon is clear—and comes to Agamemnon whom he finds putting on his shield.

Why are you arming? he asks. Will you send someone to spy on the Trojans? Who would undertake to do this alone in the dark? Agamemnon answers that they must take counsel, for Zeus has changed his mind and is now favoring Hector who has been victorious beyond all expectations. Menelaus should summon the big Ajax and Idomeneus. He himself will get Nestor to go with him to the guards and give them instructions. Nestor is the one to do this, for his son Thrasymedes and Meriones are in charge of the guard. When Menelaus has brought Ajax and Idomeneus to the place where the guards are posted, he should wait there for Nestor and himself.

After dispatching Menelaus, Agamemnon (as he has twice announced) goes off to Nestor whom he finds lying outside his hut. Hearing him coming, Nestor raises himself on his elbow and asks who goes there and why. Agamemnon reveals his identity and says how dreadfully he fears for the Achaeans. He and Nestor should go to the guards and see whether they are doing their duty. The enemy are nearby and may decide to fight even at night. Nestor agrees to go, saying that Zeus will not fulfill all the expectations of Hector who will be plagued with future sufferings if only Achilles will give up his wrath. But he suggests that they rouse Diomedes and Odysseus, and the little Ajax and Meges, and send someone to summon the big Ajax and Idomeneus whose ships are farthest away. And he blames Menelaus for sleeping when he should be helping Agamemnon. Agamemnon of course can defend his brother who is now on his way to summon the big Ajax and Idomeneus, as Nestor has just suggested be done. We are reminded of earlier scenes, in Books 4 and 7, where Agamemnon showed a protective attitude toward Menelaus. Nestor apologizes and, dressing himself in a warm wooly outfit—he will not be one of the spies—and taking his spear, goes off with Agamemnon.

This scene also, like that between Agamemnon and Menelaus, gives us a view of things to come. We now expect to see Diomedes and Odysseus and the little Ajax and Meges, as well as Agamemnon, Nestor, Menelaus, the big Ajax, and Idomeneus, made a part of the meeting.

In the rest of this book Nestor overshadows Agamemnon as leader. They go first to Odysseus whom Nestor wakes by calling him out of his hut. Odysseus agrees to follow them to rouse another leader (Diomedes), and returns to his hut to put on his shield. Willcock 1978.288 remarks that Odysseus here and Diomedes later in this book are described as coming to the meeting more or less unarmed in order that when they have been chosen to be the spies they may borrow equipment for their expedition (*prooikonomia*).

Odysseus goes off with Nestor and Agamemnon, and they find Diomedes sleeping outside his hut. Nestor, using his foot, nudges him awake. Diomedes asks, in a playful, admiring tone (we are reminded of how they interacted with each other in Books 8 and 9), whether there are not some younger men who might be going around in the night and rousing the leaders. Nestor allows that there are.

> But a mighty need has come upon the Achaeans.
> For now it stands for all on the razor's edge
> whether the Achaeans will grievously perish or live.   (172-74)

Diomedes should go and summon the little Ajax and Meges. And so Diomedes does after putting on a lion-skin and taking his spear.

We now have a complex picture of three different groups of three leaders each moving toward the guard post. Menelaus is coming with the big Ajax and Idomeneus, Nestor with Agamemnon and Odysseus, Diomedes with the little Ajax and Meges. The last group parallels the first in that both were formed by the dispatch of a leader (Menelaus by Agamemnon, Diomedes by Nestor) to summon two other leaders. Special emphasis has been put on Nestor's summoning of Odysseus and Diomedes who are going to be the spies.

When they have arrived at the guard post, the leaders find to their relief that the guards are awake. Nestor tells them to keep up the good work. Then he passes over the trench, followed by those who have just arrived, and also by Thrasymedes and Meriones. They stop to hold the meeting of their special council on the spot from which Hector turned back when his victory was interrupted by the coming of the present night at the end of Book 8. Their advance into the danger zone seems strange, but they are separating themselves from the more than seven hundred men on guard. Their action will be paralleled by Hector's holding his council in a spot withdrawn from the mass of his men.

Nestor speaks first. He asks if someone will volunteer to go into Trojan territory and try to catch one of the enemy and learn

> what they are planning among themselves, whether
> they will stay out here in the plain or return
> again to their city since they have defeated the Achaeans.   (208-10)

That the Trojans should return to Troy seems very unlikely, but, as Klingner 1940 has pointed out, this reason parallels that given by Hector for the Trojan spying mission (to determine whether the Achaeans will try to set sail for home during this night). Nestor goes on to promise that the other leaders will each give the volunteer a black ewe and a lamb and invitations to dinner. This will also be paralleled on the Trojan side by the reward Hector promises.

At first Nestor's speech meets with silence, but then Diomedes volunteers. He suggests, however, showing his good sense, that someone should go with him, a man of keen intelligence; two heads are better than one. Immediately six men step forward, Menelaus and Odysseus among them. Then Agamemnon, because of his fear for Menelaus (240), tells Diomedes to choose the best man without any consideration of rank.

Diomedes chooses Odysseus (an older, more experienced man) because he is a favorite of Athena (as is Diomedes) and excels in thought. Odysseus says that they should be off immediately since the night is almost over. And so they arm themselves. Thrasymedes gives Diomedes his sword and shield and a special helmet. Meriones gives Odysseus his bow and quiver and his sword and the special boar's-tusk helmet which comes with a pedigree going back to Autolycus, Odysseus' maternal grandfather.

Diomedes and Odysseus are about to set out when Athena sends a heron on the right, a good omen. Odysseus asks her to help him now if she has ever helped him before (as of course she has). Diomedes asks her to help him now as she helped his father Tydeus when he slew the Thebans in an ambush (an expedition referred to at 4.396 and 5.803), and vows to sacrifice a special ox to her in return for her aid. We are then told (295) that Athena hears their prayers, and so we can expect their expedition to be successful. Odysseus and Diomedes go out like lions into the night "through the slaughter, corpses, shields, and black blood" (298). There has been no burial of the dead after the second day of battle. It is a ghastly scene. We feel a shudder of fear for what may happen next.

Preparations on the Trojan Side, 299-337

Having started the Achaean spies on their way, the poet now turns to the Trojans to describe how they send out a spy (really a simultaneous action; Zielinski's law). We should note the contrast between the complex council of the Achaeans with all its different characters and that of the Trojans which is dominated by Hector. Hector does not allow the Trojan leaders to sleep but calls them to a meeting (at the tomb of Ilus, some distance toward Troy from where the Trojans are bivouacked, as we later learn, line 415). He asks for a volunteer, promising the reward of the best team of horses among the Achaeans to him who will go as a spy and find out whether the Achaeans are mounting guard or are deciding to flee in their ships this night. At first his speech, like Nestor's, meets with silence, but finally Dolon speaks up. Dolon is introduced as a wealthy, ugly, swift-footed man, a herald's only son among five daughters; in other words an unattractive, spoiled man who is better at running away than at making a stand. His name is connected with *dolos,* "trickery."

He will undertake this mission if Hector will promise to give him the horses and chariot of Achilles. Hector swears by his scepter, which he raises to Zeus, to do this. But this is a false oath, as the poet, foreshadowing disaster for Dolon, comments. Hector will never be able to give the horses and chariot of Achilles to anyone.

Dolon is dazzled by the hope of this reward and immediately takes up his bow and clothes himself in a fox-skin and weasel-skin cap—these animals seem very unheroic in contrast to those with which the Achaeans are associated—and seizes his spear. Thus, as the poet comments,

he set out to go to the ships from the camp, but he was not
destined to return from the ships and report to Hector.   (336-37)

He goes off like a blinded tragic figure, but he is too low and laughable a character
to be truly tragic. He is more like Thersites or Pandarus, who also had a foolish
love of horses.

The Success of the Achaean Spying Mission, 338-579

Odysseus sees Dolon and tells Diomedes that they should hide among the
corpses and let him pass in order to be able to cut him off from the Trojans. As
soon as he is past them some distance, they chase after him. At first he stops,
hoping (a sign of cowardice) that Hector has sent someone to call him back, but
when he realizes the truth, he runs. Then Diomedes, inspired with strength by
Athena, brings him to a halt by hurling his spear in front of him.

Dolon begs to be taken alive and promises that his father will pay a rich
ransom for his release. He says that Hector has persuaded him to be very foolish
by promising him the horses of Achilles if he will discover the plans of the
Achaeans. The last four lines of his speech (396-99) repeat the last four lines of
Hector's speech (309-12).

Odysseus smiles at his presumption in imagining that he can control the
horses of Achilles, and asks him about the disposition of the Trojan forces and their
intentions. The last three lines of his speech (409-11) repeat the last three lines of
Nestor's speech (208-10). Dolon replies that Hector is with the leaders of the
council at the tomb of Ilus (that is, in a protected area, 415) and that guards, as
shown by the watchfires, are guarding the Trojans (therefore they will not be easy
targets for Odysseus and Diomedes to attack) but that the allies are sleeping
unprotected, having posted no guards. Then he gives a more detailed description of
the disposition of these allies, emphasizing that Rhesus and his Thracians, who are
newly arrived (434), are nearby and that Rhesus has a pair of very beautiful white
horses. We are thus being directed to the culminating event.

Dolon ends his speech by begging for mercy. But Diomedes rebuffs him and
cuts off his head. Odysseus strips him of his cap, hide, bow, and spear, and
offers these things to Athena, holding them up and praying for her to help them in
their attack on the Thracians. Then he hides Dolon's gear in a bush, making a
marker of reeds and branches so as to be able to find it when they return.

Thus ends the Dolon phase of their adventure. It is told in 131 lines (338-
468) and is therefore considerably longer than the climactic Rhesus phase which is

told in 57 lines (469-526). The Rhesus phase has been added unexpectedly, having grown out of the Dolon phase.

Odysseus and Diomedes now proceed to the camp of the Thracians "through the armor and black blood" (469). They immediately come to the camp of the sleeping Thracians. Rhesus is in the middle of his men, his horses near him. Odysseus, the guiding intelligence of the Achaean expedition, gives Diomedes the choice of killing the men or capturing the horses, and Diomedes, inspired by Athena, begins to do the former. He kills twelve men, and Odysseus pulls the bodies out of the way in order to leave a path for the horses to go through without being frightened. When they reach Rhesus, Diomedes kills him while Odysseus unties the horses from their chariot and binds them together with the reins. Then he drives them off, whipping them with his bow—an amusing incident, on which Leaf I.59 comments that Odysseus "never fights from a chariot, and hence, perhaps, forgets the whip." Odysseus signals with a hissing sound for Diomedes to come along. Diomedes is debating with himself whether to kill more Thracians or to carry off the chariot, and does not obey Odysseus until Athena has appeared to him and told him to get moving. We are reminded of how it took the thunderbolts of Zeus and the advice of Nestor to turn him from his youthful daring in Book 8.

Fenik 1964 has convincingly argued that Book 10 shows an adaptation of an older Rhesus story (reconstructed with the help of the much later tragedy *Rhesus* and references in the scholia on Book 10). In this story an oracle apparently predicted the defeat of the Achaeans if Rhesus survived the night of his arrival at Troy. Book 10 twice (434 and 558) mentions that Rhesus and the Thracians are "newly arrived," and such a prediction would help to explain the panic of the Achaean leaders (as shown, for instance, by Nestor's assertion, in line 173, that things are now for the Achaeans on the razor's age). Moreover, it would have pleased the Greek audience to be reminded of how the Achaeans, who are destined to be defeated by the Trojans on the next day of battle, had averted this other threat of defeat. The fact that the poet has omitted to mention the oracle may have been due to his dislike of such an irrational motif (compare his replacing of the magical log with the mother's curse in the Meleager story).

As Diomedes and Odysseus start back to the ships, Apollo, who has noticed Athena helping the Achaeans, comes and rouses a relative of Rhesus, Hippocoon (probably Rhesus' charioteer; his name means "Horse-guider"), who calls the Trojans to witness what has happened; and they rush with loud cries to see the terrible, memorable deeds of the Achaeans (524-25). Thus the Rhesus episode ends with a brief notice that the Trojans learned about the massacre of the Thracians; there is no mention of Hector, and nothing is said about Dolon.

The account of the Achaean reaction is much fuller. Diomedes and Odysseus return to the ships by the same route as they came. When they reach the gear of Dolon, Diomedes dismounts, and gathers it up and hands it to Odysseus. Nestor, hearing the hoofbeats, hopes (as if for a miracle) that they are returning so soon on horseback, but fears that they have been killed. Before he can finish speaking, however, they have arrived and are being greeted joyously. Then Nestor asks Odysseus how they got possession of these marvelous horses which he has never seen before. Are they the gift of some god? Odysseus replies with a summary of their adventures in reverse. Then they drive the horses over the trench and put them with Diomedes' horses (Odysseus has none, nor does the big Ajax, their island homes being no places to rear them); and Odysseus offers the spoils of Dolon to Athena; and they wash themselves in the sea and take baths in bathtubs and have a meal (Odysseus' third this night), pouring libations of wine to Athena; and then to bed again.

SUMMARY OF PART 1

In the first nine books of the *Iliad* the poet sets the stage for the rest of the action by giving an outline of the plot and introducing his main characters. We learn to know the Achaean leaders: the youthful, fiery-tempered Achilles, the greatest hero on either side; Agamemnon, the diffident and easily discouraged commander-in-chief, a good soldier but also something of a bully; Nestor, the talkative wise old adviser; Diomedes, young, strong, and wise (though sometimes he needs help in this regard); and Ajax, the bulwark of the Achaeans, a man of few words. On the Trojan side we especially learn to know Hector, the protector of Troy who loves his wife and son dearly but is easily misled by success. As the instrument of Zeus to fire the ships, he becomes arrogantly certain of victory (at the end of Book 8), and this is how he will appear throughout the great day of battle and into the day of Achilles' *aristeia* until, too late, he comes to his senses.

In Book 1 we are told how the wrath arises and that Zeus is going to support it by causing countless Achaeans to be slain by the Trojans; and in Book 2 Zeus by inspiring Agamemnon through a false dream sees to it that the Achaeans resolve to do battle. But in Books 3-7, which describe the first day of battle, there is a long retardation. The pro-Achaean and pro-Trojan gods are allowed to help their respective sides, and the Achaeans are shown to be superior to the Trojans even without Achilles. Thus it is necessary for Zeus to play an active role in the action and prevent the other gods from taking part. This he does in Book 8 in which on the second day of battle he reaffirms his purpose of fulfilling his promise to Thetis. Although again the story is not brought to the expected climax, we feel the poet moving toward it with a new determination. Moreover, Book 8 prepares us for Book 9 in which Achilles reaffirms his wrath.

The retardation in Books 3-7 has its own structure. In its center is the narrative of the *aristeia* of Diomedes in Book 5 where with the help of Athena he wounds first Aphrodite and then Ares. This centerpiece is surrounded by two pairs of responsive episodes, for the duel between Paris and Menelaus in Book 3 is answered by the duel between Hector and Ajax in Book 7, and Paris' withdrawal from battle to be with Helen at the end of Book 3 is answered by his leaving her and returning to the battle with Hector at the end of Book 6.

In Books 2-7 the action of the *Iliad* begins very slowly. Book 2 with its catalogues of the Achaean and Trojan forces introduces the fighting in Book 3 which is broken off almost as soon as it has begun by the truce for the duel between Menelaus and Paris. In Book 4 a new beginning is signaled by the council of the gods in which Zeus spurs Athena to bring about a resumption of hostilities; then comes Pandarus' wounding of Menelaus which is followed by the Review, an echo of the marshaling of the troops in the Achaean catalogue in Book 2; then the resumption of hostilties. We are back to where we were at the beginning of Book 3. In Book 5 Achaean success is made vivid by the *aristeia* of Diomedes, and this results in Hector's mission to Troy in Book 6. In Book 7 when he returns to the battlefield, accompanied by Paris, the Trojans are encouraged to counterattack, and Athena and Apollo agree to bring the fighting to an end with the inconclusive duel between Hector and Ajax.

Several times in these first books we are reminded of events before the time of those of the *Iliad*. For instance, the Achaean catalogue in Book 2, a catalogue of ships, is reminiscent of the armada that set sail for Troy at the beginning of the war, and in Book 3 Helen's being led to bed by Paris after his duel with Menelaus reenacts her original abduction.

Even more important is the motif that Troy is destined to fall. In Book 2 we are told of Calchas' prophecy that Troy will fall in this, the tenth year of the war. At the beginning of Book 4, in the council of the gods, Zeus promises Hera that she may destroy Troy, and sends Athena to see to it that the truce is broken, thus preventing the possibility of a peaceful settlement. In Book 5 Diomedes' wounding of the pro-Trojan gods portends the fall of Troy. In Book 6, in the scene with Andromache, Hector envisions his own death and the destruction of his city. In Book 7 Ajax shows the superiority of the Achaeans in his duel with Hector, and the refusal of the Trojans to honor the terms of the truce means that the fate of Troy is sealed.

There is, however, because of Zeus' promise to Thetis (that is, because of the wrath of Achilles), a "not yet" motif connected with the motif of the inevitable fall of Troy. In Book 2, when Agamemnon prays to Zeus that he may take Troy on this day, and in Book 3, at the ceremony before the duel, when the Achaeans and Trojans pray for those who break the truce to be destroyed, the poet tells us that Zeus will "not yet" be answering these prayers.

Closely related is a "almost" motif used of the Achaeans who in Books 1-7 several times "almost" give up the war and go home, either because they have been forced to do so or because they have made peace with the Trojans. (On this motif see Reinhardt 1961.107-8.) In Book 1 the plague would have forced the Achaeans to return home if Hera had not put it into Achilles' mind to call a meeting of the assembly; and the expedition against Troy would have been brought to an end if Athena, sent by Hera, had not persuaded Achilles not to kill Agamemnon. In Book

2 the Achaeans rush to their ships in order to return home, but again Hera intervenes by sending Athena to earth: now Athena inspires Odysseus to bring the Achaeans to order. Finally, there is the duel in Book 3 for the purpose of ending the war peacefully. Menelaus is clearly the winner, and thus the Trojans should give back Helen and the possessions carried off by Paris, and the Achaeans should abandon the war and return home; but this does not happen because the gods at the beginning of Book 4 decide that the war must continue.

In Book 8 (the second day of battle; the same is true of the third day of battle described in Part 2) this "almost" motif is transformed, because of the wrath of Achilles, into an expression of fear for the Achaean ships: the Trojans almost set fire to the ships and so almost destroy the ability of the Achaeans to return home. As if in anticipation of this change, the poet has Book 7 (at the end of the first day of battle; the retardation) end with the Achaeans building a wall around their camp and digging a trench in front of it—like stage props for future use (an example of *prooikonomia*). In Book 8 the Trojans almost cross the trench and break through the wall to fire the Achaean ships, but are stopped by the intervention of Hera who inspires Agamemnon to exhort his men. On the great day of battle in Part 2, in order to prevent the ships from being fired, Hera will intervene again, and Achilles will send out Patroclus in his place and finally return to the action himself—but almost too late.

Book 8 looks forward by creating contrasts with the action of the retardation. It begins with another council of the gods in which Zeus, in contrast to his urging of Athena at the beginning of Book 4, prohibits the other gods from taking part in the action—a prohibition that will remain in effect during the great day of battle. Then Hector twice drives the Achaeans back behind their wall, in parallel narratives which contrast with the parallel narratives of Book 5 in which Diomedes prevailed against the Trojans. Finally, the attempt of Athena and Hera to come in their chariot to the aid of the Achaeans is a reversal of the scene at the end of Book 5 in which they were successful in doing this. Their attempt in Book 8 ends with Zeus predicting the course of the next day's battle.

Moreover, many of the actions of Book 8 parallel, on a smaller scale, those to be described in Part 2, Books 11-18. As in Book 8, so in Book 11, at the beginning of the great day of battle, Zeus will go down to Mount Ida to direct the fighting, and in Book 18, at the end of this day, will return to Olympus (now, at long last, having fulfilled his promise to Thetis). As in Book 8 the Trojans twice drive the Achaeans back behind their wall, so they will do in Books 12-15. In the second battle narrative in Book 8 Teucer and Ajax try in vain to ward off the

Trojans, the former shooting his arrows from behind the latter's huge shield; this looks forward to their vain attempt to defend the ships in Book 15. As in Book 8 Hera tries in vain to get the cooperation of Poseidon in aiding the Achaeans and she and Athena are prevented by Zeus from aiding them, so in Books 13-15 she and Poseidon will succeed in staging an Achaean counterattack—but only for the short time that Zeus is asleep.

Book 9 looks back to Books 2 and 1. For instance, Agamemnon's proposal to sail home, which he makes earnestly in tears, is a verbatim repetition of his speech in Book 2 where he made the same proposal in order to test the troops. And his attempt to appease Achilles by sending the embassy looks back to the beginning of their quarrel and Achilles' withdrawal in Book 1. The going of the envoys—especially the two heralds—to Achilles' hut with their offer to return Briseis reminds us of the coming of the two heralds to his hut in Book 1 in order to take Briseis from him.

The main function of Book 9 is to reaffirm the wrath of Achilles, but it also anticipates the narrative about him in Part 2. The envoys, who fail in their mission, look forward to Patroclus who succeeds in persuading Achilles to give up his wrath to the extent of allowing him, Patroclus, to lead out the Myrmidons. Moreover, in the speech of Phoenix in Book 9 the poet has apparently adapted an inherited story about Meleager to fit his story of the wrath of Achilles: for instance, the name and role of Cleopatra, Meleager's wife, seem to have been created for the purpose of foreshadowing Patroclus' role.

In Book 9 we are also made aware of two different sides of Achilles' character which will be of great importance in the coming narrative. First, there is his capacity for maintaining his wrath beyond what is normal or right, a capacity for pitilessness to the point of cruelty, a willingness to sacrifice his own people in order to satisfy his anger against Agamemnon. There is, however, another side to his character, for he also can be—or at least has been in the past—tender and yielding and able to pity. This is seen in his answer to Odysseus, who has reported Agamemnon's offer, when he says that before his wrath he had cared for the Achaeans like a mother bird for her fledglings. We are reminded of Andromache's earlier comment, in Book 6, on his kindness toward her dead father. In Book 9 Achilles' double-mindedness is also shown by his slightly different, increasingly lenient reactions to each of the three men who plea for his return.

We have treated Book 10, in which a successful Achaean night raid against the Trojans is described, as an interlude to give the Achaeans new spirit for the war and—more imporant—to salve the feelings of the pro-Achaean Greek audience.

Already in the first sentence of the *Iliad* the wrath of Achilles is described as a curse upon the Achaeans, and Homer's Greek audience must have felt this with special pain. We can imagine that they enjoyed the retardation of Books 3-7 in which the Achaeans are shown to be naturally superior to the Trojans, but that Book 8, in which Zeus reaffirms his promise to Thetis and sees to it that the Achaeans are driven back into their camp, and Book 9, in which Achilles reaffirms his wrath, were much less to their liking. Now they know, as at the end of Book 8 Zeus' prediction of the events of the the next day of battle makes clear, that they are going to hear on the next day of recitation the description of the consummation of the wrath in a horrible Achaean defeat. Accordingly, it must have relieved them to end this first day of recitation with the amusement of Book 10.

PART 2

THE GREAT DAY OF BATTLE

2. Achilles Treating a Wound of Patroclus—from a red-figure vase of around 500 B.C., Antikenmuseum Berlin, Staatliche Museen Preussischer Kulturbesitz, F 2278. Notice that Patroclus is the older man. This incident is not mentioned in the *Iliad*, but *Il.* 11.831-33 shows Patroclus using the knowledge of medicine taught him by Achilles.

BOOK 11: ZEUS BEGINS TO FULFILL HIS PROMISE

Introduction, 1-66   *3rd day of battle*

Now Zeus sets about causing a defeat of the Achaeans in fulfillment of his promise to Thetis. When the two armies go out to battle, he rains blood to show that a defeat of the Achaeans is imminent. There follows a series of Achaean woundings. First Agamemnon is wounded after a brief *aristeia*, then Diomedes, then Odysseus. These, the chief leaders of the Achaeans, are thus put out of action except as advisers, men of good counsel, for the rest of this day (and also for the day of Achilles' *aristeia;* they will reappear fully healed at the funeral games of Patroclus). Two other Achaean woundings, those of Machaon and Eurypylus, are important for connecting the narrative (examples of *prooikonomia*) with Patroclus and Achilles. Zeus further shows his direction of events by sending Iris to Hector to tell him to stay out of battle until Agamemnon is wounded and withdraws. This day will be the day of Hector's *aristeia,* for Zeus will use him as his main instrument in accomplishing his purpose.

When dawn rises, Zeus sends Eris (Strife) with a portent of war in her hands to the ship of Odysseus in the center of the Achaean camp. Emitting a horrifying war-shriek Eris

> put great strength into each of the Achaeans,
> into each heart, to war and fight without ceasing.
> And immediately war became sweeter to them than
> to return in their hollow ships to their dear native land.   (11-14)

(Compare 2.451-54 where Athena inspired the Achaeans with fighting spirit at the beginning of the first day of fighting.)

Agamemnon arms himself; he is about to have his *aristeia.* His breastplate was the gift of the king of Cyprus; his round shield has on it representations of the Gorgon's head and the demons Fear and Rout. The points of his two spears flash up to heaven, and the pro-Achaean Athena and Hera thunder in his honor (46)—a portent of his coming success.

The two armies are marshaled for battle, first the Achaeans (47-55) and then the Trojans (56-66). The Achaean horsemen form on foot in front of the trench with their charioteers and horses behind them.

> And Zeus, son of Cronus,
> drove evil Confusion among them and sent from on high

out of the bright sky dew wet with blood, because he was going
to hurl down to Hades the heads of many brave men.   (52-55)

These lines look back to the proem of the *Iliad* (1.1-5). They refer only to the Achaeans, for the marshaling of the Trojans is not described until later (in accordance with Zielinski's law). Now, finally, Zeus is going to fulfill his promise to Thetis. By putting Confusion into the Achaeans he will cause them to flee to their camp. The rain of blood portends their defeat.

In the description of the marshaling of the Trojans six leaders are mentioned: Hector, Polydamas, Aeneas, Polybus, Agenor, and Acamas. Hector will play an important role beginning in this book; the others with the exception of Polybus will appear later, in Book 12. Hector goes among the men shining like the baleful star Sirius or the lightning of Zeus (62 and 66, type 1 similes). These comparisons look forward to his *aristeia*; his great deed will be the driving back of Ajax and the firing of one of the ships (see Krischer 1971.30-35). A Sirius simile is used elsewhere of Diomedes at 5.5 and of Achilles at 22.26-27 at the beginnings of their *aristeiai*.

The *Aristeia* of Agamemnon, 67-283

On Olympus Zeus is watching the battle, but the other Olympians remain in their homes, obeying his prohibition made at the beginning of Book 8. At midday the Achaeans, by their own strength (90; they are naturally superior) break through the Trojan ranks. The routing of the Trojans is described in terms of Agamemnon's *aristeia*. He is compared to a lion from whom a mother deer runs after he has devoured her fawns (113-121, simile type 4: flight and pursuit). Agamemnon slays thee pairs of the enemy (fighters and their charioteers) with mounting fury; his assault culminates in his cutting off the arms and head of his last victim and sending the trunk rolling among the Trojans.

Agamemnon is like a wildfire sweeping over a bushy plain (155-57, simile type 3: the hero's attack). But Zeus is keeping Hector from harm, for in spite of the present Achaean success he will fulfill his promise to Thetis. The Trojans flee across the plain to the Scaean Gate, pursued like a herd of cows by the lion Agamemnon (162-76, another type 4 simile).

But when he is about to reach the walls of Troy, Zeus comes down to Mount Ida and sends Iris to Hector.

Go, swift Iris, and give this order to Hector.

So long as he sees Agamemnon, the shepherd of the people,
rushing in the vanguard and destroying the ranks of men,
let him withdraw and command the rest of the army
to fight with the enemy in the strong encounters of war.
But when struck by a spear or an arrow Agamemnon
mounts his chariot in flight, then do I grant him
the power to kill till he reaches the well-benched ships
and the sun goes down and the sacred darkness comes.   (186-94)

Iris delivers this programmatic message almost verbatim (202-9=187-94): after Agamemnon withdraws, Hector is destined to be the victor of this day, which he will end at the ships. Now he obeys by dismounting and exhorting the Trojans to turn and face the enemy; thus a situation of even battle is reestablished (lines 211-14=5.494-97 and 6.103-6).

Again (216-17=91-92) Agamemnon is the foremost Achaean fighter. The poet signals the importance of the moment by calling on the Muses (218-20) to tell which Trojan first opposed him. It was Iphidamas, a son of Antenor, the good Trojan adviser. Agamemnon misses him with a spear-cast; Iphidamas stabs Agamemnon ineffectually with his spear. Then Agamemnon, like a lion, pulling him toward himself by means of this spear, hits him a deathblow on the neck with his sword, and, having stripped off his armor, is carrying it off when Coon, Iphidamas' brother, being stricken with grief (*penthos*, 249), comes alongside Agamemnon and, without being noticed, stabs him through the lower arm. The fact that Agamemnon is wounded while not in a fighting stance by a sneak attack helps to maintain his glory in defeat; and he continues to fight. (Thus the poet shows his pro-Achaean sympathies, as he will do with the other Achaeans wounded in this book.) Coon is trying to drag Iphidamas' body away, but Agamemnon stabs him under the shield and cuts off his head over his brother—another gruesome, climactic death.

Agamemnon fights on as long as he can, but the pain forces him to withdraw. Commanding his charioteer to drive him back (273-74), he orders a general retreat to the ships, saying that Zeus has forbidden him to fight the whole day (276-79). Leaf I.486 notes the characteristic despondency, but Agamemnon rightly interprets his wounding.

Other Achaean Leaders Are Wounded. Ajax's Slow Retreat, 284-595

Hector, seeing Agamemnon depart, moves into action in accordance with Iris' instructions. He exhorts his forces, saying that Zeus is giving him the victory (286-90). His blind certainty is characteristic, but, like Agamemnon, he correctly states the plan of Zeus for this day. The Trojans respond by going on the offensive like dogs urged on by a hunter against a wild boar or lion; Hector leads them like a whirlwind (297-98, simile type 2: the hero's advance into battle). The poet calls on the Muses to tell who first, who last was slain by Hector "when Zeus gave him glory" (300).

This is the beginning of the *aristeia* of Hector. He attacks like a wind causing the sea to foam (303-8, simile type 3), and we are given a brief picture of him slaying unimportant Achaean leaders and routing the mass of the Achaeans. They would have been driven back to their ships if Odysseus had not exhorted Diomedes to help him make a stand. Diomedes of course is ready to do this.

> But only for a short while
> will we succeed, for cloud-gathering Zeus is granting
> superior power to the Trojans in preference to us.   (317-19)

Again the recognition that Zeus is favoring the Trojans, but Diomedes, characteristically, will fight on anyhow.

He and Odysseus slay two men (a fighter and his charioteer) and then wreak havoc among the mass of the Trojans, like two wild boars scattering hunting dogs (324-25, simile type 3). Then they kill two other pairs, after which Zeus reestablishes a situation of even battle (336). Hector, having noticed Diomedes slaying Agastrophus, comes against him and Odysseus. Diomedes shudders and, after calling on Odysseus for help, hurls his spear at Hector and hits him in the helmet. Hector is dazed and forced to withdraw into the throng of the Trojans. Diomedes taunts him and then returns to stripping the armor off Agastrophus. But while he is doing this Paris, shooting from a hiding place, hits him in the foot with an arrow. Like Agamemnon, Diomedes is wounded by a sneak attack. (Compare Pandarus' wounding of Diomedes in Book 5.) Diomedes taunts Paris with not having fought him man-to-man (385). Then, being protected by Odysseus, he extracts the arrow and, the pain being great, commands his charioteer to drive him back to the ships. Lines 399-400 repeat lines 273-74 describing the withdrawal of Agamemnon; the repetition impresses upon us the reversal of Achaean fortunes.

Odysseus is left alone and debates with himself whether to retreat with the others. He decides to resist, for this is the heroic thing to do. The enemy surround him like hunting dogs against a wild boar (414-18, simile type 7: resistance). After several successful encounters, he slays Charops, the brother of Socus. Then Socus, stabbing him through the shield and breastplate, takes the skin from his side; Athena protects him from death. Although Odysseus is not caught off guard like Agamemnon or Diomedes, his being completely surrounded by the enemy has put him at a great disadvantage. And, as with Agamemnon, he fights on and slays the man who wounded him. Then he extracts the spear from his flesh, causing the blood to spurt forth. The enemy move in for the kill. He shouts for help, and Menelaus comes to the rescue with Ajax. The Trojans are like jackals who, having run down a bleeding deer, scatter at the approach of a lion (474-81, simile type 8: retreat). Ajax protects Odysseus with his huge shield while Menelaus has his charioteer (Odysseus has none) take him out of the action.

We are left with the picture of Ajax, like a river in flood (492-95, simile type 3), wreaking havoc among the Trojans. Then we shift to the left (western) flank where the Achaean defense is being led by Nestor and Idomeneus. They are under heavy pressure from the enemy led by Hector. But it is not until Paris wounds the physician Machaon with an arrow in the shoulder that the battle is turned against the Achaeans (509). Fearing that Machaon may be captured—a physician is worth many men—Idomeneus tells Nestor to carry him in his chariot back to the ships, and so Nestor does.

At this point Hector, having been exhorted by his charioteer to stop Ajax, comes to the center and wreaks havoc among the Achaeans. But he avoids combat with Ajax; it is Zeus who causes Ajax to retreat by giving him the spirit of rout (544). Ajax retreats like a lion from a sheepfold (548-55, simile type 8), not fearing for himself but for the ships, "being grieved" (*tetiemenos*, 556); or like an ass driven by boys from a pasture with great trouble (558-62, another type 8 simile; contrast both these similes with the unflattering one used of the retreating Trojans at 474-81 above). Fenik 1978.76 remarks that the situation of Ajax—one man facing a mass of the enemy—repeats that of Odysseus, in what he calls "emphatic parallelism." We are impressed by the stubborn heroism of the Achaeans as they are being forced to retreat.

Then Eurypylus, having come to help Ajax, kills one of the enemy, but while stripping him is wounded in the thigh with an arrow by Paris—a sneak attack from a distance. Eurypylus is the last Achaean leader in this book to be wounded and forced to withdraw. Before he goes he exhorts the others to turn and make a stand around Ajax. Thus the Achaeans are fighting back bravely as they slowly retreat (compare their retreat in Book 17 during the battle over Patroclus' body) while we shift behind the lines to the huts of Achilles and Nestor.

Nestor's Advice to Patroclus, 596-848

Achilles, standing on the stern of his ship, sees Nestor carrying someone from the battle and calls Patroclus from his hut. Patroclus comes, which, as the poet comments, is "the beginning of evil for him" (604). Achilles says:

> Noble son of Menoetius, dear to my heart,
> now I think the Achaeans will come to my knees
> in supplication, their extremity no longer bearable.
> But go now, Zeus-dear Patroclus, and inquire of Nestor
> who is the man he is carrying wounded from battle.
> He looked from behind in every respect like Machaon,
> the son of Asclepius, but his face wasn't visible,
> so swiftly the horses ran past me eagerly forward.   (608-15)

Patroclus obeys. His obedience will result in his supplication of Achilles in Book 16 and lead to his death.

During the brief Achilles-Patroclus scene, Nestor and Machaon arrive at Nestor's hut. We are given a leisurely description of their arrival (618-43). Hecamede, a woman captured when Achilles sacked Tenedos and given by the Achaeans to Nestor because he surpassed all others in good counsel, prepares them a refreshing snack, and Nestor drinks from a beautiful golden goblet. (Machaon's wound will not be treated until the beginning of Book 14 when Nestor returns to the battlefield.) Then Patroclus appears in the doorway.

When Nestor urges him to have a seat, Patroclus refuses, saying he must hurry back to Achilles. But then, in spite of this haste, he listens to Nestor's very long speech; later he will stop off to help the wounded Eurypylus. We are reminded of how Hector in Book 6, in spite of his haste, visited with his relatives in Troy.

Nestor's speech can be divided into three parts. First he describes the present desperate situation and blames Achilles for not pitying his comrades.

> Is Achilles lamenting (*olophuretai*) so for the sons of the Achaeans,
> for any who has suffered some hit? He doesn't by any means
> know the grief (*penthos*) the army has suffered, for the best men

now lie at the ships either hit from a distance or stabbed.
Hit is Tydeus' son, brave Diomedes,
stabbed are spear-famed Odysseus and Agamemnon.
Hit is also Eurypylus in the thigh with an arrow.
This one just now I have carried out of the battle,
hit by an arrow shot from a bow. But Achilles,
though noble, has no care or pity (*ou kedetai oud' eleairei*) for the Danaans.
Is he waiting until our swift ships near the sea,
despite all we Argives can do, are blazing in hot flames
and we're being killed one after the other?   (656-69)

The wounding of their leaders makes the return of Achilles all the more necessary. Patroclus will repeat lines 656-662 (with minor changes) at 16.23-27 when he supplicates Achilles to return.

The central part of Nestor's speech is the long paradigm of his heroic behavior as a young man, the story of the war between the Pylians and the Epeans (668-761), beginning with his wish that he was still so young and strong. Achilles should behave now as he, Nestor, did then. Pedrick 1983 suggests that Nestor's lengthy account of his early exploits is a substitute for an *aristeia*, for which he is now too old. Moreover, at the present moment in their fortunes this seems the only kind of *aristeia* of which any of the Achaeans is capable.

Finally, Nestor asks Patroclus to remember the advice that he and Achilles had heard from their fathers when setting out for Troy.

The old man Peleus commanded his boy Achilles
always to excel and be the strongest in battle.
And Actor's son, Menoetius, commanded you thus:
My son, Achilles was born stronger than you,
he's much stronger, but you're the older man,
and so should counsel him wisely, give him advice,
be his commander; he will obey for his own good.
Thus your old father spoke but you are forgetful.
Yet still you might try to persuade wise-hearted Achilles.
Who knows whether you with the help of some god may succeed
in persuading him? A friend's persuasion's a good thing.
But if he is shunning some prophecy he knows on his own
or his queenly mother has brought him some message from Zeus,

at least let him send you out and the rest of the men,
the Myrmidons, that you may be of some light to the Danaans.
Let him grant you to wear his beautiful armor in battle
so that the Trojans may think you are he and hold off from battle
and give the warlike sons of the Achaeans a respite
in their distress; respites from battle are precious.
Easily might you being rested drive the tired enemy
back to their city away from our ships and our huts.   (783-803)

Patroclus will take Nestor's advice to heart, for he will repeat lines 794-803 (with minor changes) to Achilles at 16.36-45. Nestor's speech, especially in the demand that Achilles should pity the Achaeans, reminds us of the speeches of the envoys in Book 9. Lohmann 1970.263-76 finds detailed correspondences between Nestor's earlier adventures and Phoenix's story of Meleager.

Patroclus leaves Nestor in a hurry to return to Achilles, but he meets the wounded Eurypylus. Being filled with pity (*oikteire*, 814), he says:

Ah wretched men, leaders and counselors of the Danaans,
so you were destined far from your dear ones and your native land
to glut in Troy the swift dogs with your white fat.
But come, noble hero Eurypylus, tell me
whether the Achaeans can somehow resist monstrous Hector
or must they now succumb to his spear and die?   (816-21)

Eurypylus answers that the Achaeans will fall at the ships, for all their best men are wounded (compare the beginning of Nestor's speech; Patroclus is having the dire straits of the Achaeans impressed upon him). Then he asks Patroclus to treat his wound: the other physicians are unable to do this, and Achilles has taught Patroclus a knowledge of medicine, having learned it himself from the centaur Chiron (831-32). Patroclus agrees to do this, and so we leave him at the end of this book in the hut of Eurypylus using the healing art of Achilles. The role of Eurypylus might be said to be in emphatic parallelism with that of Machaon. Both men are wounded by arrows shot by Paris and forced to withdraw, and the woundings of both move Patroclus to act.

Later on this day Nestor and Patroclus are going to return to the action from where we leave them in this book, but at different times. Nestor will return at the beginning of Book 14 when the Achaean wall is first breached, Patroclus in the middle of Book 15 (line 390) at the second breaching of the Achaean wall. It seems likely that one of the reasons for the Patroclus-Eurypylus episode is to prepare (*prooikonomia*) for the return of Patroclus and Nestor at different times. If Patroclus had remained with Nestor, it would have caused the audience to ask why he did not move into action with Nestor at the first breaching of the Achaean wall. Of course, the Patroclus-Eurypylus scene serves other purposes too. It adds to the emphasis on the disaster now being suffered by the Achaeans, shows us the sympathetic soul of Patroclus, and reminds us that Achilles has a gentler side to his character.

BOOK 12: THE BATTLE AT THE ACHAEAN WALL

Polydamas' First Admonition.   Asius Attacks on the Left, 1-194

The Trojan attack on the Achaean wall builds up in two phases, each of which is divided into two strands. The strands of the first phase are closely parallel narratives: first, Asius, disobeying the advice of Polydamas not to use his chariot, attacks the left gate unsuccessfully; then Hector, having scorned the warning of Polydamas that the day will end badly for the Trojans, unsuccessfully attacks in the center. The strands of the second phase, which describe how the wall is broken through, also stand in close relation to each other. First, Sarpedon breaches the wall near the center and, though his men are unable to take advantage of this opening, causes the defense in the center to be weakened. Then Hector, empowered by Zeus, breaks open and leaps through the central gate. We are apparently being asked to compare Hector, a pious man blinded by the certainty of victory as announced to him by Zeus through Iris in the last book, with Asius, an impious and blind man, and Sarpedon, a noble and clear-sighted leader.

The poet, looking into the future, tells us that the Achaean wall, since the Achaeans built it without sacrificing to the immortals, is going to be breached by the Trojans and, after the Trojan War (beyond the action of the *Iliad*) destroyed by divine intervention.

> While Hector was still alive and Achilles was wrathful (*meni'*)
> and the city of King Priam was as yet unsacked,
> for so long a time the great wall of the Achaeans stood,
> but when all the best men of the Trojans had died
> and many Argives had perished but some had survived
> and Priam's city in the tenth year of war had been sacked
> and the Argives had sailed in their ships for their dear native land,
> then did Poseidon and Apollo together destroy
> the wall by directing the rivers of Troy against it.   (10-18)

The first line mentions the two phases of the war covered by the *Iliad*, Achilles' wrath and his vengeance against Hector, in inverse order, the culminating event, as often in Greek poetry, being put first. Leaf I.526 notes that "the *menis* is mentioned as the distinguishing mark of the period which required the building of the wall; it is the *terminus a quo* of the wall, just as the sacking of Troy mentioned in the next line is the *terminus ad quem*." It must have been reassuring to the Greek

audience, at this moment of imminent Achaean defeat, to be reminded that
eventually the Achaeans won the Trojan War. Compare our comment on the same
prediction at 7.445-63. Moreover, the present passage shows how great an
obstacle the wall now poses for Hector and the Trojans.

> Thus in the future Poseidon and Apollo were going
> to obliterate it. But now loud battle was blazing
> over the well-built wall, the timbers were echoing
> with hits, and the Argives, overcome by the scourge of Zeus,
> were being constrained, pent in, by their hollow ships
> in fear of Hector, the mighty deviser of flight.   (34-39)

Hector is continuing to fight like a whirlwind (40, simile type 3: the hero's attack;
cf.11.297) or a wild boar or lion at bay who turns in different directions trying to
break though the circle of his attackers and whose high spirits kill him (41-48,
another type 3 simile)—probably a foreshadowing of Hector's death (so Willcock
1978.313). And he urges his men to cross the trench.

> But his swift-footed horses
> dared not do this but loudly neighed as they stood
> at the sheer edge, greatly frightened at the sight of the trench,
> so wide it was and not to be leaped, not to be passed through
> easily, for the banks everywhere overhanging
> rose on both sides, fitted above with stakes,
> sharp ones, which the sons of the Achaeans had put there,
> thickly set and long, to keep off the enemy.   (50-57)

This description of the trench introduces the speech of Polydamas, the wise Trojan
adviser, who tells the Trojans that they must not try cross it in their chariots.

Polydamas makes two speeches in the present book, a third in Book 13, and a
fourth in Book 18. Hector obeys him here and in Book 13, but later in this book
and in Book 18 will disobey him. Now Polydamas, addressing the whole army,
says that he is hopeful of a Trojan victory if Zeus is really on their side, but that he
fears they may have to retreat suddenly and disastrously from the area of the ships.
Because of the trench they should leave their chariots behind and, being properly
armed (and marshaled), follow Hector on foot. He ends by remarking that the
Achaeans will not hold out if really they are fated to perish (79), showing that,
unlike Hector, he has doubts about this.

Hector immediately leaps from his chariot, and the other Trojan leaders except Asius follow suit. They marshal their men in five divisions. It is like a new beginning of battle (so Hainsworth1966.58-66). Each division has three leaders. The first and most important division is led by Hector, Polydamas, and Cebriones, Hector's charioteer, whom Hector orders to leave their horses and chariot with someone else; the second is led by Paris, Alcathous, and Agenor; the third by Helenus, Deiphobus, and Asius; the fourth by Aeneas, Archelochus, and Acamas; and the fifth, which comprises the allies, by Sarpedon, Glaucus, and Asteropaeus. Our attention is drawn to Asius, whose horses are described, and to Sarpedon, the most outstanding man among the allies, and so we can expect these two to play prominent roles along with Hector in the coming action.

Only Asius disobeys Polydamas and remains in his chariot.

> The fool (*nepios*), he was not destined to avoid evil death
> and come, rejoicing with horses and chariot, back
> again from the ships to the windy city of Troy,
> for accursed fate was going to overwhelm him
> by the spear of Deucalion's son, Idomeneus.   (113-15)

Idomeneus will kill him in the next book. Asius leads his men against the left gate, through which some of the fleeing Achaeans are passing.

> Here Asius aimed his horses, and his men
> shrilly shouting were following him, thinking the Achaeans
> no longer would put up a fight but fall at the black ships,
> fools (*nepioi*), who found at the gate two of the best men.   (124-27)

This gate is being defended by the two Lapiths, Polypoetes and Leonteus, who stand like great oak trees, having flashed out in front of the gate like wild boars against hunters and dogs (132-34 and 145-50, type 7 similes: resistance). The foolish expectations of Asius are answered by those of his men.

The battle is fiercely fought.

> As snowflakes fall to earth
> which a stormy wind driving the dark clouds
> pours down thickly upon the nourishing land,
> so the missles poured forth from the hands of Achaeans
> and Trojans.   (156-60, simile type 6: even battle)

Then Asius, beating his arms on his thighs in frustration, cries out to Zeus.

> Zeus Father, it is clear now that you are a lover of lies
> completely, for I didn't think the Achaeans would put up
> a fight against our strength and invincible hands.
> But like wasps with bright-colored waists or bees
> who make their homes by the side of a rocky way
> and do not leave their hollow abodes but stay
> and defend their children from the approach of hunters,
> so these, though only two, are unwilling to leave
> their gate, choosing instead to kill or be killed.   (164-72, simile type 7:
>   resistance)

Asius is apparently referring to Zeus' promise to Hector in the last book (11.207-9), and wrongly assumes that victory is in the power of any Trojan, including himself, to win. But Zeus, as the poet comments (173-74), is reserving for Hector the glory of breaking through the wall. Asius has not understood the mind of Zeus.

Lines 175-94 give a general description in which the poet voices his inability to describe the battle fully; only a god could do this. The Achaeans, are grieved (*achnumenoi*, 178), as are the pro-Achaean gods (*akacheiato*, 179). This characterizes the Achaeans for us on the entire great day of battle, during Achilles' absence. Nevertheless, they are fighting bravely to defend their ships, and each of the two Lapiths slays several of the enemy. We (the Greek audience) can thus switch to the center with the feeling that the Achaeans are holding their own on the left.

Polydamas' Second Admonition. Hector Attacks in the Center, 195-289

In the center Hector and his men are still on the Trojan side of the trench and have not yet begun their attack. (It is unrealistic for the Trojans not to attack all at once along the wall, but this is in keeping with Zielinski's law, according to which first one strand of the narrative is told and then another; cf. Willcock 1978.317). An omen is causing the delay, an eagle sent by Zeus on the left with a snake in its talons. The eagle is bitten by the snake and drops it into the middle of the Trojan forces. Immediately Polydamas, speaking to Hector, advises against fighting at the ships (216-27). Though the Trojans, like the eagle, may be successful to some extent, that is, they may break through the wall, they, again like the eagle, will fail in the end and return from the ships in disorder with many men killed. Whereas Polydamas' first speech was concerned with the trench, this one is concerned with the wall.

Hector replies:

> Polydamas, you no longer say what is pleasing to me;
> you're able to think up better advice than this.
> But if you truly, in all seriousness, mean what you say,
> the gods have evidently destroyed your wits, for you
> urge me to forget loud-thundering Zeus' will,
> the promises he himself made to me and agreed to,
> when you advise me to trust in long-winged birds,
> of which I take no thought and have no care
> whether they go on the right toward the sun and the dawn
> or on the left toward the shadowy darkness of evening.
> But let us obey the will of powerful Zeus
> who rules as king over all immortals and mortals.
> One bird omen is best, to fight for one's country.   (231-43)

He ends by charging Polydamas with cowardice and threatening to kill him if he sees him shirking or persuading others to shirk. Hector is relying on the promise of Zeus announced to him by Iris in the last book. This is understandable. And his rejection of bird omens is also understandable, although it seems likely that the poet had a different view, for Polydamas' interpretation will prove to be right. Hector's reply shows his courage, but also his inability to see that Zeus may allow him to be the victor of this day only and at the cost of losing many good men.

In response to his speech, the Trojans with loud shouting follow him in an attack against the wall, and Zeus sends a whirlwind from Mount Ida driving dust toward the ships. This bewilders the minds of the Achaeans, and no doubt confirms Hector in his blindness. Accordingly, he and the Trojans

> putting their trust in the omens and might of Zeus
> tried to break through the high wall of the Achaeans.   (256-57)

There follows a general account of how the Trojans in the center try to tear down the wall, which is described in some detail (258-60), as the trench was earlier when it was the main obstacle.

But not yet were the Achaeans yielding from the way.   (262)

Notice the "not yet"; the Achaeans are going to be forced to yield. Their defense
against Hector is being led by the two Ajaxes who exhort their side (269-76) to
show their courage and press forward in the hope that Zeus will allow them to drive
the enemy back to Troy.

The present section ends with a long simile describing the hotly fought even
battle.

> Just as snowflakes fall thickly upon the land
> on a day in winter when Zeus of the Counsels stirs it
> to snow, displaying to men the strength of his shafts—
> having stilled the winds, he snows steadily until
> he has covered the mountain tops and jutting peaks
> and meadows growing in clover and men's fertile farmlands;
> snow is poured over the gray sea, on harbors and beaches,
> the wave splashing forward restrains it, but everything else
> is enveloped completely when Zeus storms heavily down—
> so the rocks were flying thickly from both sides.   (278-87, simile type 6:
>   even battle)

Our vision is being expanded over the whole battle along the wall. We are
reminded of the snowstorm simile used at the end of the last section (156-60) to
describe the situation of even battle on the left. The poet is apparently using these
two similes to synchronize his very similar narratives of the fighting on the left and
in the center. Both narratives are introduced by an admonition of Polydamas which
a Trojan leader (Asius, Hector) rejects, and in both two Achaean heroes (the two
Lapiths, the two Ajaxes) are featured as defenders of the ships (so Winter
1956.39). Also, there is the contrast between the complete blindness of Asius and
the partial blindness of Hector regarding the will of Zeus for this day of battle.

Sarpedon Tears Down a Part of the Wall Near the Center, 290-429

> Then the Trojans and glorious Hector would not yet
> have burst through the gate in the wall and broken its long bolt
> if Zeus of the Counsels hadn't driven his son Sarpedon
> against the Argives like a lion among horned cows.   (290-93)

Again we should notice the "not yet," and also the role of Zeus in directing events; Zeus is going to help Hector break through the central gate. By having Sarpedon attack the wall near the center, he will cause the Achaeans opposing Sarpedon to call Ajax and Teucer to their aid and so leave the central gate an easier target for Hector.

Striding forward against the wall in the spirit of a lion attacking a sheepfold (299-306, simile type 2), Sarpedon exhorts Glaucus in a speech ending with the words:

> Ah friend, if only after escaping this battle
> we were to be unaging immortals for ever,
> I would not fight in the forefront myself nor would I
> urge you into the fighting where men win renown.
> But since countless death-demons are standing around us
> which no one can flee or avoid, let us go fight,
> whether to die and give glory or kill and obtain it.   (322-28)

Sarpedon's clear-headedness contrasts with Asius' total, and Hector's partial, delusion.

The Achaean defender at this part of the wall is Menestheus who at the approach of Sarpedon and Glaucus looks for help and sends Thootes to bring from the center either the two Ajaxes or at least the big Ajax and Teucer. Thootes repeats verbatim (344-50=357-63) Menestheus' words to the two Ajaxes; and the big Ajax, after telling the little Ajax that he will return as soon as possible, goes off with Teucer and Teucer's bow-carrier.

When he has arrived at the area near the center, Ajax kills a companion of Sarpedon with a rock so huge that a man of the present time could lift it only with difficulty, and Teucer hits Glaucus with an arrow. Glaucus leaps back, but Sarpedon, though striken with grief (*achos*, 392), continues to fight. (Sometimes grief can so overwhelm a man that he is unable to fight.) He kills an Achaean and pulls down part of the wall, thus creating a breach, but his men are unable to take advantage of it. Ajax and Teucer both strike him, Ajax with his spear, Teucer with an arrow, but Zeus protects Sarpedon, his son, preventing him from dying at the ships (402-3). We are thus put on notice that he will die later (in Book 16) in the open plain. Now he withdraws and exhorts his men to try to break into the Achaean camp, but the Achaeans oppose them in close formation. And so the present episode ends in an even battle, the sides being compared (421-29, simile type 6: even battle) to two men with measuring rods arguing over the boundary between their properties.

Sarpedon always appears in the *Iliad* in close association with Hector. In Book 16 Hector will slay Patroclus after Patroclus has slain Sarpedon. In Book 5 Sarpedon's encounter with Tlepolemus, when Zeus saved him from being slain, was followed by the description of Hector driving back the Achaeans. The present episode, in which Sarpedon is again saved by Zeus, is followed by the description of Hector breaking into the Achaean camp.

Hector Breaks Through the Central Gate, 430-71

Another type 6 simile (433-35), that of a woman weighing wool in a balance, describes the even battle along the entire wall before Zeus gives the glory to Hector. Hector, with the help of Zeus, easily picks up a huge stone which two men now could hardly raise onto a wagon.

> As when a shepherd easily carries a ram's fleece,
> taking it in one hand, and the weight doesn't bother him,
> so Hector raised and bore the rock straight on
> against the gate with its closely, well-fitted leaves,
> doubly secured and high; two cross bars within
> on this side and that were holding them, fastened by one bolt.
> He came and stood very near and aimed for the middle,
> taking a wide stance so that his throw might be strong,
> and hit and broke off both hinges. The rock fell within
> heavily, and the gate gave a loud resounding roar;
> the cross bars failed, and the leaves were split apart
> under the crash of the rock. Bright Hector leaped in,
> his face like the coming of swift night; he gleamed
> in frightening bronze, with which he was clothed, and brandished
> two spears. No one but a god could have stopped him
> as he leaped through the gate, his eyes blazing with fire.   (451-66)

Now the gate is described, as were the trench and the wall, each in its appropriate place. Hector and the Trojans pour into the camp; the Achaeans flee back among their ships. The din of loud shouting reaches to heaven. So ends Book 12.

It is noteworthy that Hector is not opposed by any named hero when he breaks open the gate. The poet has withdrawn his main opponent of this day, the big Ajax, to the part of the wall being attacked by Sarpedon. Thus, as in Book 11 and later in the description of this day, we are being kept in suspense to see the encounter of Hector and Ajax.

BOOK 13: POSEIDON INTERVENES

Zeus is Diverted and Poseidon Inspires the Achaeans in the Center, 1-205

This day's battle, in which the Trojans will set fire to the Achaean ships in fulfillment of Zeus' promise to Thetis and Hector will slay Patroclus and Achilles will return to the action, is the longest and most complicated battle in the *Iliad*. In Books 11 and 12 we have move steadily forward toward the expected defeat of the Achaeans, but now there occurs a lengthy retardation in Books 13 through 15.389, in which against the will of Zeus, who is diverted and put to sleep, the Achaeans mount a successful counterattack until, Zeus having awaked and seen to it that the Trojans prevail again, the situation is restored to essentially what it was at the end of Book 12. This at-first-sight unnecessary retardation can be seen to serve a number of purposes. It emphasizes the importance of this most important battle, lets the poet exercise his skill at creating variety, and shows his "impulse to allow the Achaeans some glory even in their defeat" (Whitman and Scodel 1981.1-2). The culminating event of the retardation will be the big Ajax's wounding of Hector in Book 14. We remember that this is the day of Hector's *aristeia,* as promised to him by Zeus in Book 11, and that the wounding of the hero is a regular feature of an *aristeia.*

Edwards 1987.241 has remarked on Book 13 that it deals with heroes of the second rank and that "though it contains some passages of much interest, a reader who finds uninterrupted battle scenes boring might well consider it the dullest in the poem." Idomeneus, Meriones, and Deiphobus are listed by Edwards as heroes of the second rank appearing here. We might add Menelaus who does his best to maintain his cause during this day of battle. All the great leaders of the Achaeans except the big Ajax (Achilles of course is not to be counted) have been wounded (in Book 11) and forced to retire from the fighting. But is this book so boring? Perhaps; let the reader be warned. It seems likely, however, that an ancient Greek audience would have enjoyed hearing at length how the Achaeans, in the face of inevitable defeat, found the inspiration and courage to make a stand. The morale of the Achaean army is a major concern in the retardation in Books 13 and 14. How can the Achaeans, faced with defeat, rally their spirits?

At the beginning of the present narrative Zeus turns his gaze to more distant scenes, not expecting (*eelpeto,* 8) any god to intervene. He is being treated like a fallible human being, a theme which will be brought to a climax in Book 14 when he is beguiled by Hera. "But the glorious earth-shaker was keeping no blind watch (*alaoskopien*, 10)." Poseidon seizes the opportunity. He has been watching the war from the topmost peak of the island of Samos, feeling pity (*eleaire*, 15) for the Achaeans and great anger toward Zeus. Immediately he gets his horses and comes in his chariot across the sea to Troy. The moment of his arrival is described as follows:

> The Trojans all like a raging fire or a whirlwind
> were eagerly following Hector, the son of Priam,
> with roaring and loud shouting; they expected (*elponto*) to seize the ships
> of the Achaeans and there to kill the best of their men.
> But Poseidon, the earth-holder, the earth-shaking god,
> stirred up the Argives, having come from the deep sea
> and taken the form and weariless voice of Calchas.   (39-45)

The Trojans, like Zeus, are going to be disappointed in their expectations.

Poseidon-Calchas comes first to the Ajaxes in the center—the big Ajax has returned to this position—and tells them that he fears for the Achaeans, especially here where Hector, who claims to be a son of Zeus, is attacking. He ends with the following wish:

> Would that one of the gods might put it into your minds
> to stand firmly yourselves and exhort the others to stand firm.
> Then Hector would have to withdraw from the swift ships, though eager
> for battle and though even Zeus himself is behind him.   (55-58)

This is an ironic wish of course, for it describes what Poseidon is actually doing now. Then touching the Ajaxes with his scepter, which Calchas as a prophet can be thought to have with him, he fills them with new fighting spirit and departs with the swiftness of a hawk. The Ajaxes rightly suspect that he was a god in disguise. The big Ajax says that he is eager to fight Hector; this prepares us for his later encounters with Hector (so Janko 1992.53).

Meanwhile Poseidon, going behind the lines, finds the younger Achaean leaders who are weeping in grief (*achos*, 86) at the sight of the Trojans coming over the wall. Among them are Teucer, Thoas, Deipyrus, Meriones, and Antilochus who will figure prominently in the fighting of this book. Poseidon-Calchas tells them that it is unbelievable that the Trojans, who earlier were afraid to come out of their city, are now at the ships.

> They're fighting away from their city at the hollow ships
> because our leader is no good and so our men
> in their anger at him are withdrawing. Unwilling to try
> to defend the swift ships, we're meeting our deaths beside them.
> But granted that our leader, the son of Atreus,
> wide-ruling Agamemnon, is entirely to blame
> because he dishonored the swift-footed son of Peleus,
> still we shouldn't withdraw from the battle, by no means.
> Let us, like good men, be quickly reconciled with him.   (107-15)

As Michel 1971.39 has pointed out, these words seem especially appropriate to Calchas who spoke out against Agamemnon in Book 1. Poseidon ends his speech by emphasizing the danger to the ships where Hector has broken in. Accordingly, the younger leaders come and take their stand with the two Ajaxes in the center. Neither Ares nor Athena could have found fault with their battle formation (compare the similar statement at 4.539-44 about the beginning of even battle).

Hector has the momentum of a great rock that rolling down a mountain comes to a halt in the plain (137-42, simile type 3: the hero's attack). As Janko 1992.62 says, this simile "presages the failure not of this attack only, but of Hector's entire drive to the sea." Hector boasts that the Achaeans will yield if Zeus is with him, as he understandably believes is the case.

In the first encounter Meriones breaks his spear on Deiphobus' shield and goes off to his hut to get another. This is preparation (*prooikonomia*) for his meeting with Idomeneus in the next section. Moreover, Meriones' indecisive attack on Deiphobus "prefigures" how he will later wound him (Janko 1992.39).

There follows a chain-reaction battle. Teucer kills Imbrius and rushes in to strip him of his armor. Hector hurls a spear at Teucer but hits Amphimachus instead. Ajax forces Hector back with a spear-thrust in the shield. The Achaeans having gained possession of both bodies, the Ajaxes carry off Imbrius, like two lions with a deer; and the little Ajax, in his anger over the slaying of Amphimachus, cuts off Imbrius' head and hurls it into the crowd of the Trojans so that it lands at Hector's feet—a terrible scene of vengeance bringing to a climax this description of the fighting in the center.

Hector has backed off from the big Ajax; the fact that their meeting here has been aborted raises our expectations of a later decisive encounter (so Michel 1971.47). This is in accord with the technique, pointed out by Schadewaldt 1938.93, whereby the poet leads his audience to expect what is going to happen by describing how it almost happened or was unsuccessfully attempted. Another example, which we have just seen, is Meriones abortive attack on Deiphobus.

Idomeneus and Meriones on the Left, 206-672

The slaying of Amphimachus has a further result, for Poseidon, his grandfather, is also angered by his slaying and so goes back among the huts and ships to stir up other Achaeans. Taking the form of the youthful Thoas (a leader of the Aetolians who will organize an orderly retreat in Book 15; Willcock 1984.238 well describes him as "a man of authority"), Poseidon meets the middle-aged Idomeneus who, having withdrawn from the fighting to attend to a wounded man (compare Idomeneus' concern for the wounded Machaon in Book 11), is on his way to his hut to arm himself. Idomeneus is "abruptly introduced" (Janko 1992.73), but we can deduce that the poet has been looking forward to an episode in which he plays a leading role from the statement in Book 12 that Asius will die at his hands, and from the preparation in this book for a meeting between him and Meriones by having the latter go behind the lines to get a new spear. Poseidon-Thoas asks him what has happened to the threats of the Achaeans. Idomeneus says that their present plight is the fault of Zeus, and urges him to exhort others. So Poseidon-Thoas departs for the battle after cursing shirkers and telling Idomeneus to get his armor.

Idomeneus comes from his hut armed like the lightning of Zeus (242-44, simile type 1: the gleaming of the hero's armor). This is the beginning of his *aristeia*. He meets Meriones and asks why he has left the battle (a reproach is implied). Meriones answers that he has come for a new spear and would like to take one from Idomeneus' hut if any are available. Idomeneus is glad to oblige him, saying that he has many spears taken from the enemy—a proof of his own prowess in battle. Meriones explains that that he too has many such spears but that his hut is too far off to fetch one quickly. Then Idomeneus, realizing that he has hurt his friend's feelings, praises his courage at length (speaking in coarse good humor; see Janko 1992.83) and exhorts him to take one of his spears. This little scene shows how sensitive to the charge of being a shirker the Achaean leaders could be, and it is a variation on the general theme, so important in Books 13 and 14, of how the Achaeans can find the spirit to resist the apparently irresistible Trojans.

Thus Idomeneus and Meriones set off for the front, like Ares and his son Phobos (Fright) (298-300, simile type 2: the hero's advance into battle). Idomeneus decides that they should go to the left since the Ajaxes and Teucer are able to handle Hector in the center; not even Achilles is a better defensive fighter than the big Ajax. But then the poet, before turning to the fighting on the left, gives us a general view of the even battle.

> Thus were opposed the two mighty sons of Cronus
> devising terrible pains for the heroes to suffer.
> Zeus was planning victory for the Trojans and Hector
> so as to glorify swift-footed Achilles but without
> destroying entirely the army of the Achaeans at Troy;
> he was glorifying Thetis and her strong-hearted son.
> But Poseidon, come from the gray sea, had gone to the Argives
> whom he was stirring up secretly, for he was grieved (*echtheto*)
> to see them defeated, and terribly angry (*enemessa*) with Zeus.
> These two were sons of the same family, of the same parents,
> but Zeus was the earlier born and superior in wisdom.
> Therefore Poseidon avoided aiding the Achaeans
> openly, but disguised as a man inspired them
> continuously. Zeus and Poseidon pulled this way and that
> the rope of strong strife, even battle, over both armies,
> unbreakable, unlooseable, death-bringing to many.   (345-60)

This general description of even battle is now made specific by the deeds of Idomeneus which are told in a chain-reaction battle. Exhorting the Achaeans, he leaps out in front and slays Othryoneus. Asius tries to avenge Othryoneus, but Idomeneus slays him in front of his horses and chariot, and Antilochus slays his charioteer. Asius should have followed Polydamas' advice in Book 12. A simile (389-93=16.482-86 used of Sarpedon; type 9: the hero falls) likens him to a tree cut down for planks to build a ship.

Deiphobus, being grieved (*achnumenos*, 403) over the death of Asius, aims at Idomeneus but hits Hypsenor instead; he boasts that he has given Asius someone to accompany him into the underworld. Grief (*achos*, 417) seizes the Achaeans, especially Antilochus who sees to it that Hypsenor is carried to safety. Then Idomeneus kills Alcathous whom Poseidon has demobilized, and boasts to Deiphobus that now he has slain three to Deiphobus' one.

Deiphobus reacts by deciding to seek the aid of Aeneas. Having found him in the rear, he persuades him to avenge Alcathous, his brother-in-law. And so Aeneas comes against Idomeneus, who awaits him like a wild boar against dogs and hunters (471-74, simile type 7: resistance).

Idomeneus shouts for help, saying that if he were as young as Aeneas he would meet him in single combat (485-86); and Aeneas likewise calls on the Trojans. Thus the battle rages over the body of Alcathous. Aeneas throws at Idomeneus but misses. Idomeneus, apparently missing Aeneas, slays Oenomaus, but is unable to strip him of his armor, for he is overwhelmed by the missiles of the enemy and forced to withdraw. Janko 1992.111 remarks that Idomeneus' miss is left unmentioned in order to give the impression of Achaean success. As Idomeneus departs, Deiphobus, angry at Idomeneus' taunt, hurls his spear at him but hits Ascalaphus.

Thus ends the fighting of Idomeneus, cut short without a single combat with his main opponent Aeneas. Such a curtailed *aristeia* is suited to the time when Poseidon is helping the Achaeans secretly, before in Book 14 he leads them openly on the offensive. It is no shame for Idomeneus who is middle-aged and not one of the best Achaean fighters to yield before the much younger Aeneas who is second only to Hector in prowess among the Trojans.

The poet comments (520-25) that Ares, who is staying on Olympus in obedience to Zeus, is not yet aware of the death of his son Ascalaphus. This "not yet" looks forward to a passage at the end of the retardation (15.110ff.) where Ares will be told of Ascalaphus' death by Hera, but then it will be too late for him to do anything about it, for Zeus will be awake and in charge.

The battle rages around the body of Ascalaphus. Deiphobus, trying to seize the helmet, is stabbed in the arm by Meriones; we remember how Meriones' spear earlier broke on his shield. The withdrawal of Deiphobus is described at length: he is carried from the battlefield groaning (538); Janko 1992.113 contrasts the more dignified withdrawals of Odysseus and Agamemnon in Book 11. Then Trojan (Aeneas) slays Achaean (Alphareus); Achaean (Antilochus who is being protected by Poseidon) slays Trojan (Thoos); Achaean (Meriones) slays Trojan (Adamas); Trojan (Helenus) slays Achaean (Deipyrous). These balanced slayings show a situation of even battle. In lines 550-59 Antilochus is pictured in slow retreat, assailed by the enemy on three sides; this situation of a lone hero retreating before many men—the hero is never slain—is elsewhere used of other Achaeans but never of a Trojan (Janko 1992.114). The death of Deipyrus gives grief (*achos*, 581) to Menelaus who stabs Helenus and forces him to withdraw in the care of Agenor. Now Peisander advances against Menelaus with a battle ax, but Menelaus with his spear crushes in his head, causing his eyes to fall out onto the ground (a climactic death). As he strips him of his armor, Menelaus makes the following speech:

> Thus you will leave the ships of the swift-horsed Danaans,
> you arrogant Trojans, insatiable of the terrible war cry,
> who already have committed the shameful outrage
> of what you did to me, evil dogs, nor did you
> fear at all the harsh wrath of thundering Zeus,
> the guardian of friendship, who will destroy your steep city.
> You have taken my wife and many of my possessions,
> outrageously carrying her off after being her guests.
> And now it's our seafaring ships that you want to destroy
> with baneful fire and kill the heroic Achaeans,
> but you will be checked no matter how eager for war.
> Zeus Father, you have a mind of wisdom surpassing
> all gods and men, and everything here is your doing.
> How can you favor men who are guilty of outrage,
> these Trojans, whose desire is without any limit,
> who can't get enough of the din and killing of warfare.
> One can get sated with anything, with sleep or with love,
> with hearing sweet music or dancing in orderly motion,
> things most people would much rather do than fight,
> but fighting is something the Trojans can't get enough of.   (620-39)

Troy is destined to fall because of the wrongdoing of the Trojans. How can Zeus continue to let them fight on? How can they have the heart to fight on?

Then, as if to confirm the insatiable appetite of the Trojans for battle, the poet gives us two other encounters. Harpalion, after stabbing at Menelaus ineffectively, is hit by Meriones with an arrow in the buttock as he tries to withdraw. Harpalion's death is pathetic: having breathed out his last in the arms of his companions, he lies stretched out on the ground like a worm, his black blood wetting the earth; they put him on a chariot and, grieving (*achnumenoi*, 658), take him back to Troy, his father, weeping, going with them (we are reminded of Priam mourning Hector); there will be no payment in requital for this death. Scholars have complained that this father, Pylaemenes, was slain by Menelaus at 5.576; the poet has apparently nodded, perhaps carried away by his desire to call forth the sympathy of his audience and to create a parallel with the father in the next scene.

Paris, being angered (*cholothe*, 660) by Harpalion's death, strikes Euchenor dead with one of his arrows. Euchenor, having been told by his father, a seer, that he was destined to die in battle at Troy or of sickness at home, had chosen the former fate (we are reminded of Achilles' choice). Paris' activity here prepares us (*prooikonomia*) for the scene in the next section in which Hector will wrongly taunt him with not doing his part in the fighting. The deaths of Harpalion and Euchenor echo the tone of Menelaus' almost philosophical speech and fill us with a feeling of sadness about the war.

Scholars have speculated that the present section was created in order to honor the Cretan heroes Idomeneus and Meriones. But, as Whitman and Scodel 1981.6-7 point out, whatever the truth of this theory, the main function of this section is to retard the action in the center while allowing the Achaeans to slay or wound many of the Trojan leaders on the left—an equivalent to the wounding of the Achaean leaders in Book 11.

Polydamas' Third Admonition.   Hector Unites his Forces, 673-837

Hector is not aware of how Poseidon is stirring up the Achaeans on the left, for he is in the center where he leaped through the gate. Here, where the wall is built farthest inland, are the ships of the little Ajax and Protesilaus. It is Protesilaus' ship which Hector will eventually set on fire.

We are given a brief catalogue (685-700) of the Achaean forces in the center: the Boeotians, the Ionians, and the Locrians. The little and the big Ajax are fighting together with their spears, like two hard-working plow-oxen; the Locrians are shooting their arrows from the rear. Thus the Trojans in the center (as well as those on the left) are being thrown into confusion and are almost forced to retreat with serious losses.

At this point Polydamas makes his third speech. After blaming Hector for not listening to good advice and after describing their present desperate situation, he says:

> But let us withdraw and call all the best men here.
> Then we might carefully consider what we should do,
> whether to make an attack on the many-oared ships,
> to see if the divine power may grant us the victory
> or force us to retreat from the ships with losses. For my part
> I fear that the Achaeans may repay us for yesterday's defeat,
> since there's a man at the ships insatiable of battle

who, if I'm right, will no longer stay out of action.   (740-47)

Hector should call the Trojan leaders to a conference in the center for the purpose of discussing what they should do. Polydamas himself (as in his second speech in Book 12) clearly hopes that they will decide to retreat, for he fears Achilles' return to battle.

Hector, following this advice and seeking leaders to consult, goes off to the left—gleaming in his armor like a snowy mountain—in search of Deiphobus and Helenus (who have just been wounded) and Asius and Adamas (who have just been slain). Finding Paris, he taunts him with being a lady's man and no real fighter. Paris defends himself, as we know he can, and tells Hector about the casualties on the left. Then they return to the center to find the other leaders gathered around Polydamas and create with them a new Trojan front. A short catalogue of names answers to the much longer Achaean catalogue at the beginning of this section (so Winter 1956.113). A simile (795-801; simile type 2) compares the bright oncoming ranks of the Trojans to a succession of curling, roaring waves rolling over the sea. Hector, gleaming in his armor, is leading them like Ares (802, simile type 2; cf. lines 298-300).

The Achaeans are standing fast in close formation, led by Ajax who strides forward and challenges Hector, saying that the present defeat of the Achaeans has been the work of Zeus (812) and predicting that Troy will fall and that Hector will pray to Zeus to escape. This speech is followed by an omen—an eagle on the right—which emboldens the Achaeans. Has this omen been sent by Zeus, in spite of the fact that he is now willing a victory for the Trojans and has had his attention diverted? It is hard to accept this inconsistency. The omen sent by Zeus to Agamemnon at 8.245-52 was less difficult to explain, for there Zeus was fully aware of events on the battlefield. Two things seem certain, however, that the poet is using the present omen, whether sent by Zeus or not, to give an effect of climax and to confirm Ajax's prediction (so Michel 1971.64-65).

Hector responds by saying that he only wishes it was as certain that he might be the son of Zeus as it is that this day will bring destruction to the Achaeans and to Ajax in particular. This prediction is not answered by any omen. We are reminded of how Hector reacted in Book 12 to the omen of the eagle and the snake which was the occasion of Polydamas' second admonition.

We expect a single combat between Ajax and Hector, but, as has happened before, this is postponed. Instead, the two armies clash with loud shouting. In the present book Poseidon, by his secret intervention, has inspired the Achaeans to resist and has reestablished a situation of even battle. In Book 14, after he has inspired the wounded Achaean leaders to marshal their forces (and Zeus has been put to sleep), he will act openly and in his own person lead the Achaeans in a counterattack.

BOOK 14: POSEIDON LEADS THE ACHAEANS IN A COUNTERATTACK

Nestor Confers with the Wounded Achaean Leaders. Poseidon Inspires Them, 1-152

Whitman and Scodel 1981 have well described how the retardation in Books 13 through 15.389 has been composed in accordance with Zielinski's law, which they summarize (p. 3) as follows : "no two actions in the epic are ever presented as simultaneous, for the narrative never twice traverses the same temporal space." Moreover, as they emphasize, we must keep in mind the distinction Zielinski made between "scheinbare" and "wirkliche Handlung," that is, apparent and real sequence, at points in the retardation where new episodes are introduced by shouting. These shoutings can be thought of as occurring at the same time as an earlier shouting (real sequence), usually that at the end of Book 12 when the wall was first broken through, but the poet is always giving us the illusion that they are later (apparent sequence).

In Book 13 Poseidon, disguised as a human being, inspired the Ajaxes and other Achaean leaders with new fighting spirit. Now he continues to do this for Agamemnon, Odysseus, and Diomedes, whom he encounters behind the lines where they and Nestor have met. We remember that in Book 11 Agamemnon, Odysseus, and Diomedes had to withdraw because of their wounds, and Nestor withdrew to take care of the wounded Machaon.

In the opening scene of Book 14 we shift to Nestor as we left him at the end of Book 11 in his hut with Machaon. On hearing the shouting (which we naturally assume to be that of the clashing armies at the end of Book 13; apparent sequence), he leaves Machaon to see what has happened and discovers that the wall has been breached and that the Trojans are pouring through it. Thus the shouting he hears must be (in real time) that which arose when the wall was breached at the end of Book 12, and his meeting with the wounded Achaean leaders, and their being inspired by Poseidon, must belong to this earlier time, with Poseidon's inspiration of the other leaders at the beginning of Book 13.

Nestor debates with himself what he should do, his indecision being like swelling waves on the open sea before they break; he finally decides to go to Agamemnon. On the way, however, he meets Agamemnon in company with Diomedes and Odysseus. They too have heard the shouting and come from their ships to see what has happened, being grieved (*achhnuto*) at heart. The sight of

Nestor—why has he left the battle?—tends to confirm their fears. Agamemnon
says:

> Nestor, son of Neleus, great glory of the Achaeans,
> why have you left man-slaying war to come here?
> I fear that mighty Hector will now fulfill
> the threat he made in his speech to the assembled Trojans,
> that he would not return from the ships to Troy
> before he had burned our ships and slain us ourselves.
> Thus he spoke and all these things will now happen.
> Alas, it's true that the other well-greaved Achaeans
> are heartily angry with me, just like Achilles,
> and are unwilling to fight at the sterns of the ships.   (42-51)

We can compare how, in Book 13, Idomeneus asked Meriones why he left the
front. Agamemnon assumes that Hector is fulfilling his threat made in the Trojan
assembly in Book 8, and that the Achaeans are refusing to fight out of anger with
him (compare the words of Poseidon-Calchas at 13.111-14).

Nestor answers that Agamemnon's fears have indeed been realized: the wall
has been breached and the Achaeans are being routed. Accordingly, although they
are unable to fight because of their wounds, they should try to think of some
helpful plan of action.

This reply further disheartens Agamemnon, who says:

> Nestor, since they are fighting at the sterns of the ships,
> since the wall and trench we made is of no use,
> which we labored a great deal to build, hoping
> to find it an unbreakable protection for the ships and ourselves,
> I think that almighty Zeus has destined us
> to perish here without glory far off from Argos.
> I knew when he was willing to be our defender,
> and know now when he is glorifying them like gods
> and binding our strength and laming the force of our hands.   (65-73)

He goes on to make the discouraging proposal, as in Books 2 and 9, that they
should sail home. Odysseus opposes him, saying that they must fight on, even in
the face of certain death, for this is the heroic thing to do; Agamemnon's proposal
will only further demoralize the men. Agamemnon accepts this rebuke. He will not

order the men to sail home against their will. Somebody else, an old man or a
young one, should try to make a better proposal.   *Diomedes*

This is the cue for the young man Diomedes to speak up, as he did in Book 9.
He begins diplomatically by implying that, though they are older than he is, they
should be willing to listen to him, for he is the son of Tydeus who had died bravely
in similar desperate circumstances in the Theban War. He proposes that, since (as
Nestor has said) they are unable to fight because of their wounds, they should
exhort the others to fight.

> Thus he spoke, and they promptly did as he said
> and started to set out with King Agamemnon leading them.   (133-34)

They are setting out to exhort the troops, but we wonder how they will be
able to do this effectively in view of their demoralizing assumption that Zeus is
against them.   Then, as if in answer to this question, Poseidon enters the scene.
"But the glorious earth-shaker was keeping no blind watch" (135=13.10, where he
first intervened). He takes the form of a nameless old man; not Calchas, as at the
beginning of Book 13, for Calchas is unsuited to encourage Agamemnon (compare
Book 1). Seizing Agamemnon by the hand (a gesture of reassurance), he says:

> Son of Atreus, surely now the accursed heart of Achilles
> is rejoicing in his breast at the sight of the slaughter
> and flight of the Achaeans, for he is completely mindless.
> May he perish, may some divinity destroy him.
> Not all of the blessed gods are angry with you,
> but the leaders and the commanders of the Trojans still
> may raise the dust on the broad plain, and you shall see them
> fleeing from the ships and the huts back to their city.   (139-46)

Poseidon, speaking with dramatic irony as he did to the Ajaxes in Book 13, begins
by blaming Achilles in order to win the favor of Agamemnon. Then he gives
Agamemnon the hope that the gods (Zeus is not mentioned) will help the Achaeans
defeat the Trojans.

We are not told how Agamemnon responds to this encouragement. Instead,
Poseidon ends his speech, as he moves out toward the front, with a miraculously
loud shout.

> As loud as the shouting of nine or ten thousand men

when they are joining in battle, the conflict of Ares,
so loud was the shout emitted by the lordly earth-shaker,
which was putting great strength into each of the Achaeans,
into each heart, to war and fight without ceasing.   (147-52)

Compare how Eris, shouting at the beginning of this day of battle, filled the two
armies with spirit; lines 151-52 above=11.11-12.

The present section brings to a climax the narrative of Poseidon's secret
exhortation of Achaean leaders. There are clear similarities between his inspiration
of the Ajaxes and the younger leaders behind the lines at the beginning of Book 13
and his inspiration of the Achaean leaders at the beginning of this book. The
present episode acts as a climactic parallel with that one. The return of the great
Achaean leaders who withdrew in Book 11 gives a sense of closure and underlines
the completion of this first stage of Poseidon's intervention. Now he will act
openly. But at this point, when he is apparently throwing off the mask of the old
man, the scene shifts to the beguilement of Zeus.

Hera's Beguilement of Zeus Enables Poseidon to Act Openly, 153-391

Poseidon's loud shout seems likely to recall Zeus' attention to the battlefield.
At any rate Zeus must be put out of action more thoroughly than by merely having
him turn his gaze elsewhere; and this is accomplished by Hera. But, as Whitman
and Scodel 1981 point out, the shout of Poseidon really takes us back again to the
end of Book 12 and so is identical with the shouting heard by Nestor, in spite of the
fact that for narrative purposes it is treated as later. Thus, in real time, Hera's
intervention here is simultaneous with Poseidon's at the beginning of Book 13.
Looking down from Olympus, she sees Poseidon and rejoices, sees Zeus and
thinks how much she dislikes him. She decides to deceive him. Her deception of
him will bring to a climax his self-deception in turning his eyes away from the
battlefield at the beginning of Book 13. Thus Hera's intervention creates a climactic
parallel with that of Poseidon at 13.15ff. when seeing that Zeus was diverted he
came to aid the Achaeans.

As Poseidon went to get his horses and chariot, so she goes to her bedroom
to dress herself. In both cases we have a substitute for the arming motif at the
beginning of the hero's *aristeia*. She dresses herself to look her most seductive.
The perfume of her dress reaches to heaven; she glitters with grace. Then she gets

from Aphrodite a magic girdle to make her irresistibly lovely. The additional power she thus gains is like that given the hero at the beginning of his *aristeia*.

Being so prepared, she descends from Olympus to the island of Lemnos, not far from Troy, where she finds Hypnos (Sleep). The poet will have her overpower Zeus by love—and sleep (cf. line 353). She persuades Hypnos to put Zeus to sleep after she and Zeus have made love, implying that this will help the Achaeans but not instructing him specifically to urge on Poseidon. When she offers him an elegant chair with footstool in return for his services, he refuses, reminding her of how Zeus had earlier tried to punish him for putting him to sleep. But then she wins him over by promising to give him the youngest of the Graces, whom he has always desired. He makes her solemnly swear to uphold her end of the bargain.

This incident is very amusing, as is the whole beguilement. But why does Hera need Hypnos? Might not Zeus simply have fallen asleep as men often do after sexual intercourse (so Anchises in the *Hymn to Aphrodite*)? The poet apparently wanted to make vivid the power of sleep, as he did that of love, in the person of a deity. This seems the most important reason for the presence of Hypnos. But it is also true that, after Zeus has fallen asleep, someone is needed to tell Poseidon that he now has a free hand in helping the Achaeans, for Hera will stay in the arms of Zeus, and Poseidon will be unable to see through the cloud of invisibility in which Zeus and Hera are wrapped. Although it is easy to assume that Hypnos understands what he should do, scholars have often remarked that he informs Poseidon without any specific instructions from Hera. Why did the poet not have her tell him to do it? Perhaps because thus in Book 15 she will be able to swear to Zeus, without perjuring herself, that she is not responsible for Poseidon's activity.

When Hypnos has arrived at Mount Ida, he takes the form of a bird and sits on the highest tree. Hera goes to Zeus, who is immediately inflamed with passion and urges her (as she had planned) to make love right then and there. This she finally agrees to do after some humorous hesitation, and so they lie together under a golden cloud, created by Zeus to make them invisible, upon beautiful golden flowers which grow up spontaneously. Then Zeus falls asleep.

> So the Father was asleep on the top of Mount Ida,
> subdued by love and sleep, embracing his wife.
> And sweet Hypnos went off to the ships of the Achaeans
> to take his message to earth-holding, earth-shaking Poseidon;
> he went and stood by him and addressed him in winged words.
> Now, Poseidon, give help to the Danaans at will

> and grant to them glory, though but for the short time Zeus
> is still sleeping the soft deep sleep I've poured over him
> after Hera beguiled him to lie with her in love.
> So speaking, having stirred up Poseidon to aid the Danaans
> even more, he went on his way among humans.   (354-62)

The theme of exhortation begun before the beguilement is continued (we remember Poseidon's loud shout which was inspiring the Achaeans with new fighting spirit), for Hypnos not only informs Poseidon of the beguilement but exhorts him to act with complete freedom. And so Poseidon (who apparently has been acting in his own person since the time of his great shout) exhorts the Achaeans, telling them that they will not need Achilles if only they bestir themselves and exhort each other to fight (368-69); and he proposes that they exchange armor with each other, the best armor being given to the best fighters. This proposal has been criticized on a realistic level, but it is meant to put the men on their mettle and rouse their spirits (the theme of exhortation): men with good armor will be ashamed to admit that they are unworthy to keep it. Finally, Poseidon says that he will lead them in their counterattack.

Immediately the wounded leaders, Agamemnon, Odysseus, and Diomedes, marshal the troops and see to the exchange of armor. And, as is customary in marshaling troops, they exhort them, as they were planning to do before Poseidon's intervention. No mention is made of Nestor. It is as if his sole purpose in Book 14 were to introduce the informal council of Achaean leaders before the beguilement and to help create with them the climactic scene in the first, secret phase of Poseidon's intervention.

Now the Achaeans, under the leadership of Poseidon, advance against the enemy.

> When they had clothed themselves in gleaming bronze,
> they began to advance, and earth-shaking Poseidon led them,
> holding a terrible sharp-edged sword in his strong hand,
> like a lightning-bolt, which no one would dare to encounter
> in painful battle, no one would dare to come near.
> Opposite them gleaming Hector was marshaling the Trojans.
> Now the most terrible strife of battle was being
> stretched by black-maned Poseidon and gleaming Hector,
> this one helping the Argives, that one the Trojans.   (383-91)

These lines remind us of 13.345-60 where Poseidon and Zeus were described as pulling the cord of evenly fought battle between the two sides, in the first phase of Poseidon's intervention. But then Poseidon still had to act secretly; now he is acting openly, taking the place of the wounded Agamemnon as commander-in-chief of the Achaeans. Now the Achaeans will win the upper hand. *Poseidon*

Ajax Wounds Hector and the Trojans Are Put to Flight, 392-522

> And the sea was washing against the huts and the ships
> of the Argives, and the armies were clashing and loudly shouting.
> Not so loud is the roar of the waves on the shore
> stirred up on the sea by the troublesome blowing of Boreas,
> not so loud is the roar of a blazing fire
> in a mountain vale when it rushes to burn up the forest,
> not so loud is the wind in the leafy high oak trees
> which roars the loudest of all things when it is angry,
> as was the noise and the cries of the Trojans and Achaeans
> rushing with terrible shouting to encounter each other.   (392-401)

The sea in sympathy with its lord miraculously washes against the huts and ships, showing his favor toward the onrushing Achaeans. The simile describing the noise made by the clashing armies seems created in response to that at 13.795-801 (a type 2 simile) in which the oncoming Trojans were likened to waves rolling over the sea. But now the poet is concerned with both armies and the point of comparison is different. Moreover, the present simile is more complex, a threefold comparison, and is made in negative terms—the only such simile in the *Iliad*. The shouting here takes us back to 13.833-37 where the imminent single combat between Ajax and Hector failed to develop as the two armies clashed with loud shouting. As Whitman and Scodel 1981.5-8 point out, there are clear similarities between the narratives describing the beginning of conflict in both places, and these prevent us from supposing, as we can elsewhere in the retardation, that the present shouting is to be identified in real time with that at the end of Book 12. The single combat between Ajax and Hector is the climactic event of the retardation, and now it is finally about to occur.

Hector throws at Ajax but hits him ineffectively where his sword and shield straps cross. Then, as Hector pulls back in fear, Ajax hits him in the chest with a huge stone, making him spin like a top. Hector falls like an oak struck by the lightning of Zeus (414-17, simile type 9), and the Trojans and their allies move in to protect him. They carry him, groaning heavily, back to the ford of the Scamander River, where they stop and douse him with water. He sits up and spits out blood, but then collapses again. The poet emphasizes this scene in preparation for Hector's miraculous recovery in the next book, where Apollo will come to him at almost the same moment as we leave him here.

The wounding of Hector encourages the Achaeans. There follows a chain-reaction, even battle in which vengeance-demanding grief alternates from one side to the other. The little Ajax stabs Satnius, around whose body a struggle arises. Polydamas, having with his spear hit Prothoenor in the right shoulder, boasts over him: now Phothoenor will have something to lean on as he goes into Hades. This speech gives grief (*achos*) to the Achaeans, especially the big Ajax. Having hurled his spear at Polydamas and hit Antenor's son Archelochus instead, he shouts to Polydamas that this man seems a worthy exchange for Prothoenor—words that fill the Trojans with grief (*achos*). And Acamas, having stabbed the Boeotian Promachus, boasts that he has avenged his brother Archelochus, and so fills the Achaeans with grief (*achos*), especially Peneleos, who rushes at Acamas. But Acamas withdraws, and Peneleos stabs Ilioneus instead, driving his spear into his eye and out through the back of his head—a climactic kill. Then, having cut off his head with his sword, he waves it on his spear like a poppy, showing it to the Trojans and telling them to go and tell the mother and father of Ilioneus to wail in mourning, for the wife of Promachus will not rejoice when the Achaeans return from Troy. (Compare 13.202-5, where the little Ajax cut off the head of Imbrius and hurled it into the throng of the Trojans, to stop at Hector's feet.)

As Winter 1956.124-25 has pointed out, we have felt the wounding of Hector as a sign that the Achaeans will gain the advantage, and so it comes as no great surprise that now Peneleos' gruesome act causes the Trojans to turn and flee. The poet calls on the Muses at this critical turning point (so Willcock 1984.234) to say which Achaean first despoiled one of the enemy when Poseidon inclined the battle against the Trojans. In a brief closing passage (511-22) we are told that the big Ajax was first, then came Antilochus, Meriones, Teucer, and Menelaus, and finally, last but not least, the little Ajax, distinguished for slaying most since he is swiftest in pursuit. Thus the Achaeans, led by Poseidon acting openly and in disregard of Zeus, have wounded Hector and are putting the Trojans to flight.

BOOK 15: ZEUS GIVES VICTORY TO THE TROJANS

Zeus

He Awakes and Takes Control, 1-238

The Trojans are fleeing over the trench to where they left their chariots at the beginning of Book 12 when they were about to attack the wall, Polydamas having advised them to go on foot because of the trench. This is as far as the poet will have them flee, for at this critical moment Zeus awakes and sees what is happening. Now Zeus will cause the Trojans to break through the wall again and so restore the situation to what it was at the end of Book 12 before the retardation. Seeing what has happened and being filled with pity for the wounded Hector (*idon eleese*, 12), he upbraids Hera and threatens to punish her, but she mollifies him by swearing that she has not urged Poseidon to help the Achaeans. Then he tells her to call Iris and Apollo to him

> that Iris my go to the army of the bronze-chitoned Achaeans
> and carry my command to lordly Poseidon to leave
> the battlefield and return to his own abode;
> and that Phoebus Apollo may stir up Hector
> by giving him new fighting spirit and healing that pain
> with which he is still tormented, and inspire
> the Achaeans to turn and flee in impotent panic.
> So they in flight shall come to the many-oared ships
> of Achilles, Peleus' son, and he shall send forth
> his comrade Patroclus, whom gleaming Hector shall slay
> with the spear before Troy, after Patroclus has slain
> many heroes, among them Sarpedon, my godlike son.
> Then in his anger (*cholosamenos*) shall godlike Achilles slay Hector,
> and I from that time on shall see to it that
> the Achaeans shall always be driving the Trojans back
> until they take steep Troy by the plans of Athena.
> But I shall not cease from my anger (*cholos*) nor shall I allow
> any of the other immortals to give aid to the Danaans
> before I have brought to fulfillment the desire of Achilles,
> the promise I made when I nodded my head in assent
> to the plea of divine Thetis who taking hold of my knees
> begged me to honor Achilles, sacker of cities.   (56-77)

We should compare Zeus' prediction to Hera after her abortive attempt to help the Achaeans at the end of Book 8. Now, after telling how he intends to use Iris and Apollo (a programmatic statement for this book), he gives us a more detailed look into the future: the Achaeans will be driven back upon their ships; Achilles will send out Patroclus who will slay Sarpedon and be slain by Hector; Achilles will slay Hector and the Achaeans will take Troy. Zeus describes his support of Achilles' wrath as a prosecution of his own anger.

Hera goes off to Olympus, moving quickly in obedience to Zeus. Her speed is compared to that of the mind of a man remembering the places he has visited. Similes will also be used to illustrate the swiftness with which Iris and Apollo obey Zeus. The poet seems at pains to let us know that, in spite of his lengthy description, it actually took very little time to turn back the Achaeans from the point at which we have just left them.

The gods, assembled in the palace of Zeus, rise at Hera's approach, and Themis, the goddess of law and order, gives her a cup of greeting and asks whether Zeus has been frightening her. Hera answers that Zeus' tyrannical character is well known, and that not all of them will like what he has decided will happen. Ares, for instance, must endure the death of his son Ascalaphus.

Ascalaphus was slain by the Trojan Deiphobus in Book 13. Thus Ares, a pro-Trojan god, in order to avenge him, must go against the Trojans. We can compare how later, in Book 22, Poseidon, though pro-Achaean, will save the Trojan Aeneas. Now Ares is eager to avenge his son, but Athena, a more sensible divinity of war, stops him. She takes off his armor piece by piece and puts his spear to rest (the reverse of the arming of the hero in preparation for his *aristeia*). Ares' demobilization stands for the inability of all the other gods to oppose Zeus' purpose. Moreover, this episode introduces a theme—the acquiescence of a god in the death of his son—which will be most poignantly illustrated in the next book where Zeus will grant to Hera that Sarpedon must die (so Thalmann 1984.45).

Then Hera, having called Apollo and Iris out of the assembly, tells them to go to Zeus "as quickly as possible" (146). In spite of her hasty obedience to Zeus the scene on Olympus has taken some time. Compare the "haste" of Iris-Polites in Book 2, who is used to exhort the Trojans to meet the oncoming Achaeans; and that of Hector in Book 6, the success of whose mission in Troy is meant to stop the attacking Achaeans; and that of Patroclus in Book 11, who remains inactive during the assault on the wall in Book 12 and during the retardation in Books 13 through 15.389, in spite of the fact that the safety of the ships depends upon his supplication of Achilles.

When Apollo and Iris have come before Zeus, Zeus tells Iris to order Poseidon off the battlefield. She obeys swiftly, going to the plain like falling snow or hail. When Poseidon asserts his right to act independently of Zeus, she reminds him of the respect due to an older brother; and so he yields, saying, however, that Zeus must not try to prevent the ultimate defeat of the Trojans.

Not until the Iris strand of the narrative is completed does Zeus turn to Apollo and give him his commission (an example of Zielinski's law; see Introduction, p. 6). Now that Poseidon has left, Apollo should revive Hector and, using the aegis, should put the Achaeans to flight; later he, Zeus, will contrive a respite for the Achaeans (by means of Patroclus and then Achilles). Apollo obeys with the swiftness of a hawk, the swiftest of birds.

Apollo Revives Hector and, Leading the Trojans, Breaks Down the Wall, 239-389

Apollo finds Hector already being revived by the "mind of Zeus" (242) and tells him to take courage, for he is Apollo sent by Zeus to be his protector. Hector should command his charioteers to drive toward the ships, for he, Apollo, will level a way for them (by creating a passage over the trench and through the wall) and turn the Achaeans to flight. So saying, he breathes great strength into Hector, so that Hector returns to the action like a well-fed stallion who has broken his tether to run in the meadow (263-68, simile type 2: the hero's advance into battle). The same simile was used of Paris at 6.506-11 when he was returning to battle after his refreshing visit with Helen.

A second simile describes the effect of astonishment that Hector's reappearance has on the Achaeans. It is as if they were hunters who while pursuing a deer or a goat are suddenly faced by a lion (271-76; cf. type 8 similes: retreat). We can contrast (so Winter 1956.136) how the wounding of Hector in Book 14 boosted their spirits. Their reaction is further shown by a speech of Thoas who says that some god must have saved Hector and that Zeus must be supporting him now. The miraculous healing of Hector is the first of several indications that Zeus is willing victory for the Trojans. Accordingly, Thoas proposes that the Achaeans should retreat in good battle formation behind their wall. And so the Ajaxes, Idomeneus, Teucer, Meriones, and Meges oversee the creation of a line of defense while the mass of the men start to retreat. Thus, as Janko 1992.258 notes, "the poet returns the Greeks to the ships without a shameful, uncontested rout."

The Trojans press forward, led by Hector and Apollo holding the aegis of Zeus. The present attack of the Trojans is a reversal of the counterattack of the Achaeans led by Poseidon with his lightning-like sword (so Winter 1956.139).

> As long as Apollo was holding the aegis motionless,
> the missiles of both sides were hitting and heroes were dying,
> but when he looked straight-on at the swift-horsed Danaans
> and shook it and shouted against them terribly, then they
> lost all spirit to fight and forgot to be valorous.   (318-22)

The Achaeans flee like a herd of cattle or flock of sheep stampeded by the sudden appearance of two wild animals (Hector and Apollo; 323-25, simile type 4: flight and pursuit). Hector kills a man; Aeneas two; and Polydamas, Polites, Agenor, and Paris each kill one. They strip the dead, thus giving the Achaeans time to get behind their wall.

Hector, noticing this, commands the Trojans to attack and leads the way for the other charioteers. Notice that they are using their chariots, not abandoning them as in Book 12, for they can trust Apollo to see them safely over the trench. They come on with loud shouting (355, like that at the end of Book 12 when they first breached the wall); and Apollo, going before them, kicks in the trench, thus creating a passageway extending the length of a spear-cast made by a man showing his mettle; and he breaks down the wall.

> He threw down the Achaean wall
> very easily, as when a boy near the sea who has made
> a sandheap to play with, delighting his childish mind,
> playfully destroys it again with his hands and his feet;
> so you, goodly Phoebus, destroyed what with labor and pain
> the Achaeans had built and filled them with panic fear.   (361-66)

Thus Apollo, miraculously, does so much more easily and so much better what it took Hector and the Trojans great trouble to do in Book 12.

The Achaeans make a stand at the sterns of the first row of ships (drawn up on the shore with their prows toward the sea). They are exhorting each other and praying to the gods. Nestor prays Zeus to save them from destruction; and Zeus thunders in answer, showing that he will not allow them to be completely destroyed. But the Trojans, taking this as an omen in their favor, come through the wall with loud shouting like waves pouring over the sides of a ship (381-83, simile type 3: the hero's attack).

> Thus the Trojans with great shouting came through the wall,
> driving their horses, and now at the sterns of the ships
> were fighting with broad-bladed spears close-in from their chariots,
> while the Achaeans, having mounted their high black ships,
> were fighting with long pikes, found there ready for use,
> ship-pikes, jointed, their points being covered with bronze.   (384-89)

The shouting here reminds us of that at the end of Book 12 when the wall was first breached. We have returned to the same point, and the retardation begun in Book 13 is over. The mention of fighting with ship-pikes here prepares us (Willcock 1984.240 uses the term "foreshadows") for Ajax's later using a ship-pike to defend the ships.

Patroclus Sets Out to Return to Achilles.   The Battle at the Ships, 390-591

Now we switch to Patroclus in the hut of Eurypylus where we left him at the end of Book 11. Hearing the noise of the fleeing Achaeans and realizing that the wall has been breached, he says:

> Eurypylus, no longer am I able to stay here with you,
> though you are suffering, for a great crisis has arisen.
> Let your attendant care for your wound. I must
> hasten to Achilles in order to stir him to battle.
> Who knows whether I with the help of some god may succeed
> in persuading him? A friend's persuasion's a good thing.   (399-404)

(Lines 403-4 repeat Nestor's words to Patroclus at 11.792-93). And so Patroclus sets out to return to Achilles.

The present shouting and breaching of the wall are re-creations of the first shouting and breaching at the end of Book 12. But to which breaching is Patroclus responding? "On the surface, it must be the second . . . , but it is not a problem that he has failed to notice the first, for the two are essentially the same" (Whitman and Scodel 1981.9). As we commented on the Patroclus-Eurypylus scene in Book 11, Patroclus' being with Eurypylus instead of with Nestor enables the poet to bring him back into action after Nestor without raising the question of timing.

When we return to the battle (with which the Patroclus strand of the narrative is being interwoven), the charge of the Trojans has been stopped, but the Achaeans, though outnumbering the enemy, are unable to drive them back (for Zeus is favoring the Trojans). The even battle is compared to a carpenter's line for cutting a plank straight (410-12, simile type 6: even battle).

Hector and Ajax are fighting over one of the ships (416), probably that of Protesilaus over which they will fight at the end of this book. Willcock 1984.240, following Schadewaldt, speaks of "a technique of the oral poet to adumbrate in general terms what will later be treated more specifically." Ajax slays Hector's cousin Caletor. Hector aims at Ajax but hits Ajax's attendant Lycophron. Then Ajax calls on Teucer to use his bow against Hector to avenge their companion, and Teucer responds by shooting a barrage of arrows. He hits Polydamas' companion Cleitus, but when he aims at Hector, Zeus causes his bowstring to break. Teucer complains:

> Alas, some god has cut off my devices of fighting
> entirely, for he has cast my bow from my hand
> and broken my new-strung bowstring which I bound on it
> this morning for bearing the frequent shooting of arrows.   (467-70)

Ajax tells him to get his shield and spear (for fighting at close quarters), and so he does.

The breaking of Teucer's bowstring is another sign that Zeus is favoring the Trojans, and Hector, seeing it, exhorts his men (485-99). It is clear, he says, to whom Zeus is giving the victory; and they are fighting for their native land, for which it is not shameful to die. Ajax in turn exhorts the Achaeans (502-13). It is better for them to risk all in a brief hard-fought battle than to be beaten down gradually by these inferior men.

There follows a description of fighting at close quarters (515-45). Hector kills Schedius; Ajax Laodamas; Polydamas Otus. Meges aims at Polydamas (whom Apollo is protecting—since he is his priest according to Ameis-Hentze on 522) but hits Croesus. Dolops, Hector's cousin, darts forward to attack Meges, but Meges lops off part of his helmet, and when Dolops foolishly presses on leaving his back unprotected (so Janko 1992.288), Menelaus kills him from the rear with a spear through his shoulder and chest. Notice how the slayings of Trojans and Achaeans alternate, as is typical of even battle. Special emphasis, however, is put on the slaying of Dolops.

Now Hector exhorts Melanippus (553-58): they must try to protect the body
of their cousin Dolops. And again Ajax exhorts the Achaeans (561-64; compare
Agamemnon's exhortation at 5.529-32), who create a strong defense in front of the
ships; but Zeus is driving on the Trojans. Then Antilochus, urged on by Menelaus,
rushes forward and hurls his spear at the enemy. He hits Melanippus and springs
upon him, like a dog upon a wounded deer (579-81, simile type 5: the victor and
his victim), to strip him of his armor. But Hector forces Antilochus to withdraw,
like a wild animal who having slain a dog or shepherd retreats before a company of
men (586-88, simile type 8: retreat). The Trojans and Hector, with loud shouting,
send their missiles after him.

Hector Breaks Through the Achaean Defenses, 592-652

At this point we are given a view of the action from Zeus' perspective..

> The Trojans were like flesh-rending lions as they rushed
> toward the ships in fulfillment of the commands of Zeus,
> who always was driving them on and rousing their spirits,
> but was bewitching the Argives and depriving them of glory.
> For he was planning to grant the glory to Hector,
> the son of Priam, to throw blazing fire to burn up
> the beaked ships and so to fulfill the unreasonable prayer
> of Thetis completely. For Zeus the Counselor was waiting
> to see before him the bright light of a ship being burned.
> From that time on he was going to cause the Trojans
> to retreat from the ships and give the Danaans glory.
> In furtherance of this plan he now urged to the hollow ships
> Hector, Priam's son, who was already eager to go,
> raging like spear-wielding Ares or as baneful fire
> rages in the thickets of deep woods in the mountains.
> The mouth was white with foam, the eyes gleaming
> under the frightening brows, the helmet shaking
> terribly over the temples of him as he fought on,
> Hector, for there had come from on high as his helper
> Zeus, who was granting to him alone among many
> honor and glory, for Hector was destined a short time
> to live, since Pallas Athena was already preparing
> the day of his death at the hands of Peleus' son.   (592-614)

Zeus is in control, waiting, as we are, for Hector to fire a ship, with the result that Achilles will return. In line 598 Thetis' prayer is called *exaisios*, "unreasonable" (Leaf II.598). No doubt the Greek audience, at this moment of Achaean defeat, felt very much out of sympathy with Achilles.

The Trojans are attacking, but the Achaeans are still standing firm, like a sheer rock against the waves of the sea (618-21, simile type 7: resistance), until Hector leaps into their midst like a wave falling into a ship (624-28, simile type 3: the hero's attack). Now they are thrown into confusion like a herd of cattle before a lion (630-36, simile type 4: flight and pursuit). One of them trips on his body shield as he tries to turn to flee, and Hector slays him. This is Periphetes, the son of Copreus, the messenger of Eurystheus to Heracles; he seems an ad hoc invention. His men, fearing Hector, can do nothing to protect him in spite of their grief (*achnumenoi*, 651). Since Periphetes is killed only because he stumbles, his slaying gives Hector no glory (so Janko 1992.298).

Ajax Defends the Ship of Protesilaus against Hector, 653-746

The Achaeans are forced to fall back into the spaces between the first row of ships (so Winter 1956.165). Their exhortations of each other are exemplified by a speech of Nestor (661-66) comparable to his prayer to Zeus which was answered by the omen of the thunder at the beginning of the present battle. Now Athena responds by taking the mist from the eyes of the Achaeans, enabling them to see the entire battle clearly. We can compare how later, at 17.645-50, Zeus removes the mist of battle in answer to Ajax's prayer.

Ajax, having retreated, takes a position on the stern-deck of one of the ships, wielding a ship-pike twenty-two cubits long (compare the use of ship-pikes at 15.388-89); and he jumps from one ship to another, like an acrobatic horseman leaping over the backs of a team of four horses. Hector, urged on by Zeus, is coming against the Achaeans like an eagle against waterfowl (690-92, simile type 5).

After a brief description of hotly fought even battle, the narrative centers on the ship of Protesilaus. They are using battle-axes and hatchets; the ground is flowing with blood. Hector, his hand on Protesilaus' ship, exhorts the Trojans.

> Bring fire and all together raise the war cry.
> Now Zeus has given us a day worth all our days,
> to take the ships which have come here with the gods' disapproval
> and put many pains upon us, because of our elders'

cowardice, who forbade me to fight at the sterns of the ships,
though I was eager to do so, and kept back the army.
But if wide-seeing Zeus then blighted our brains,
now he is driving and leading us on himself.   (718-25)

This speech shows Hector's blindness, for the true reason why he is fighting at the ships for the first time in the Trojan War is that Achilles is absent.

Again, and for the last time in this battle, Ajax, who has been forced to withdraw to the midship-plank of Protesilaus' ship, answers Hector's exhortation. He tells the Achaeans that, with the sea at their backs, their only hope is to fight—a clear-sighted assessment of their no-exit situation. And suiting his action to his words, he successively stabs, in the closing lines of this book, twelve Trojans as they try to fire Protesilaus' ship.

The fighting at the ships has become increasingly desperate for the Achaeans. First they retreated to a position in front of the row of ships farthest inland (367). Then they were forced back into the spaces between these ships (655). Finally, Ajax withdrew onto the sterns of the ships (676) and then to the midship-plank of Protesilaus' ship (728). As the battle has progressed the distance withdrawn has become shorter, and Ajax has become more isolated. We now expect to see the ship of Protesilaus being fired. But this will not happen immediately, for at this moment of highest suspense we shift to the Patroclus-Achilles scene.

The present book describes one of the two main defensive actions of the Achaeans in the *Iliad*; the other occurs in Book 17 during the battle over Patroclus' body. We shall see that these narratives show definite similarities (for instance, Protesilaus' ship as the object being fought over can be equated with Patroclus' body), and that they introduce the parallel episodes of Achilles' two momentous decisions, to send out Patroclus in Book 16 and to return to battle himself in Book 18.

BOOK 16: THE *ARISTEIA* OF PATROCLUS

Achilles Sends Out Patroclus to Save the Ships. The Fulfillment of Zeus' Promise, 1-418

In this book Achilles gives up his wrath to the extent of allowing Patroclus to lead out the Myrmidons to save the ships. The strand of the narrative dealing with him and Patroclus is interwoven with that describing the battle over the ship of Protesilaus, the two being closely connected. There is a strong theme of pity. Patroclus, a naturally sympathetic person, tries, as Nestor in Book 11 has urged him to do, to prevail upon Achilles to pity the Achaeans, but Achilles lacks sufficient pity. Patroclus will enter the battle wearing the armor of Achilles, as his substitute, and drive the Trojans from the ships. His great deed, the central episode of this book, will be the slaying of Sarpedon; but then he will be slain by Hector. Thus Achilles' present decision will lead inevitably to his decision in Book 18 to renounce his wrath completely. In our comments on Book 18 we shall try to specify some of the ways in which that narrative creates a climactic parallel with this one.

When Patroclus comes to Achilles, he is weeping like a dark spring (3-4) because of his sympathy for the Achaeans (the same simile occurred at 9.14-15 to describe Agamemnon weeping in self-pity). Achilles pities (*okteire*, 5) Patroclus, comparing him to a little girl who runs weeping beside her mother and begging to be picked up. Has one of their fathers died? Or is he lamenting over the Achaeans who are dying because they have wrongly sided with Agamemnon? This all seems a little sarcastic.

Patroclus answers, groaning, that Achilles should not be angry with him, for great grief (*achos*, 22) has come upon the Achaeans. He goes on to describe this grief in the same way as Nestor has done to him (23-27=11.658-62), and blames Achilles for being set in his anger (*cholos*, 30), pitiless (*apenes*, 35); the sea and rocks must have been his parents. He ends by repeating (with minor variations) the concluding words from Nestor's speech:

> But if you are shunning some prophecy you know on your own,
> or your queenly mother has brought you some message from Zeus,
> then send me out quickly at least and the rest of our army,
> the Myrmidons, that I may be of some light to the Danaans.
> Grant me to wear that armor of yours on my shoulders
> so that the Trojans may think I am you and hold off from battle

and give the warlike sons of the Achaeans a respite
in their distress; respites from battle are precious.
Easily might we who are rested drive the tired enemy
back to their city away from out ships and our huts.   (36-45=11.704-803)

And the poet comments:

Thus he prayed, greatly foolish (*nepios*), for he was destined
to ask for an evil fate of death for himself.   (46-47)

Achilles answers:

Alas, noble Patroclus, what are you saying?
Neither am I bothered by any prophecy I know of
nor has my lady mother revealed to me a divine word.
But a terrible grief (*achos*) has come on my heart and spirit
since a man has wanted to deprive me, his equal,
and take back again the reward won by my own strength
—a terrible grief (*achos*)—after I had suffered in battle.
The girl the Achaeans chose out to be my reward,
my spear-prize seized when I sacked her well-walled city,
King Agamemnon took back out of my hands,
Atreus' son, treating me like a worthless day laborer.
But let us let bygones be bygones; it wasn't after all
possible to be angry (*kecholosthai*) forever. Admittedly, I'd thought
that I wouldn't cease from my wrath (*menithmon*) until the moment
the shouting of battle and warfare came to my own ships.
But you now put on your shoulders my glorious armor
and lead out the war-loving Myrmidons to battle.   (49-65)

Achilles is modifying his decision at 9.650-55 not to return until Hector reaches his
own ships. He goes on to say that Patroclus should attack the Trojans, but only to
drive them off, for he fears that some god, like Apollo (a foreshadowing of
Apollo's role in Patroclus' slaying), might help them. He ends by making the
impossible wish (97-100) that only he and Patroclus, of all the Trojans and
Achaeans, might survive to take Troy, thus showing his lack of pity for his own
people as well as the enemy.

Now we switch back to the battlefield. The mind of Zeus and the Trojans are overpowering Ajax; and the poet calls on the Muses to help him describe what is happening.

> Hector, coming near, struck Ajax's ashen shaft
> with his huge sword behind the socket of the spear-point
> and broke it off. So Telamonian Ajax
> brandished ineffectively his cut-off shaft; the bronze
> spear-point falling to the ground loudly resounded.
> Ajax recognized in his heart with a shudder the working
> of divinity, that high-thundering Zeus was cutting off his devices
> of fighting entirely and willing the Trojans the victory.
> He withdrew from the missiles; the enemy set fire to the swift ship,
> immediately covering it with inextinguishable flames.   (114-22)

We are reminded of how Zeus caused Teucer's bowstring to break, which was an earlier signal of the Achaean failure to defend the ships. There (15.467-68) Teucer said , "Alas, some god has cut off my devices of fighting entirely." Here (lines 119-20) the poet underlines the similarity—a climactic parallel—by having Ajax use the same words. The shattering of Menelaus' sword in Book 3 is also comparable, but this occurred in an altogether different context.

Immediately we return to Achilles and Patroclus. Achilles, slapping his thighs (a sign of frustration, also made by Patroclus at 15.397), orders Patroclus to arm himself while he marshals the Myrmidons. This is a great moment in the narrative. Zeus has fulfilled his promise to Thetis by having Hector set fire to Protesilaus' ship; and Achilles is giving up his wrath to the extent of sending out his men under the leadership of Patroclus dressed as himself. The poet holds this moment in suspense with a long description (130-256) of the arming of Patroclus and the marshaling of the Myrmidons.

Patroclus puts on the armor of Achilles, but does not take up his spear, for he is incapable of playing the role of Achilles this far (so Armstrong 1958). Moreover, the fact that his armor is not said to shine, as is usual at the beginning of a hero's *aristeia*, apparently shows his coming death (so Krischer 1971.29). Then Automedon, Achilles' charioteer, harnesses Achilles' two immortal horses to the chariot and adds a third mortal trace horse, which is destined to be killed. As Edwards 1987.260 says: "the mortal horse, like Patroclus, will die in this battle."

Meanwhile Achilles is marshaling the Myrmidons. Arming like ravening wolves (156-63; cf. the simile at 352-55), they form into five groups (168-97). Latacz 1977.59-63 has argued that this passage was omitted from the Catalogue of the Achaean Contingents in Book 2 since Achilles had taken the Myrmidons out of the battle. The listing of them here underlines the fact that he is giving up his wrath.

He exhorts his men, reminding them of how during the time of his wrath (*menithmon*, 202) they had blamed him, imagining them saying:

> Stubborn son of Peleus, your mother nursed you on bile (*cholos*),
> pitiless (*nelees*), who keep us against our will at the ships.
> Let us go home again in our seafaring ships,
> since such an evil anger (*cholos*) possesses your soul.   (203-6)

We (the Greek audience) can fully sympathize with this expression of disaffection. It is easy to believe that Achilles' own men have lost patience with him, as we have seen that Phoenix and Patroclus have done.

Then Achilles fetches a beautiful cup and, in front of his hut, pours a libation as he prays to Zeus for Patroclus' success.

> Truly you have answered my earlier prayer
> and given me honor by smiting the army of the Achaeans.
> So even now fulfill my present petition.
> I shall myself stay behind in the camp by the ships
> but send my comrade out with my many Myrmidons
> to battle. Give glory, far-thundering Zeus, to him,
> strengthen his heart in his breast, that Hector may know
> whether he, my comrade, has the ability to fight
> when left to himself or if his hands are invincible
> only when I have entered the turmoil of Ares.
> But when he's driven from the ships the fighting and war cries,
> may he come back unhurt to me at the swift ships
> with all of his armor along with our close-fighting men.   (236-48)

Thus he prayed, but, as the poet comments (249-50), Zeus while granting him one request denied him the other. Patroclus will not return safely from battle. Achilles, by saying that his prayer (made through Thetis in Book 1) has been fulfilled, acknowledges that the time has come for his wrath to end, but now he takes his stand at his hut to view the battle.

The Myrmidons advance with loud shouting. Patroclus exhorts them to fight so well that Agamemnon will realize his foolishness in dishonoring Achilles, the best of the Achaeans. And so they fall upon the Trojans, who start to flee, thinking that Achilles has given up his wrath (*menithmon*, 281). Patroclus charges into their center and, slaying Pyraechmes ("Fire-spear"; his name suits the moment), drives them from the half-burned ship of Protesilaus. The Achaeans are given a breather, described by a simile (297-302, type 4: flight and pursuit) of Zeus causing the sky to shine after driving away a thick cloud (the enemy). But the Trojans continue to resist, though in disarray.

In lines 306-51 the Achaeans gradually push them back and gain the victory. Nine Achaeans, beginning with Patroclus, each slays a Trojan. The final, climactic slaying, by Idomeneus, who stabs his victim in the mouth, is especially horrible. The Achaeans are compared to wolves attacking sheep (352-55, simile type 5: victor and victim; cf. the wolf simile at 156-63). The Trojans think only of flight. Ajax moves against Hector, who, though he recognizes that the battle has turned against the Trojans, is holding his ground in the hope of saving his comrades.

But soon the Trojans and Hector are fleeing in disorder, like a great billowing storm-cloud sent by Zeus into the sky (364-65, simile type 4: flight and pursuit). The Trojan horses are disabled by the trench, but not so the horses of Patroclus as he rides in pursuit. The roar of the Trojan horses in flight is compared to the roar of rivers swollen by a great rain sent by Zeus to punish men (384-92, another type 4 simile).

Patroclus pursues the Trojans onto the open field, thus disobeying the order of Achilles. He cuts off their retreat to the city and avenges the death of many (398; thus, as Willcock 1984.250 notes, fulfilling the prediction of Polydamas at 13.745.) He slays Pronous, and then Thestor, Pronous' charioteer; stabbing Thestor in the jaw, he draws him from his chariot like a fish (406-8, simile type 9: the warrior falls) and lets him fall on his face. Then in quick succession he slays eleven others, apparently Lycians, for Sarpedon is moved to enter the action.

Patroclus Slays Sarpedon, 419-683

Sarpedon, after exhorting the Lycians and saying that he will oppose this man and find out who he is, leaps from his chariot. And, Patroclus having leaped from his, they attack each other like vultures.

At this point we switch to Zeus and Hera (on Mount Ida, to which we must suppose that Hera has returned). Zeus, seeing them and being filled with pity (*idon eleese,* 431), wants to save his son Sarpedon; Hera says no.

> O most awesome son of Cronus, what are you saying?
> Do you want to bring back from ill-omened death
> a man who is mortal, one long fated to die?
> Do it, but we other gods won't all be applauding.   (441-43)

The other gods would want to save their favorites too. Sarpedon must die.

> But when his soul and life have departed from him,
> commission Thanatos (Death) and sweet Hypnos (Sleep)
> to carry him off to his home in the land of broad Lycia,
> where his relatives and friends will bury him properly
> with mound and stone, for this is the right of the dead.   (453-57)

Lines 441-43 will be used later, at 22.178-81, by Athena to Zeus when he complains of Hector's death. Now he weeps tears of blood for Sarpedon, "whom Patroclus was destined to slay" (460-61). Patroclus' slaying of Sarpedon shows parallels with Hector's slaying of Patroclus later in this book and with Achilles' slaying of Hector in Book 22. Kirk 1976.209-17 has a good analysis of how these death-scenes are similar to each other, especially the latter two, and how the poet has created a climax (a climactic parallel) in the death of Hector.

As we return to the battle, Patroclus, missing with his spear, hits Sarpedon's charioteer. Sarpedon, missing Patroclus, kills the mortal trace-horse, and Automedon cuts it loose. Then Patroclus and Sarpedon attack each other again. Sarpedon, having missed a second time, is hit in the heart by Patroclus' spear and falls like a tree cut down in the mountains (482-86=13.389-93 describing the death of Asius; simile type 9: the warrior falls). Then another simile compares the roaring of Sarpedon to that of a bull being slain by a lion (487-89; another type 9 simile). He dies calling on Glaucus to take command of the Lycians and not to allow the Achaeans to gain possession of his armor. "When he had spoken thus, the end of death covered him" (502). This line recurs in two other places, at 16.855 of Patroclus and at 22.361 of Hector. Kirk 1976.210 points out that these are the only death-scenes in which a mortally-wounded man speaks, and also notes that the death-scenes of Patroclus and Hector, for which we are told how their souls go down to Hades, elaborate upon that of Sarpedon: the soul leaves Sarpedon's body as Patroclus extracts his spear. The Myrmidons capture Sarpedon's horses.

Glaucus feels terrible grief (*achos*, 508), but is unable to protect Sarpedon's body because of the wound he suffered at 12.388. Accordingly, he calls on Apollo, who heals him and gives him new strength. Then, after exhorting the Lycians to fight over Sarpedon's body, he reproaches the Trojans for neglecting their allies. He fears that the Myrmidons may disfigure the body in their anger (*kecholomenoi*, 546) at all the Achaeans who have been slain. His words produce great grief (*penthos*, 548) in the Trojans, and Hector leads them to save Sarpedon's body, being angered (*choomenos*, 553) over his death.

Patroclus urges on the Ajaxes, saying that the man who was first to leap through the Achaean wall is now dead, and that they should try to get hold of his body in order to disfigure it. On both sides the motivating force is the anger of grief, the desire to avenge the dead by slaying the enemy and stripping him of his armor and disfiguring his body—a theme which will come to a climax in Achilles' slaying of Hector.

Lines 562-68 give a general view of the even battle over Sarpedon's body (Zeus covers the area with a miraculous darkness in order to increase the terrible conflict), followed, in lines 569-643, by a detailed description. Hector slays Epeigeus, a Myrmidon who was reared by Peleus and Thetis. This gives grief (*achos*, 581) to Patroclus and, being angered (*kecholoso*, 585), he goes against the Lycians like a hawk putting jackdaws and starlings to flight (582-83, simile type 4: flight). He hits Sthenelaon and causes the Trojans to fall back the distance of a spear-cast. When Glaucus slays Bathycles, the son of a wealthy Myrmidon, great grief (*achos*, 599) seizes the Achaeans. Meriones, after slaying the son of a priest of the Zeus of Mount Ida, is forced to dodge a spear thrown by Aeneas. Then they exchange insults; and Patroclus (completely forgetful of Achilles' command) admonishes Meriones for speaking instead of fighting. The sound of the fighting over Sarpedon's body is like that of woodmen cutting down trees (633-34, simile type 6: indecisive battle). Not even a very observant person could recognize Sarpedon, so covered is he with blood and dust and missiles. They are fighting over the body like flies swarming around a milk pail in spring (641-43, another type 6 simile).

In line 644 we return to Zeus who, like us, is watching intently. He is debating with himself whether to let Hector slay Patroclus now over the body of Sarpedon or later before the walls of Troy. Deciding on the latter course, he puts fear into Hector.

Hector mounts his chariot and urges the others to flee. He recognizes that the scales of Zeus are against him. The Lycians also flee. And so the Achaeans are able to strip the armor from Sarpedon's body and take it to the ships (to be a prize at the funeral games of Patroclus at 23.798-810).

At this point Zeus on Ida intervenes, commanding Apollo (who like Hera earlier is conveniently there) to save Sarpedon's body and have Thanatos and Hypnos carry it to Lycia for proper burial. Lines 674-75 repeat lines 456-57 of Hera's speech (ring composition, giving a pleasing sense of completion). There follows a brief but moving account of how Apollo obeys. The way Sarpedon's body, by divine intervention, is saved from being disfigured and is returned to his own people is like what is going to happen to the bodies of Patroclus and Hector.

Hector Slays Patroclus, 684-867

Patroclus, urged on by Zeus, leads the Myrmidons in pursuit of the Trojans; and the poet asks who was the first and who the last he slew "when the gods were calling you to death" (693; used again only at 22.297 of Hector). In quick succession he slays seven men, and the Achaeans would have taken Troy if Apollo had not intervened. Three times Patroclus is repulsed by Apollo as he attacks a corner of the Trojan wall. The fourth time Apollo cries out:

> Yield, noble Patroclus, you are not fated
> to take with your spear the city of the glorious Trojans,
> nor is Achilles, who is much stronger than you.   (707-9)

Similar, at 5.440-42, is Apollo' rebuke of Diomedes, the surrogate of Achilles in Part 1. We should remember Achilles' wish, at 97-100, that only he and Patroclus might survive to take Troy (so Edwards 1987.258).

Patroclus yields, and we turn to Hector who is pondering at the Scaean Gate whether to command a retreat within the walls of Troy. This is the same decision he will have to make at the end of Book 18 about the next day of battle. In both instances he chooses to remain and fight on the open plain. Now he is helped to this decision by Apollo who comes to him in the form of his uncle Asius and exhorts him to go against Patroclus, promising that Apollo will give him the victory (724-25).

Accordingly, Hector commands Cebriones to drive their horses against Patroclus. Patroclus leaps from his chariot to meet them and with a large stone, missing Hector, hits Cebriones in the head, knocking his eyes out and causing him to fall from his chariot like a diver (742, simile type 9). Patroclus makes a vaunting speech, comparing him to a man diving for molluscs (745-48, simile type 9), and advances to take possession of the dead body like a wounded lion whose spirit causes it to be slain (752-53, simile type 5: victor and victim; this surely portends the death of Patroclus). Hector leaps from his chariot and seizes the head of Cebriones while Patroclus seizes a foot; they are like lions fighting over a slain deer (756-58, simile type 6: indecisive battle). The fighting rages like a battle of the winds (765-69, another type 6 simile) over Cebriones' body. We feel a repetition, boding ill for Patroclus, of the same situation we had in the open plain over the body of Sarpedon when Zeus debated with himself whether to let Hector slay him.

Finally, when the sun begins to move from the zenith toward evening, the Achaeans, "beyond what was fated" (780), gain the upper hand. They as well as Patroclus should not be pressing their offensive so far. They obtain the body of Cebriones and strip him of his armor while Patroclus leaps into the Trojan lines three times—again a repetition boding ill for him. The fourth time Apollo, being invisible, meets him and strikes him on the back with the flat of his hand, dazing and disarming him.

> Rolling among the horses' hoofs the magnificent
> helmet resounded; its flowing crests were befouled
> with blood and dust. Earlier it was not permitted
> that this horse-haired helmet should be so befouled,
> for it protected the beautiful head and brow
> of godlike Achilles. But now Zeus gave it to Hector
> to wear on his head since death was imminent for him. (794-800)

Euphorbus (a foppish young man, the brother of Polydamas), taking advantage of the situation, hits Patroclus with a spear-cast in the back. Patroclus tries to withdraw into the protection of the Achaean lines, but Hector stabs him in the stomach and finishes him off, like a lion killing a wild boar (823-26, simile type 9). Janko 1992.408-10 has persuasively argued that the roles of Euphorbus and Apollo in the slaying of Patroclus are modelled on the roles of Paris and Apollo in the slaying of Achilles; the poet (so H. Mühlestein, *Homerische Namenstudien* 1987.808-11n.) has created Euphorbus as a doublet of Paris. Patroclus' death greatly grieves (*ekache*, 822) the Achaeans. It would take a very insensitive member of Homer's audience not to burn with indignation at the way he has been slain; the poet is preparing us to understand the reaction of Achilles (so Owen 1946.163).

Hector boasts over the dying Patroclus, blaming him for his foolishness in thinking that he could sack Troy and imagining that Achilles has told him to try to kill him. Patroclus answers that the gods, Zeus and Apollo, and then Euphorbus have had a hand in his slaying before Hector. Clearly this slaying has given Hector very little honor; the great deed of his *aristeia* is his victory over Ajax at the ships and the firing of Protesilaus' ship. Now Patroclus, as he dies, predicts that Achilles will soon slay Hector.

> Truly you yourself will not live long, but already
> death and strong fate stand near you; you're destined to die
> at the hands of Achilles, Aeacus' blameless descendant.   (852-54)

And the poet continues:

> When he had spoken thus, the end of death covered him,
> his soul fleeing his limbs went down to Hades,
> bemoaning his fate, leaving his manhood and youth.   (855-57)

In Book 22 Hector's death will be described in much the same way. He as he dies will predict Achilles' death. The first line above, 855, which was used of Sarpedon, will be used of Hector at 22.361; and lines 856-57, which are an elaboration on the idea of the life-soul leaving the body in the Sarpedon death-scene, will be used again of Hector at 22.362-63.

Hector answers that he may slay Achilles instead. Then, kicking Patroclus free from his spear, he rushes to attack Automedon, whom the immortal horses of Achilles carry away. Hector's pursuit will be continued in the next book, where it will become clear that these horses are not for him. The fact that he is unable to have them will be a portent of his coming death.

BOOK 17: THE BATTLE OVER PATROCLUS' BODY

The Increasing Fury of the Struggle, 1-423

We look forward now to Achilles' hearing the news of Patroclus' death, but the poet delays this scene until the beginning of the next book by a long description of the battle over Patroclus' body. "Like so many story-tellers after him, Homer thinks the great moment comes more tellingly from being delayed" (Owen 1946.164). The battle over Patroclus' body is the longest battle over a body in the *Iliad* and, with that in Book 15, one of the two longest defensive actions of the Achaeans. We are made to feel the swelling tide of grief over Patroclus' death in preparation for Achilles' learning of it. Like Sarpedon, Patroclus will lose his armor—but not his horses—to the enemy, and his body eventually will be saved by a miraculous intervention (in the next book when Achilles glorified by Athena appears at the trench).

In the present book Hector is three times rebuked by a leader of the allies or Apollo disguised as such, and is once exhorted by Aeneas who has been rebuked by Apollo in human form. We can compare Glaucus' rebuke of Hector in the last book. The Trojan allies are inclined to be disaffected and blame Hector. On this pattern of rebuke see Fenik 1968.159-89. We shall find that these rebukes are used to create parallel episodes in the battle over Patroclus' body and help to impress us with its increasing intensity.

When Patroclus was alive, he and the Myrmidons led the Achaean attack. Now that duty devolves on Menelaus especially, but also on the Ajaxes, Idomeneus, and Meriones. Agamemnon, Diomedes, and Odysseus are still unable to fight because of their wounds.

While Hector is chasing after the horses of Achilles, Menelaus comes to protect Patroclus, like a cow her newborn calf (4-5), and is opposed by the youthful and brash Euphorbus who, as the first to stab Patroclus, lays claim to his body and armor. Wondering at his audacity, Menelaus reminds him of how, at 14.516, he slew his brother Hyperenor. Euphorbus answers:

> Now, god-nourished Menelaus, you will pay
> for my brother's death and for your boasting over him and
> making his wife a widow in their new marriage-chamber
> and giving unspeakable mourning and grief (*penthos*) to my parents.
> I'd give relief to these poor mourning ones, noble
> Phrontis, my mother, and Panthous, my father, by bringing

your head and your armor and throwing them into their hands.
But let us no longer put off this labor of fighting
and leave untried the issue of victory or flight.   (34-42)

He thrusts ineffectively at Menelaus' shield, and Menelaus kills him with a stab through the neck. The youth, his hair plaited and pinned with gold and silver, lies bloodied in the dust, like a well-watered olive tree torn up by a great wind (53-58, simile type 9: the hero falls). Menelaus, as he begins to strip him of his armor, is like a lion enjoying a cow and frightening the dogs and herdsmen (61-67, another type 9 simile; Euphorbus' comrades can do nothing to help him). We pity and at the same time blame Euphorbus for his youthful presumption; he could never have slain Patroclus in a fair fight.

Menelaus might have stripped him if Apollo, in the form of Mentes, a leader of the Ciconians, one of the Trojan allies, had not rebuked Hector for running after the horses of Achilles and told him of Euphorbus' death. Hector is stricken with grief (*achos*, 83) and immediately rushes against Menelaus, like fire in his fury (88-89, simile type 2: advance into battle). Menelaus debates with himself (91-105) whether to retreat, feeling ashamed to do so since Patroclus has died fighting for his, Menelaus', honor, but he is about to be surrounded by the Trojans and he knows that Hector is favored by the gods. He wishes that he could find Ajax, for the two of them might carry the body back to Achilles. This is where the narrative is headed—back to Achilles.

He goes off, then, against his will, with a chill in his heart, like a lion retreating from a steading before dogs and men (108-12, simile type 8: retreat). He finds Ajax on the left exhorting the Achaeans, whom Apollo has filled with the spirit of flight. Menelaus says:

Good Ajax, let us hasten to fight for Patroclus and try
to carry his body back to Achilles, at least
his bare body; bright-helmeted Hector possesses his armor.   (120-23)

Line 123 is full of pathos. Menelaus will repeat it to Antilochus toward the end of this book, and Antilochus will repeat it to Achilles at the beginning of the next book. Menelaus' message rouses the spirit of Ajax (causing him grief), and they go against Hector.

Hector, having taken the armor of Patroclus, is trying to drag off the corpse in order to cut off the head and throw the body to the dogs (127-28), but when he sees

Ajax approaching he withdraws and hands over the armor to his men to carry to Troy. Then Ajax bestrides the body, like a lioness with glaring eyes protecting her cubs from hunters (133-36). Menelaus is beside him, his breast swelling with grief (*penthos*, 139). We remember the earlier scene in which Menelaus alone tried to protect the body as a cow her calf (4-5), and feel the emphatic parallel. Now, with Ajax to help him, there is a much better chance that the body , though stripped of its (that is, Achilles') armor, can be saved.

We switch to Hector whom Glaucus is rebuking for withdrawing. They should try to gain possession of Patroclus' body in order to exchange it for Sarpedon's. (Glaucus is unaware that Sarpedon's body has been carried back to Lycia.) Patroclus, he adds, is the friend of the best of the Achaeans (Achilles), whom he contrasts with Hector who is afraid to go against Ajax. Hector replies by showing his readiness to fight and, after exhorting the others, goes to put on the armor of Achilles. "He is not only going to attack Ajax, but he is going to flaunt his triumph in the face of the defenders of the body" (Owen 1946.169). He is going to dare to rouse their grief and anger even more.

As Hector puts on the armor of Achilles, Zeus sees what is happening and once more predicts his death, saying that Andromache will not receive this armor from him returning from battle. Now, however, Hector appears among his men filled with new spirit and exhorts a group of allied leaders, among them Glaucus, saying that they should prove themselves worthy of the gifts he has given them.

So they attack.

> They greatly hoped (*elpeto*)
> to drag the body from Telamonian Ajax,
> fools (*nepioi*), many of whom he was going to kill. (234-36)

First, however, Ajax orders Menelaus to call for help, and Menelaus does so, reminding the Achaean leaders of how well he and Agamemnon have entertained them. Many answer his call, among them the little Ajax, Idomeneus, and Meriones. First it was Menelaus alone who tried to protect the body, then Ajax and Menelaus, now many others. Menelaus' address to the Achaean leaders parallels Hector's call on the Trojan allies. The Trojans come on with the roar and force of a river in flood (263-65, simile type 3: attack), but the Achaeans stand firm. Zeus pours over them a mist to prevent the Trojans from gaining possession of the body and to show his grief for Patroclus as he had done for Sarpedon (so Edwards 1991.89)—though he is giving the victory to Hector on this day. As schol. T on 272 say: "This forecast encourages us (the Greek audience) to endure the perilous situation by informing us of its outcome." We know that Patroclus' body is going to be saved.

At first the Trojans push the Achaeans back and begin to drag off the body. But Ajax, quickly rallying the men, charges into the Trojan lines like a wild boar (281-83, another type 3 simile) and slays Hippothous; Hippothous—a pathetic touch—will not repay his parents for rearing him. Then Hector hurls a spear at Ajax but hits Schedius; and Ajax slays Phorcys over the body of Hippothous. The Trojans withdraw, and the Achaeans strip Hippothous and Phorcys.

At that time the Achaeans would have driven the Trojans back into Troy— contrary to the will of Zeus (321)—if Apollo, taking the form of a herald belonging to the family of Aeneas, had not rebuked Aeneas, asking him why he refrained from battle when Zeus was giving the Trojans the victory. Aeneas, having recognized Apollo, in turn rebukes Hector, saying how shameful it is for the Trojans to be fleeing when, as a god has just told him, Zeus is helping them. They must not let the Achaeans retrieve Patroclus' body without a fight.

Hector responds by leaping out in front of his men, and the Trojans rally to oppose the enemy. In the ensuing battle (344-65) Aeneas stabs Leiocritus. Then Lycomedes, Leiocritus' companion, being filled with pity (*eleesen,* 346), strikes Apisaon, thus calling forth the pity (*eleesen,* 352) of the latter's fellow Paeonian Asteropaeus, who tries to avenge him. But Asteropaeus is unable to penetrate the shields and spears of the Achaeans. The ground is drenched with blood as many fall on both sides, but there are many fewer Achaean casualties,

> for they were always
> each of them guarding the other to ward off destruction.   (364-65)

As schol. A on 364 say, these lines praise the Achaeans greatly.

In the middle, where the battle over Patroclus' body is raging, darkness covers the field, and Nestor's sons Antilochus and Thrasymedes, who are fighting elsewhere in the light, do "not yet" (377) know of Patroclus' death. This "not yet" foreshadows Menelaus' informing Antilochus of Patroclus' death later in this book.

Then we are given a similar passage about Achilles' ignorance. The battle over Patroclus is like a piece of hide being stretched taut (389-93, simile type 6: even battle)—we think again of the darkness covering it—and Achilles does "not yet" (401) know what has happened. This is another foreshadowing "not yet," for Antilochus, sent by Menelaus, will inform Achilles of Patroclus' death at the beginning of the next book. Now Achilles does not suspect (*elpeto,* 404) that

Patroclus is dead. The Achaeans are saying: May the earth swallow us before we let the Trojans have Patroclus' body. The Trojans are saying: If need be, let us all die fighting over Patroclus.

Hector Vainly Pursues the Horses of Achilles, 424-542

> Thus they fought on, and the iron-like noise of their fighting
> went through the shimmering brightness up to the bronze sky.
> But the horses of Achilles were standing apart from the battle
> and weeping, having learned that their charioteer
> lay dead in the dust, the victim of man-slaying Hector.   (424-28)

This episode, which creates an interruption in the narrative of the battle over Patroclus' body, continues the theme of grief. Moreover, it makes clear the blindness of Hector. He is blindly infatuated to try to catch the horses of Achilles, for he is no match for Achilles. He is destined to be victorious only on this day.

The above lines are followed by a passage which shows the grief of the immortal horses. Automedon is unable to make them move. They stand like grave stones, weeping with lowered heads. Zeus, seeing and pitying them (*idon eleese*, 441), regrets that the gods ever gave them to the mortal Peleus; he will not allow them to be saddened further by being taken by Hector, for whom it is quite enough to have Achilles' armor. Zeus will give the horses the strength to flee from the Trojans, to whom, however, he

> shall grant
> the power to kill till they reach the well-benched ships
> and the sun goes down and the sacred darkness comes.   (453-55)

These words are repeated from Zeus' instructions to Hector at 11.192-94 and 207-9. Hector has almost reached this goal, for the sun will set soon.

So the horses are inspired to move in spite of their grief. Running everywhere over the battlefield, they carry Automedon into the fighting, though he is grieving (*achnumenos*, 459). Eventually, he is helped by Alcimedon, who becomes the charioteer. Hector tells Aeneas that they, he expects (*eelpoimen*, 488), can capture the horses of Achilles, and so they advance against Automedon and Alcimedon with Chromius and Aretus, who are filled with the same false hope (*elpeto*, 495),

> fools (*nepioi*), they were not destined to return unbloodied again

from Automedon.   (497-98)

Automedon prays to Zeus and is filled with strength. Then, having told Alcimedon to hold the horses nearby and having called on the Ajaxes and Menelaus for help, he spears Aretus, who falls dead on his back like a slain ox (520-22, simile type 9: the hero falls). Hector misses with his cast at Automedon. Then they would have come to close quarters with their swords if the Ajaxes had not arrived and forced Hector and the others to withdraw, leaving behind Aretus dead, over whom Automedon says:

> Now truly I've eased the pain of my grief (*achos*) a little
> by slaying this lesser man for Patroclus slain.   (538-39)

Then taking the armor of Aretus he mounts the chariot with bloody hands and feet, like a lion who has devoured a bull. We are reminded of how Euphorbus hoped to relieve the grief of his mother and father by throwing Menelaus' head and armor into their hands.

The Achaeans Retreat with the Body to the Ships. Antilochus Is Sent to Achilles, 543-761

We return to the battle over Patroclus' body as Zeus sends Athena (she comes like the rainbow) from heaven to stir up the Achaeans. Zeus' "mind has turned" (545), that is, he will now have Hector end this day in victory at the ships as promised in Book 11, but at the same time he will have Athena see to it that the Achaeans save the body of Patroclus. Athena appears to Menelaus in the form of Phoenix (who is naturally concerned) and urges him to save the body. Menelaus, saying how grief-stricken he is, shows his willingness if only Athena would grant him the power, but Zeus is giving the victory to Hector. This answer pleases her, and she fills him with the persistence of a blood-sucking fly. He bestrides the body and kills Podes, Hector's close friend, and drags him off.

News of Podes' death is brought to Hector by Apollo in the form of Phaenops, an ally of the Trojans and Hector's dear friend. Apollo rebukes him for not attacking Menelaus. Hector, being filled with grief (*achos*, 591), advances with his men. We are reminded of how, at the beginning of this book, Apollo, in the form of the ally Mentes, rebuked Hector by telling him of Menelaus' slaying of Euphorbus; and we feel the repetition as the signal of a climax in the narrative.

At this moment Zeus, intervening directly, shakes the aegis from Mount Ida with thunder and lightning to frighten the Achaeans, showing them that he is giving the Trojans the victory. (We should compare Apollo's shaking the aegis in 15.320-22; so Fenik 1968.185.) The first of the Achaeans to flee, Peneleos, is hit a grazing blow by Polydamas. Thereupon Hector wounds Leitus in his spear hand, causing him to flee. Idomeneus tries to stop Hector, but his spear breaks on Hector's breastplate. The Trojans shout with joy: such an incident shows whom the god is favoring. (We can compare the breaking of Teucer's bowstring in Book 15 and of Ajax's spear in Book 16.) When Hector throws at Idomeneus, who has mounted a chariot to flee, he hits Coeranus, the charioteer. But Meriones, coming to the rescue, urges Idomeneus to whip the horses back to the ships since it is clear that the victory is no longer theirs. Idomeneus obeys, for fear has seized his spirit.

Ajax, faced with the Trojan onslaught, says to Menelaus:

> Alas, it's clear to see now, even a great fool (*nepios*)
> would know that Zeus Father himself is aiding the Trojans.
> All of their missiles find their marks whether shot
> by good or bad fighters—all are guided by Zeus—
> but ours are all shot in vain and fall on the ground.
> We must rely on ourselves to think of a plan,
> how we may best save the body and how we ourselves
> may also return and so give joy to our friends.   (629-36)

It is up to them to think of some plan. If only the mist would lift and they could see someone to send to tell Achilles. Speaking in tears, Ajax ends (645-47) with a prayer to Zeus to remove the mist: let them, the Achaeans, die in the light if Zeus so wills.

Zeus responds by scattering the mist. Then Ajax tells Menelaus to find Antilochus and send him to Achilles. Menelaus obeys unwillingly, like a lion leaving a sheepfold, being grieved at heart (656-64, simile type 8: retreat; this simile was used at 11.550 ff. of Ajax, the general situation of retreat and grief being the same). Before Menelaus goes, he exhorts the Ajaxes and Meriones to protect Patroclus' body.

> Ajaxes and Meriones, leaders of the Argives,
> let all remember the greatness of poor Patroclus,
> for he was gentle to everyone while he was living,
> but now death and fate have come upon him.   (669-72)

Then he goes off, like the sharp-sighted eagle, in search of Antilochus. Having found him (with his brother Thrasymedes commanding the Pylians), he tells him that, as he must know, Zeus is giving the victory to the Trojans and that, what is worse, Patroclus is dead. Antilochus must act.

> Immediately run to the ships of the Achaeans and tell
> Achilles to be very swift to save to his ship
> the bare body; bright-helmeted Hector possesses the armor.   (691-93)

Antilochus goes off, weeping and speechless. Menelaus, turning to Thrasymedes, instructs him to look after the Pylians—a parallel to his telling Ajax and Meriones to look after Patroclus' body—and then returns to the Ajaxes and Meriones to report the completion of his mission.

> Now I've sent him off to the swift ships to tell
> swift-footed Achilles. But I don't think Achilles
> will come. Enraged (*kecholomenon*) though he'll be at great Hector, he
>   won't
> be able to fight with the Trojans without any armor.
> We must rely on ourselves to think of a plan,
> how we may best save the body and how we ourselves
> may escape from death and fate in fighting the Trojans.   (708-14)

Lines 712-13 repeat lines 634-35 in Ajax's speech telling Menelaus that they must think of some plan to save the body and suggesting that they send someone to tell Achilles of their plight.

Now Ajax replies that Menelaus and Meriones should carry the body toward the ships while he and the little Ajax give them protection. Thus, on one level, the intervening episode of sending Antilochus to Achilles was unnecessary, but the poet is preparing for the Antilochus-Achilles scene with which the next book will open. At the same time he must have the Achaeans bring the body of Patroclus to the area of the ships where Hector is to end his day of victory, as Zeus promised him in Book 11.

As Menelaus and Meriones, protected by the Ajaxes, carry off the body toward the ships, the Trojans attack them like dogs pursuing a wounded boar (725-29, simile type 8: retreat). The battle rages like a city on fire (737-39, simile type 6: even battle) Menelaus and Meriones move like plodding mules (742-45, another type 8 simile). The Ajaxes protect them like a wooded hillock diverting a river in flood (747-52, simile type 7: resistance). The mass of the Achaeans, however, are fleeing before the Trojans like a flock of jackdaws and starlings before a hawk, crying in fear of death which they see coming on (755-57, simile type 4: flight). This culminating simile is comparable to that at 16.582-83 which describes Patroclus putting the Trojans to flight; the scholia (bT, cited by Edwards 1991.138) note that, whereas the mere human being, Patroclus, caused the Trojans to flee, it takes the intervention of Zeus to produce the present flight of the Achaeans. The string of similes serves to describe briefly, in a relatively painless way, the shame of their retreat.

> Many beautiful shields fell on both sides of the trench
> as the Danaans fled, and there was no pause in the battle.   (760-61)

Thus ends Book 17. The Achaeans, with Patroclus' body, have been driven back to the area of the ships. The battle continues to rage ceaselessly, but to the disadvantage of the Achaeans. Achilles is needed to save the body.

As we said at the end of our comments on Book 15, the two main defensive actions of the Achaeans in the *Iliad*, which are described there and in the present book, show clear similarities (noted by Fenik 1968.185). In both narratives a god (Apollo at 15.320-22, Zeus at 17.593-96) shakes the aegis and causes the Achaeans to flee. In both the action of a messenger (Patroclus at 15.390-405, Antilochus at 17.64-700) setting out to Achilles to try to prevail upon him to save the situation is interwoven with the description of the fighting. And both battles culminate in similar struggles over a greatly valued object (Protesilaus' ship, Patroclus' body) at the ships or at least in the area of the ships, where Zeus has promised Hector he will end this day. What is most important, however, is that these two narratives introduce the parallel episodes in which Achilles makes his two great decisions, in Book 16 to give up his wrath to the extent of sending out Patroclus dressed as himself, in Book 18 to renounce his wrath completely.

BOOK 18: ACHILLES GIVES UP HIS WRATH

He Saves the Body of Patroclus, 1-240

This book describes the momentous event of Achilles' giving up his wrath completely and returning to the action, and, as we have pointed out before (see also Frazer 1989), the present section creates a climactic parallel with the first section of Book 16 in which he gave up his wrath to the extent of sending out Patroclus in his place. Both sections open with the arrival at Achilles' hut of a messenger (Patroclus, Antilochus) who is weeping in pity and grief at the desperateness of the situation. In both sections scenes at Achilles' hut are interwoven with those describing the battle raging over the object (the ship of Protesilaus, the body of Patroclus) which Achilles is being urged to save. In both there is the theme of pity and grief. In Book 16 Patroclus blamed Achilles for not pitying the dying Achaeans; in the present book Achilles will show that he has learned pity through his grief over Patroclus' death. In both sections the appearance of the hero on the battlefield to save the threatened object is described as having a similar effect. Patroclus was a frightening figure to the Trojans when he came out at the beginning of his *aristeia* in the armor of Achilles; Achilles, though without any armor, will be even more terrifying when—a foreshadowing of his *aristeia*—he shows himself at the trench.

We switch from the battle to the hut of Achilles who speaks a soliloquy. He suspects from the flight of the Achaeans that Patroclus has been slain, for he is reminded of a prophecy of his mother that the best of the Myrmidons (that is, Patroclus, his substitute during his withdrawal, the best after himself; so Barth 1989) will die while he is still living. He calls Patroclus stubborn; he had told him only to drive the fire from the ships. This is the state of mind in which Antilochus finds Achilles when he arrives, weeping.

Antilochus says:

> Ah me, son of valiant Peleus, you are about to learn
> a very painful thing which never should have happened.
> Patroclus lies dead; they are fighting over his body,
> his bare body; bright-helmeted Hector possesses his armor. (18-21)

Line 21 is a climactic repetition of what Menelaus said to Ajax at the beginning, and to Antilochus at the end, of the last book (17.123 and 693). A black cloud of grief (*achos*) covers Achilles. He pours dust on his head and ashes on his clothes.

Tearing his hair, he stretches himself in the dust as if dead himself. Then his slave women wail in their grief (*akechemenai*, 29) and run from his hut to surround him. Antilochus takes hold of his hands to prevent him from committing suicide.

As he cries out horribly, his mother wails where she sits at the bottom of the sea. Her sister Nereids gather around her, thirty-three of whom are named with a lyrical, soothing effect. They beat their breasts as Thetis begins the lament, telling of her sorrow in bearing an ill-fated son.

> As long as he lives and sees the light of the sun
> he'll grieve (*achnutai*). I can't prevent it by going to him.
> But I shall go to see my dear child and hear
> what grief (*penthos*) has befallen him during his absence from battle. (61-64)

And so she and her sisters come out of the sea (65, a climactic parallel to the slave women coming out of the hut), they to surround him while she, taking hold of his head (the gesture of a woman mourning over the dead), says:

> Child, why are you weeping? What is your grief (*penthos*)?
> Tell me, don't hide it. Zeus has fulfilled your wish,
> the prayer you earlier made with hands upraised,
> that all the Achaeans be crowded at the sterns of their ships
> and suffer horrible woes because of your absence. (73-77)

Achilles replies that, yes, Zeus has answered his prayer, but with the result that he has lost the friend who was dearer to him than his own life. Hector has slain Patroclus and stripped him of the beautiful armor the gods had given Peleus as a wedding present. Would that Thetis had never married Peleus and that he, Achilles, had never been born.

> But, as it is, you were fated to bear countless grief (*penthos*)
> over the death of your son, whom you won't be welcoming
> home again, since now I've no spirit to live
> any longer and be among men except to see to it
> that Hector, struck down by my spear, loses his life
> and pays for slaying Patroclus, the son of Menoetius. (88-93)

Thetis, weeping, replies oracularly:

You shall die early, my child, from what you say,
for you're fated to die after Hector immediately.   (95-96)

Then Achilles, in a second, longer speech, affirms his readiness to die and
curses his wrath as he finally gives it up.

Now since I'm not returning to my dear native land,
nor was I a light to Patroclus or to those others,
my comrades, whom Hector has slain in large numbers,
but sit by the ships a useless weight on the earth,
being superior to any of the bronze-armored Achaeans
in battle though others surpass me in public speaking—
let strife perish from among both gods and men,
and anger (*cholos*) which causes even wise men to turn harsh,
which, being something much sweeter than dripping honey,
expands in the hearts of men like rising smoke.
So now King Agamemnon caused me to be angry (*echolosen*).
But let us let bygones be bygones in spite of our grief (*achnumenoi*),
subduing the anger (*thumos*) in our breasts because of necessity.
Now I shall go to meet my dear friend's killer,
Hector, and then shall accept death myself whenever
Zeus and the other immortals decide to fulfill it.   (101-16)

He ends by saying that not even Heracles, who was dearest to Zeus, was able to
escape death, and that now he will cause many Trojan women to mourn. Thus,
apparently, he consoles his weeping mother with the thought of these women. We
are reminded of how Euphorbus at 17.34-42 wanted to present the head of
Menelaus to his mother and father to make them stop grieving.

Thetis grants that it is right to fight for one's comrades, but commands him to
stay out of battle until she brings him new armor from Hephaestus the next
morning. Then she tells her sisters to return to the sea while she goes off to
Olympus to see Hephaestus. The return of her sisters rounds off the present scene
(145, creating a ring composition with 65), whereas her going to Hephaestus
prepares us for her scene with him at the end of this book.

With the departure of Thetis (at line 147) we are made to realize anew that
something extraordinary must be done to save Patroclus' body. Three times the
Ajaxes drive off Hector, but now he would have dragged off the body if Iris had

not come to Achilles (166). Sent by Hera secretly from Zeus (as if Zeus might still be angry at this though he has fulfilled his promise to Thetis), she urges Achilles to defend Patroclus, over whom they are fighting in front of the ships and whose head Hector threatens to cut off. Then she tells him who has sent her, and that his mother's command that he not enter the battle until she has brought him new armor should not prevent him from being effective now. He should show himself unarmed at the Achaean side of the trench in order to frighten the Trojans and give the Achaeans a moment to act.

> But as you are show yourself at the trench to the Trojans
> so that they may be frightened and hold off from battle
> and give the warlike sons of the Achaeans a respite
> in their distress; respites from battle are precious.   (198-201)

Lines 199-201 are repeated (with minor changes) from Nestor's speech to Patroclus at 11.800-1 and Patroclus' speech to Achilles at 16.41-43. Leaf II.263 suggested that these lines have been added here, for he thought that Achilles was not to be roused by his sympathy for the Achaeans but only by his desire to save Patroclus' body. This interpretation, however, reduces the meaning of Achilles' enlightenment. In the present passage, which is a recognition scene like that in Sophocles' *Oedipus Rex* and which corresponds to the *peripeteia* in Greek tragedy (so Rutherford 1982.145-47), Achilles finally realizes the consequences of his wrath and that he was wrong to desert his fellow Achaeans. Thus Iris' repetition of Patroclus' words in Book 16 begging him to show pity on the Achaeans seems especially appropriate to prick his conscience.

As soon as she has left, Achilles moves into action, and Athena (like Hera acting contrary to Zeus' now meaningless prohibition) protects him with the aegis and puts a golden cloud over his head, like the fire lit as a signal by an island under attack (207-13, simile type 1: the gleaming of the hero's armor). Taking his stand on the Achaean side of the trench, he shouts three times—and Athena shouts too—like the blaring of a trumpet signaling the approach of the enemy. The Trojans, twelve of whom are slain, fall back in confusion. The Achaeans recover Patroclus' body and carry it off on a litter. His companions, and especially Achilles, are weeping to see him dead. The day ends miraculously, for Hera (fearing that the Trojans may rally?) causes the sun to set before its normal time.

Thus Achilles gives up his wrath and decides to return to the action (a decision he will formally ratify in Book 19). We have already remarked on the similarities between the present scene and that at the beginning of Book 16 in which Achilles gave up his wrath to the extent of sending Patroclus into battle, but something more might be said about how a feeling of climax is created. The narrative of Achilles' second decision is longer (18.1-147 compared with 16.1-100) and more complex than that of his first decision. The Antilochus-Achilles part develops into the Thetis-Achilles part by way of the small transitional episode of the slave women who come to weep around Achilles. The climax of course is simply there in the fact that now Achilles is finally giving up is wrath completely: the old grief and anger have given way to a greater grief and anger. And this leads to his return to the action, which is parallel to Patroclus' entering the battle in Book 16. Now the narrative is shorter (18.148-240 compared with 16.101-302), but there is no more impressive sight in the *Iliad* that that of the unarmed Achilles appearing at the trench. The fact that he is acting in obedience to Iris sent by Hera adds to his glory as does the role of Athena in surrounding his head with light and shouting in sympathy with him. Patroclus' appearance in Book 16 is made longer by the descriptions of his arming and the marshaling of the Myrmidons, whereas Achilles must wait until Book 19 to arm himself and lead out his men.

Polydamas' Fourth Admonition to Hector. Achilles Vows Vengeance. Zeus Chides Hera for Supporting the Achaeans, 241-367

This section rounds off the events of this day of battle by telling us how the human beings and gods react to them. There is a Trojan assembly, as we have come to expect after a day's fighting. Polydamas gives advice to Hector for the fourth time in Part 2, his culminating admonition, and Hector disastrously refuses to obey it. There is no Achaean assembly, however; this will not occur until the morning of the next day, at the beginning of Part 3, after Achilles has received the new armor from Thetis. Instead, now we are given a scene of mourning over Patroclus in the Achaean camp. The important thing here is that Achilles is going to avenge Patroclus. On the divine level Zeus sarcastically congratulates Hera for having brought Achilles back into the action, and she affirms her right to prosecute her hatred against the Trojans. Thus, the wrath of Achilles being over, we are being prepared for the day of his *aristeia* when his slaying of Hector will symbolize the fall of Troy.

The setting of the sun comes as a welcome relief to the Achaeans (compare their relief at the end of the second day of battle in Book 8). The Trojans meet in assembly on the open plain, and Polydamas, who was born on the same night as Hector but with the gift of good counsel in contrast to Hector's gift of martial prowess, advises them to retreat into Troy. During the time of Achilles' withdrawal and anger with Agamemnon, Polydamas was not afraid to remain on the plain, but now he fears for the city. Achilles, in his armor, will attack tomorrow. If they return to Troy now, he will be unable to do any harm.

Hector rejects this advice. They spent their wealth when they were being besieged, and now Zeus has let him besiege the Achaeans. He implies that Polydamas is motivated by a concern for his personal possessions (see Willcock 1984.267 on 300-2). Now they should take their supper and keep guard. Tomorrow they will fight at the ships, and he will meet Achilles.

Hector's speech is applauded by the Trojans, whom the poet calls fools (*nepioi*, 311), adding that Athena has deprived them of their senses. Having helped to bring Achilles back into action, she is making sure that things will go bad for the Trojans. The stage is being set for the death of Hector.

And so the Trojans take their supper, whereas the Achaeans are mourning over Patroclus "all night long" (314-15). Achilles is groaning like a lioness whose cubs a hunter has taken from her lair during her absence: she goes off in fierce anger (*cholos*, 322) to find him. He had been mistaken to promise Patroclus' father to bring him home after sacking Troy; Zeus does not fulfill our every expectation. It was destined for them both to be buried at Troy. Then, addressing the body, he promises Patroclus a proper burial and to kill twelve Trojans on his pyre after he has slain Hector and brought in his armor and head. In the meantime the Trojan women whom they have captured will wail over Patroclus. The poet, by putting the Trojan assembly before this scene, has enabled us to know that Achilles can fulfill his promise. Hector is going to fight him. "Clearly the poet has arranged his scenes very well" (Rothe 1910.293).

Then Achilles commands his comrades to wash the body of Patroclus. The description of them doing this is balanced, ceremonial; and they cover the body with a linen cloth and a white robe. "All night long" Achilles and the Myrmidons mourn over Patroclus (354-55, creating a ring composition with 314-15, where we were told that the Achaeans mourned over Patroclus "all night long.").

We now switch to a conversation between Zeus and Hera (356-68). The tone of Olympian aloofness and indifference to human affairs contrasts sharply with that of the previous scene. When Zeus, who knows what Hera has done, chides her sarcastically, good-humoredly, she answers that, as his wife, she ought to be allowed to create evil for those with whom she is angry, that is, the Trojans. Although Zeus does not answer, he apparently acquiesces in the destruction of Troy, as at the beginning of Book 4. The hiatus caused by the wrath of Achilles is

now at an end, and the war can take its inevitable course. In the previous two
scenes we have been made aware that on the next day Achilles will kill Hector; and
we know that Hector is the mainstay of Troy, that his death will mean Troy's
destruction. We are thus prepared on both a human and a divine level for the events
of the next day.

The scene between Zeus and Hera is sometimes treated as an interpolation,
but there is a similar scene between them at the end of the second day of battle, at
8.434-84; and we can compare the scene between Zeus and Poseidon at 7.443-62,
after the truce following the frst day of battle. Moreover, the present scene is
consistent with the activity of Hera in support of the Achaeans earlier in this book.

Hephaestus Makes New Armor for Achilles, 368-617

The scene between Zeus and Hera also makes a nice transition to that between
Thetis and Hephaestus. When Thetis arrives at Hephaestus' house, he is at his
forge putting the finishing touches on twenty tripod-cauldrons which will be able to
move automatically. We are thus impressed by his ability to create lifelike objects.

Thetis is greeted by Charis (Grace), Hephaestus' wife, who takes her by the
hand and calls her by name.

> Why, long-robed Thetis, do you come to our house,
> revered and dear one? You visit us very infrequently.
> Please come in and I'll give you something to eat.   (385-87)

So saying, she leads her in and has her sit on a fine chair with footstool, and calls
out to Hephaestus that Thetis has come and needs him. He answers (394-409) that
Thetis is especially revered by him since she, along with Eurynome, had saved him
and reared him when Hera, disgusted at seeing him born lame and ugly, had
thrown him out of heaven; he had spent nine years with Thetis and Eurynome
making marvelously beautiful jewelry for them. Therefore he is eager to do
whatever he can to help Thetis now, and Charis should entertain her until he can put
away his tools.

The reason given here by Hephaestus for him to help Thetis reminds us of
that given by Thetis in Book 1 for Zeus to help her: she had helped him in the past
(so Willcock 1976.208). Her first request introduced the wrath of Achilles, this
second one introduces his vengeance against Hector.

Hephaestus puts away his tools, washes up, dresses in fresh clothes, and
comes forth with his scepter, supported by two golden female robots. He thus

shows his respect for Thetis. Taking her by the hand and calling her by name, he greets her:

> Why, long-robed Thetis, have you come to our house,
> dear and revered one? You visit us very infrequently.
> Say what you want; I am eager to fulfill your desire
> if I am able to fulfill it and it is fulfillable.   (424-27)

Lines 423-25 repeat lines 384-86 describing how Charis welcomed Thetis. We are thus given a sense of closure and climax. Reinhardt 1961.392-94 has pointed out that Hephaestus' explanation (395-407) of his devotion to Thetis elucidates his use of "dear and revered one" and that thus this form of address seems more appropriate to him than to Charis.

Thetis answers, weeping, with a long speech (429-61) in which she gives an assessment of Achilles' life. (She has been weeping throughout this book, as she was in Book 1 when she told Achilles that she would try to win the support of Zeus for his wrath.) Having been forced to marry a mortal, Peleus, she has borne the ill-fated Achilles whom she has reared to be the best of the heroes and sent off to Troy.

> But I shall not welcome him
> coming home again to the house of Peleus.
> As long as he lives and sees the light of the sun
> he'll grieve (*achnutai*). I can't prevent it by going to him.   (440-43)

Lines 437-43, which characterize Achilles as a man of *achos*, "grief," more emphatically than any in the *Iliad*, repeat lines 56-62 in Thetis' speech of mourning to her sister Nereids: "As long as he lives and sees the light of the sun he'll grieve. I can't prevent it by going to him." She adds to these words a summary of the *Iliad* so far. Agamemnon deprived Achilles of his girl (Book 1), and Achilles ate his heart out in grief (*acheon*, 446, over the loss of Briseis). When the Trojans had pent up the Achaeans by their ships (Book 8), the Achaeans through their envoys offered Achilles gifts (Book 9), and he sent out Patroclus with the Myrmidons, who would have taken Troy if Apollo had not slain him and given the glory to Hector (Book 16). Achilles is now lying on the ground grieving (*acheuon*, 461, over the death of Patroclus), and needs new armor since Patroclus has lost his original armor to Hector.

Notice that Thetis omits the defeat of the Achaeans in Books 11-15 by having Achilles send out Patroclus immediately after the embassy. Thus she retells the story in such a way as to put Achilles in the best possible light. We can sympathize with her, as we can imagine the Greek audience did. It is time to let bygones be bygone.

But why do we have this summary at all? We should compare the summary of Achilles to Thetis in Book 1 when the wrath of Apollo was being replaced by his wrath. Now we have reached another, similar turning point: Achilles' wrath is being replaced by his vengeance against Hector.

Hephaestus, having answered that Achilles will have his armor as surely as he cannot save him from death, returns to his forge to work on the shield, which is described in the cataloguing style (see Introduction, pp. 6-8). The scenes are listed one after the other, and twice, at the beginning (483) and to introduce the two cities (490), there is a synopsis of what is to come.

The shield is round, consisting of a central disk, an outer rim, and four circular bands. We can imagine the decorations to be arranged as follows. Moving from the sky on the central disk to the circle of Ocean on the rim, we pass through the four bands, probably of decreasing width: a four-scened band for the two cities (490-540), a three-scened band for the farming year (541-72), a two-scened band for herding and shepherding (473-89), and a one-scened band for the dance (590-606). This is the usual interpretation (so Edwards 1987.280-83; cf. Willcock 1984.269-70). Philipp 1984, however, argues that the sky should be on the outermost band next to Ocean and that the cities follow on the next band, and so on until we reach the central disk on which are the dancing boys and girls.

The Shield is "part of an immensely elaborated arming scene, intended as always to honor a hero going into battle; and its scale is fitting for a hero like Achilles, for a poem the size of the *Iliad*, and for such a climax" (Edwards 1987.283-84). Moreover, the cosmos of the Shield can be thought of as placing the story of the *Iliad* in perspective (so Taplin 1980). It is like the similes in that it takes us into the greater world, thus giving us relief from the battle and the anguish of Achilles and the recklessness of Hector.

We have suggested that the successful Achaean night adventure in Book 10 was meant to salve the feelings of the Greek audience who knew that the Achaeans were going to be defeated on the next day. Now, with the return of Achilles, they can look forward to the death of Hector and the defeat of the Trojans; and so it is much easier for them to hear the story in a spirit of impartiality and detachment as represented by the universality of the Shield. Now they will be able to blame

Achilles, not for refusing to support his own people, but for carrying his vengeance against the enemy too far.

Hephaestus makes the breastplate, helmet, and greaves in short order (4 lines), and then takes the new armor to Thetis.

> And she like a hawk leaped from snowy Olympus
> carrying from Hephaestus the brightly shining armor.   (616-17)

So ends Book 18 and, as I would like to think, the second day of recitation. We retire for the night with the image in our minds of Thetis flying swiftly through the darkness with the bright new armor for Achilles.

SUMMARY OF PART 2

The major events of Part 2 (Books 11-18) were prepared for, predicted, and foreshadowed in Part 1, especially in Books 8 and 9. In Book 8, which described the second day of battle, Zeus reaffirmed his purpose of supporting the wrath of Achilles by making the Trojans victorious, and predicted to Hera that on the next day (which is described in Part 2) Hector would slay Patroclus and that Achilles would return to the action while they were fighting at the ships over Patroclus' body. In Book 9 Achilles by rejecting the embassy reaffirmed his wrath, which he maintains in Part 2 until he gives it up partially in Book 16 and completely in Book 18.

In Book 8 Zeus began by prohibiting the other gods from participating in the battle—a prohibition that still holds good for Part 2. Then he came from Olympus to Mount Ida to direct events and twice had Hector drive the Achaeans back into their camp; at the end of the first drive Hera tried unsuccessfully to persuade Poseidon to help the Achaeans. These events foreshadowed those of Part 2, which repeats the general outline of Book 8 but in a narrative that is much expanded, especially by the Poseidon retardation in Books 13 through 15.389 and by the fact that Achilles sends out Patroclus in his place. The counterattack of the Achaeans under Patroclus' leadership means that Hector must drive the Achaeans back a third time into their camp in order to end this day in victory at the ships, as Zeus in Book 11 has promised him he will do.

Book 11 is programmatic for the whole day. Zeus goes to Mount Ida to direct events, and from there sends Iris to assure Hector of victory until sunset, once Agamemnon has been wounded. Then Agamemnon is wounded, and Hector comes to the fore. This is the first in a series of Achaean woundings, which show the increasing desperateness of their situation. Next Diomedes is wounded, and then Odysseus. Then Nestor carries off the wounded Machaon, whose identity Achilles sends Patroclus to confirm. Nestor tells Patroclus a long story about how he in his youth had fought on behalf of his people, saying that Achilles should be following this good example now, and that Patroclus should persuade him to do so or at least to let him, Patroclus, do it for him. On his way back to Achilles, Patroclus stops off to care for Eurypylus, another wounded Achaean.

Book 12 ends with Hector breaking through the central gate of the Achaean wall. He and the Trojans rush in among the Achaeans, who flee back among their ships; a loud noise arises. At this moment, at the beginning of Book 13, Zeus looks away from the battlefield, and Poseidon intervenes to reorganize and inspire the Achaeans. Among those he inspires are Nestor and the wounded leaders, at the beginning of Book 14; Nestor has come from his hut to learn the cause of the noise. Then, at the end of Book 14, after Hera has beguiled Zeus, Poseidon is able to act openly; the Achaeans counterattack under his leadership, and Ajax wounds Hector. When Zeus awakes at the beginning of Book 15, he sends Iris to dismiss Poseidon, and Apollo to help the Trojans. Now it is the Trojans' turn to have a god as their leader. Apollo enables them to break trough the wall again; and again a loud noise arises, but this time it is Patroclus who is stirred to action. He leaves Eurypylus' hut to report to Achilles. The poet has carefully planned to bring back Nestor and Patroclus at different times by leaving them in different places at the end of Book 11.

Now we can expect the firing of Protesilaus' ship, Patroclus' entry into battle, and the return of Achilles. In the rest of Book 15 the Trojans drive back the Achaeans relentlessly, and at the beginning of Book 16 Hector is successful in firing Protesilaus' ship at the moment Patroclus is pleading with Achilles. Achilles gives up his wrath to the extent of sending out Patroclus in his place, and Patroclus is slain by Hector. In Book 17 there is the long battle over Patroclus' body in which the retreating Achaeans finally bring it to the Trojan side of the trench. In Book 18 Achilles, having received news of Patroclus' death, decides to give up his wrath completely in order to take vengeance on Hector. Being unarmed, but with Athena's support, by merely appearing and shouting on the Achaean side of the trench he so frightens the Trojans that the Achaeans are able to retrieve Patroclus' body.

The episodes of this day again and again build up to a climax until we reach the final great climax of Achilles' return. In Book 12 the Trojan assault on the Achaean wall is described in three stages. First Asius attacks on the left unsuccessfully; then Sarpedon almost breaks through near the center; finally Hector breaks down the central gate. In the retardation of Books 13 through 15.389 Poseidon at first acts secretly, going first to the Ajaxes, then to the younger leaders, then to Idomeneus, and finally to Nestor and the wounded older leaders (the climactic scene in this series). Then, Hera having put Zeus temporarily out of action (a climax to his being diverted by looking off into the distance), Poseidon is able to act openly and lead the Achaeans. Again, the second breaching of the wall by Apollo comes as a climax to the first breaching by Hector. Moreover, the long defense of the ships in Book 15 culminating in the fight over Protesilaus' ship shows parallels with the long battle over Patroclus' body in Book 17, and these help to create the most striking climactic parallel in Part 2, the episodes describing

Achilles' two decisions, first in Book 16 to relent from his wrath to the extent of sending out Patroclus and then in Book 18 to give it up entirely and return to the action himself.

This day of battle is the day of Hector's *aristeia*. His great deeds are the breaking-through of the Achaean wall and the firing of Protesilaus' ship (this especially), and also the fact that he three times drives the Achaeans, led by Ajax, back into their camp. His being wounded by Ajax in Book 14, during the Poseidon retardation, can be seen as a feature of his *aristeia*, for the hero of a *aristeia* is often wounded (as was Diomedes in Book 5 and Agamemnon in Book 11). We are repeatedly informed that Hector is what he is on this day as the instrument of Zeus. He is clearly no match for Patroclus, who is disarmed by Apollo and wounded by Euphorbus before he finishes him off. Nor is he the equal of the big Ajax; it is Zeus who causes Ajax to retreat and enables Hector to be victorious.

It is noteworthy how the poet postpones (the suspense of anticipation) the conflict between Ajax and Hector. Throughout Book 12 they fight in different areas. At the beginning of Book 13 Ajax forces Hector back with a spear-thrust in the shield, so that he and the little Ajax can rescue the body of one of their fallen comrades. But thereafter he and Hector are kept apart until, at the end of Book 13, they face each other at the head of their armies. Then yet again the expected conflict is delayed while we are given the climactic episodes in the first phase of the Poseidon retardation, when he is acting secretly from Zeus. Finally, as Poseidon leads the Achaeans openly at the end of Book 14, Ajax and Hector clash, with the result that Ajax wounds Hector. Again, after Hector has been revived by Apollo in Book 15, the poet builds up gradually to the encounter between him and Ajax over the ship of Protesilaus.

Hector fails to realize the temporary, conditional nature of Zeus' support, the fact that his success is due ultimately to Achilles' wrath. This is shown most graphically in his responses to Polydamas, a character who appears in the *Iliad* only on this day (in Part 2). In Book 12 Hector rejects Polydamas' advice not to fight at the ships lest the Trojans be driven back with heavy losses. Being blinded by Zeus' promise of victory, he is unable to see the possibility that the Achaeans may counterattack (as they will do twice) and slay many Trojans. Then in Book 18 he rejects Polydamas' advice to return into the safety of the walls of Troy, for he blindly believes that Zeus will continue to support him on the next day when Achilles will have returned to the fighting.

Part 2 brings to a climax themes found in Part 1. Book 11 sets the stage for the fulfillment of Zeus' promise to Thetis in Book 1. Achilles' scene with his mother in Book 18 where he gives up his wrath reminds us of Book 1 where she undertook to plead with Zeus on his behalf. Book 16 can be thought of as a continuation of the embassy in Book 9, since Patroclus can be viewed as the last of the envoys to Achilles. Also, the scene in Book 14 in which Agamemnon suggests that the Achaeans should abandon the war looks back to Books 2 and 9 where he made the same suggestion.

There are also themes which are continued from Part 1 but do not find their climax until Part 3. Most notable is the theme of Achilles return to battle. He returns in Books 16 and 18 in the sense that he sends out Patroclus and appears unarmed at the trench, but not until Books 19 and following will he enter the battle. Closely connected with this theme is that of the death of Hector. We saw this foreshadowed at the end of Book 6 in the farewell scene between him and Andromache, and in Books 11-18 we are made aware of its inevitability, especially in his two responses to Polydamas, but Hector will not die until Book 22. Finally, we might add the important theme of the fall of Troy which, begun on the first day of recitation, has continued to be emphasized in Books 11-18. In Book 18 Zeus grants Hera that, now that he has fulfilled his promise to Thetis, she may support the Achaeans and see to it that Troy falls; this reminds us of the scene between them at the beginning of Book 4. We are also told, at the beginning of Book 12, that Poseidon will demolish the Achaean wall after the fall of Troy—a fact we already know from the conversation between him and Zeus at the end of Book 7. The fall of Troy will receive even greater emphasis on the last day of recitation, where the death of Hector will portend it.

The structure of Part 2 is similar to that of Part 1. In Books 1 and 2 (ending with the catalogues of Achaean and Trojan forces) we moved forward in the expectation of an Achaean defeat, but then, beginning with Book 3, were unexpectedly given a long retardation in which the Achaeans were in the main victorious. This was the first day of battle (Books 3-7) during which Diomedes had his *aristeia* (Book 5). It was not until the second day of battle (Book 8) that Zeus took charge and made Hector victorious. Then again we moved forward in our expectations of an Achaean defeat, in Books 8 (end) through 10, which described the events of the following night. This same general scheme appears in Part 2. We continue to expect an Achaean defeat until the retardation of Books 13 through 15.389, after which the course of events leads fairly straightforwardly to the firing of Protesilaus' ship and the return of Achilles.

The most important event in Part 2 is the return of Achilles at its end, which makes a marked contrast to his refusal to return in Book 9 at the end of Part 1.

There he was blamed for his lack of pity for his fellow Achaeans. Now the death of Patroclus has brought home to him what he has done, and he rejoins the Achaeans with an awakened sense of pity for their suffering during his absence. He gives up his wrath, being eager to avenge Patroclus and his other slain fellow countrymen.

Grief gives rise to a desire for vengeance on those who have caused it. This was true in Books 1-10: Achilles' wrath against Agamemnon grew out of his grief over being deprived of Briseis. That was a question primarily of his injured honor, of his being aggrieved at being disgraced. Now his much greater grief over the death of Patroclus has brought forth his vengeful anger against Hector. This is the way Thetis describes the situation in her great summarizing speech to Hephaestus on Achilles as a man of *achos*, "grief," in Book 18 (429-61). The theme of grief over the dead and the demand to avenge them (with the closely related theme of the mutilation of the corpse; see Segal 1971) has received increasing emphasis in Books 16-18 and will be brought to a climax on the next day of recitation in Book 22 with Achilles' slaying and mutilation of Hector.

The Greek audience must have lost patience with Achilles in Part 1. They would not have liked his unpitying refusal to help his fellow countrymen and would not have been happy at the prospect of hearing a description of the Achaeans being defeated. Thus the poet may have added the successful Achaean night raid of Book 10 in order to salve the pro-Achaean feelings of his audience. During the recitation of Part 2 the Greek audience must have continued to be dissatisfied with Achilles until he returned to the action; they must have cheered his appearance at the trench in Book 18. Now they could look forward, in Part 3, to a description of the Achaeans being victorious and could afford to take a more universal view. We have suggested that the Shield, which sees the world in universal terms, was created to suit this new mood, and that thus it serves a purpose similar to that of Book 10 with regard to the different mood prevailing at the end of the first recitation. Now the Greek audience can view the battle with the impartiality of the gods and demand that Achilles show pity on Trojans as well as Achaeans.

At the end of Part 1 we knew that Part 2 was going to describe Zeus' fulfillment of his promise to Thetis, and that Achilles was going to return to the action during the battle over Patroclus' body. This has happened, and now at the end of Part 2 we expect to hear in Part 3 the *aristeia* of Achilles, how he will slay Hector and what he will do with Hector's body.

PART 3

THE *ARISTEIA* OF ACHILLES

3. Thetis Bringing Armor to the Grieving Achilles—from a red-figure vase of the early fifth century B.C., Rijksmuseum van Oudheden, Leiden, PC 88. The sympatheic friend is probably Antilochus.

BOOK 19: ACHILLES AND AGAMEMNON ARE PUBLICLY RECONCILED

Thetis Brings the Armor to Achilles, 1-39

Throughout Part 3 Achilles will be driven by his grief over Patroclus. This will be the motivating force of his vengeful anger which he will continue to maintain even after his slaying of Hector. One of the ways in which the poet shows the depth of Achilles' grief, especially in the present book, is by emphasizing his refusal to eat. Achilles will not eat until Book 23 after he has slain Hector. The theme of grieving and eating will also be prominent in Book 24 where Achilles will prevail upon Priam to eat with him in spite of the fact that they both are in mourning.

On the dawn of this fourth day of battle (which will last into Book 23) Thetis arrives with the new armor for Achilles. He is in his hut (where we left him in the last book) mourning over Patroclus; his companions are grieving with him. She comes to him and says:

> My child, we must let him so lie in spite of our grief (*achnumenoi*),
> for he is dead, slain by the will of the gods.
> But now receive from Hephaestus this glorious armor,
> so beautiful and such as no man has worn on his shoulders.   (8-11)

When she puts it down, it makes a resounding noise which frightens his companions. They are unable to look at it, but Achilles can and does. He is filled with rage (*cholos*), and his eyes blaze as he handles it with joy. He tells her that he will arm but that he fears that flies may produce maggots in the wounds of Patroclus.

She answers that she will protect the body so well that it will be safe even for a whole year, and that he must renounce his wrath publicly before returning to battle.

> Call the Achaeans into assembly and renounce
> your wrath (*menis*) against Agamemnon, the people's shepherd.
> Then arm yourself quickly for battle and put on your valor.   (34-36)

These instructions are programmatic for the rest of this book. We are reminded that in Book 1 Hera had Achilles call the assembly for the purpose of propitiating the wrath of Apollo and that there he conceived his wrath. Now Thetis has him call an assembly for the purpose of renouncing his wrath, and here he will show his eagerness to avenge Patroclus.

> Thus having spoken, she filled him with furious strength,
> and into Patroclus' nostrils instilled ambrosia
> and drops of red nectar to preserve his flesh from harm.   (37-39)

She inspires Achilles with strength (*menos*). This is the inspiring of the hero for his *aristeia*—a motif which will be repeated at the end of this book when, while he is arming, Athena instills ambrosia and nectar into him to keep him from being hungry. The arming of Achilles is the frame (ring composition) surrounding the assembly in which he renounces his wrath and announces his vengeance, and it introduces his *aristeia*, the subject of the remaining books of the *Iliad*.

Achilles goes off to call the assembly, leaving Thetis behind with the body of Patroclus. We will find her with it when we see her again, mourning, at the beginning of Book 23. The body of Patroclus will be protected from harm during the time Achilles is avenging Patroclus. We are thus to keep in mind the grief that motivates and sustains the vengeance.

The Assembly of Reconciliation, 40-275

Achilles calls the Achaeans to assembly with a loud shout, and everyone comes, including those who before had stayed away, the helmsmen and the cooks (42-46). The mention of cooks ("bread-givers") anticipates the discussion on eating. The wounded leaders Diomedes and Odysseus limp in and take front-row seats, and finally the wounded Agamemnon enters. As in Book 1, Achilles who has called the assembly speaks first, addressing Agamemnon.

> Son of Atreus, it wasn't better for either of us,
> was it, for you or for me, to be grieved (*achnumeno*) in heart
> and rage (*meneenamen*) in strife soul-consuming over a girl?
> Would that Artemis had shot her dead at the ships
> on the day I sacked Lyrnessus and took her as booty.
> Then so many Achaeans wouldn't have fallen
> under the enemy because I in wrath had withdrawn (*apomenisantos*).
> This helped the Trojans and Hector, but the Achaeans,
> I think, will sadly remember our strife for a long time.
> But let us let bygones be bygones though we are grieved (*achnumenoi*),
> subduing the spirits in our hearts out of necessity.

> Now I am ending my wrath (*cholos*)—it wasn't right
> always to rage (*meneainemen*) without yielding. But quickly now
> rouse up the long-haired Achaeans to go into battle
> in order that I may make trial, man to man, of the Trojans,
> if any should want to bivouac here at the ships.
> He'll be glad for a rest for his knees, I think,
> whoever escapes my spear and the blaze of the battle. (56-73)

Again we are reminded of Book 1 by his wish that Briseis had died before they had fought over her, and by his emphasis on his strife with Agamemnon as the cause of death for many Achaeans—the result of the wrath foreseen in the proem (1.2-7). And we remember how when, not officially but in fact, he gave up his wrath in Book 18, and when he relented to the extent of sending out Patroclus in Book 16, he used the same words, "Let us let bygones be bygones . . . " (lines 65-66 above=18.112-13 and 16.60-61). The repetition gives a sense of finality and resignation.

The Achaeans rejoice at his renunciation. And Agamemnon, rising from his seat but not going to the center (Edwards 1991.243-44 argues that Agamemnon remains seated), makes a long, nervous speech in which he puts the blame upon Zeus-sent Ate (Folly), Fate, and Erinys (Fury). We should note, however, that by blaming Ate Agamemnon does not absolve himself from responsibility, for he acknowledges that he must make amends to Achilles.

What makes Agamemnon's speech long (78-144) is the story he tells about Ate (Folly). Hera tricked Zeus into swearing that the next child to be born of his blood would rule over all. This should have been Heracles, but Hera saw to it that Eurystheus, a great-great-grandson of Zeus, was born first. When Zeus realized his folly, he was seized with grief (*achos*) and in anger (*choomenos*) cast Ate out of heaven to be among human beings. Whenever he saw Heracles laboring at the command of Eurystheus, he groaned. Similarly, Agamemnon says, whenever he has seen Hector slaying the Achaeans at the ships, he has been unable to forget how he was possessed by Ate when he wronged Achilles. Therefore, he wants to make amends by giving the gifts that Odysseus promised earlier (in Book 9). He and Achilles must be fully reconciled, and then Achilles (taking Agamemnon's position as commander-in-chief) should lead the Achaeans to battle. Edwards 1991.245 emphaszes that Agamemnon shows his dislike of Achilles by addressing him only in the third person.

Achilles answers that it is in Agamemnon's power to give the gifts—as he should—or not, but that now there must be no delay in preparing for battle. It seems that a new breach, even at this moment of reconciling the old one, is about to arise between the two men. But Odysseus intervenes. He interrupts Achilles to insist that they must eat first, for men cannot fight without nourishment.

> But command the men to disperse and prepare
> their meals, and let Agamemnon, the King of Men,
> bring his gifts into open assembly so that the Achaeans
> all may see them and you may be warmed in your spirit.
> And let him swear as he stands among the Argives
> that he has never entered her [Briseis'] bed to have intercourse,
> which is the way of men and women, O king;
> and so you will have in your breast a gladdened heart.
> Then let him give you a feast to share in his hut
> to show reconcilement, that you may be lacking no justice.
> And you, Son of Atreus, then will be juster to another
> in future, for there's no shame for a king in a quarrel
> to appease his opponent when he's been the first to be angry.   (171-83)

Odysseus suggests that there should be a delay for two reasons: to eat and to perform the ceremony for a proper public reconciliation. Although he mentions first the dispersal of the army to eat, it is clear that he intends that the men should remain in the assembly during the ceremony; then they should be dismissed, and Achilles should join Agamemnon in the latter's hut for a meal.

Why has the poet chosen Odysseus to speak here instead of, say, Nestor, as in Book 1? The parallel with Book 9 is probably the most important factor, for now Achilles is accepting the terms which were offered him there, the main difference in the situations being that the turn of events has given both him and Agamemnon a new view of what they have done. We can also compare how Odysseus in Book 2 acted as Agamemnon's spokesman, taking his scepter and using it to persuade the men to submit to Agamemnon's leadership. Also the advice on eating seems especially well suited to his character, that of "the practical, experienced soldier" (Willcock 1984.275).

Odysseus insists that Agamemnon make full restitution in a public ceremony, swearing never to have touched Briseis; and Agamemnon gladly agrees to do this. (Notice that it is Agamemnon and not Achilles who answers.) Although

Agamemnon now has said nothing about swearing an oath, in Book 9 he had promised through Odysseus to do this. He goes on to say that Achilles and the others, though eager for war, should wait until the ceremonies are completed. Odysseus should bring Briseis and the gifts, those he had promised earlier (through Odysseus in Book 9), after choosing some younger men to help him; and Talthybius, Agamemnon's herald, should bring a boar for the sacrifice. As Reinhardt 1961.416 has pointed out, by creating an official delegation of heroes led by Odysseus (instead of his own attendants) Agamemnon shows his eagerness to appease Achilles publicly.

Achilles answers Agamemnon as before, but at greater length and with greater fervor. This is no time for such a delay, for his fury (*menos*, 202; cf. 37 where Thetis filled him with *menos*) is very great. They can wait to perform the ceremony and also to eat until after they have avenged their dead. He himself will by no means eat or drink anything until he has avenged Patroclus.

> Now those lie torn and dead whom Hector slew,
> the son of Priam, when Zeus gave victory to him,
> and you two urge us to eat. But I would command
> the sons of the Achaeans to fight immediately, now,
> without eating, no food. Sunset is when we should eat,
> prepare a big meal, when we've avenged our dishonor.
> By no means will I before this take any swallow
> of food or drink, for my companion is dead,
> slaughtered, and lies in my hut torn by the sharp bronze,
> his feet being turned toward the door, and around him
> our comrades are weeping. The only thing I can think of
> is slaughter and blood and the grievous groaning of men.   (203-14)

Odysseus, answering for Agamemnon again, but at greater length (216-37), insists on the necessity of eating. Though Achilles is the best warrior among the Achaeans, he should listen to the advice of an older, more experienced man (Odysseus). Fighting is a hard business; men are soon sated with battle. This is no time to grieve over the dead with fasting. They must eat in order to fight.

Having so answered Achilles, Odysseus obeys Agamemnon's orders. With the help of some of the younger heroes he brings Briseis and the gifts into the assembly. Then Talthybius produces the boar which Agamemnon slaughters as he swears to Zeus and the other appropriate gods that he has never touched Briseis.

Talthybius completes the ceremony by throwing the carcass into the sea. Edwards 1991.263 well remarks that the ceremony is much like that in which Chryses is restored to her father in Book 1 (the end of Apollo's wrath).

Then Achilles stands up and says:

> Zeus Father, you send upon men great attacks of folly (*ate*).
> Never would the son of Atreus have stirred up in my breast
> my spirit to ceaseless turmoil, never would he,
> intractable, have led off the girl against my will,
> if Zeus had not willed to bring death on many of the Argives.
> Now let us go and eat to gather our war-strength.   (270-75)

Thus Achilles accepts Agamemnon's apology and, having submitted to the public ceremony of reconciliation, orders the men to go and eat. The assembly is over.

Achilles agrees with Agamemnon, saying that Zeus caused their quarrel in order to bring death to the Achaeans—a statement which conflicts somewhat with the fact that Zeus in the *Iliad* brings death to the Achaeans only because of the promise he made to Thetis after the quarrel. It seems unlikely, however, that this inconsistency would have bothered the poet and his audience. In early as well as later Greek thought it is a common idea that everything that happens is ultimately attributable to Zeus. Bassett 1922.54 suggests that Achilles in the present passage, whether out of politeness or conviction or both, is speaking only for himself, not for the poet.

The Laments of Briseis and Achilles over Patroclus, 276-339

The Myrmidons bring Briseis and the gifts to Achilles' hut, and she laments over the body of Patroclus whom she praises for his gentleness. Her lament is answered by the wailing of the other women as they remember their own sorrows. Owen 1946.197 notes that this scene marks the main turning point in the poem: Achilles has paid for the restoration of Briseis with the life of Patroclus, and "just as the taking of Briseis was the exciting cause of all the previous events, the death of Patroclus is the exciting cause of all that is to come."

The leaders of the Achaeans return with Achilles to his hut and beg him to eat (that is, to go to Agamemnon's hut for the meal of reconciliation), but he, groaning, refuses.

> I beg of you, dear friends, if any of you would do me a favor,
> don't ask me now to take any food or drink

to satisfy my heart, since a terrible grief (*achos*) possesses me.
I shall hold up as I am and endure until sunset.   (305-8)

Achilles will not relent until Book 23, after the slaying of Hector, when he goes to Agamemnon's hut to eat. His present brief but polite refusal reminds us of his more lengthy, ill-humored rejection of the embassy in Book 9. This is the same Achilles, but now his words show his friendship for his fellow Achaeans. All the leaders leave except Agamemnon, Menelaus, Odysseus, Nestor, Idomeneus, and Phoenix who try to cheer him in his grief (*akachemenos*, 312). But, as the poet comments, he is not to be cheered until he has entered the battle. His mind is riveted on Patroclus. The thought of food reminds him of how Patroclus used to prepare his meals, as he sobbingly says, addressing the body.

Before this, you, my ill-fated dearest friend,
you prepared warm meals for me in our hut
quickly, efficiently, whenever the Achaeans rushed forth
to bring to the horse-taming Trojans many-teared battle.
Now you lie dead, torn open, and I shall take nothing
to nourish my heart, no food or drink from our stores,
because of my longing for you.   (315-21)

He goes on to say that he would not grieve so much over the death of his father or son. Earlier he had thought that only he would die at Troy, and that Patroclus would return to Phthia (Achilles' homeland), taking Neoptolemus (Achilles' son) with him. He imagines his father Peleus now to be dead or very enfeebled by old age and waiting to hear of his death.

Thus Achilles laments, and the leaders wail in response, each of them remembering his home. We can compare, at the beginning of this section, the lament of Briseis and the responsive wailing of the other enslaved women as they remembered their own sorrows. Achilles' lament can thus be thought of as a climactic parallel to that of Briseis.

Achilles Arms for Battle, 340-424

The poet moves from the mourning in Achilles' hut to the arming of the Achaeans by way of a scene on Olympus. Seeing the scene of grief and being filled with pity (*idon eleese*, 340), Zeus suggests to Athena that she sustain Achilles by dropping nectar and ambrosia into his chest. She eagerly obeys, leaping from heaven like a swift predatory seabird (we are reminded of the hawk with which

Thetis was compared at the end of Book 18 when she brought Achilles' new armor; there are clear parallels between how Athena and Thetis help Achilles.) Athena arrives when the Achaeans—and therefore Achilles—have begun to arm, and instills nectar and ambrosia into him. Then she returns to her father's house, and we continue with the description of the Achaeans preparing for battle. As they pour out from the area of the ships and, in the brightness of their armor, come into close formation, they are like a storm of snow thickly falling (357-58, simile type 1: the gleaming of the armor); their feet make a resounding noise. Achilles is arming among them.

Athena's instilling nectar and ambrosia into Achilles is like Thetis' doing the same to preserve the body of Patroclus. The fact that Zeus sends Athena to help Achilles shows that he is now supporting him. Athena (like Thetis earlier) is acting as the inspiring divinity at the beginning of the hero's *aristeia*; we remember how she glorified him at the trench in Book 18.

Achilles' not eating is used in various ways. First, it shows his grief over Patroclus and his poignant memory of Patroclus preparing their meals. Second, it allows the gods to glorify him by protecting him miraculously from hunger. Third, by his being preserved in the same way as the body of Patroclus, it is used to identify him with his dead friend. We might compare how Patroclus' wearing of Achilles' armor and the making of Achilles' new armor are similarly used, to show the identity of Patroclus and Achilles and how the gods are glorifying Achilles.

As Achilles arms, his teeth are grinding, and his eyes are blazing (as they did when he took the armor from Thetis), because he is possessed by unendurable grief (*achos*) and is filled with fighting spirit (*meneainon*). This description, in lines 365-68, was rejected by Aristarchus as being overdone, but it describes in a very striking way the effect that Athena has had on Achilles.

There follows a detailed account of his arming. The brightness of his shield might be seen at a great distance like that of the moon or that of a fire on a mountain seen by sailors driven by storm-winds far off from their dear ones (374-78, simile type 1: the gleaming of the hero's armor; the simile is composed from the Achaean point of view—so Edwards 1991.279). Then he tests his new armor and finds that he can run in it easily, as on wings. Finally, he takes up the spear given him by his father,

> heavy, long, and strong—no other of the Achaeans
> was able to brandish it; only Achilles could do this—
> the Pelian ash which Chiron had given his father,

> from Mount Pelion, a bringer of death to heroes.   (388-91)

These lines repeat 16.141-44 where Patroclus did not take up this spear, being unable to brandish it (a foreshadowing of his death). Achilles' brandishing it now bodes ill for Hector.

Automedon as charioteer and Achilles shining like Hyperion, the sun-god (399, another type 1 simile), mount the chariot; and Achilles exhorts his two horses not to leave him dead as they had done Patroclus. One of them, Xanthus, being given the power to speak by Hera, answers that they are not to blame, for Patroclus was slain by Apollo and Hector, and that Achilles is also destined to die at the hands of a god and a man. Achilles replies:

> Xanthus, why be a prophet of death to me?
> No need of that, for I myself know I must die here
> far from my mother and father, but still I'm determined
> not to relent before sating the Trojans with war.   (420-23)

Throughout the last books of the *Iliad* Achilles will be dedicated to death, and often speak as if from the world of the dead. Now, shouting his war cry, he drives out into the forefront of the Achaeans. We can imagine how frightened the Trojans are to behold him.

Kirk 1976.207 justly describes the effect of the speeches in the present book about the necessity to eat as "rambling"; we feel that the assembly of reconciliation comes as an anti-climax after the climax of Achilles' return in Book 18. Some scholars (so Combellack 1984. 254) have seen this leisureliness as a reason for treating Book 19 as a part of the retardation in Books 20 and 21. But the events of Book 19 move steadily if slowly forward, in accordance with Thetis' programmatic words in lines 34-36, to the encounter of Achilles and Hector. Accordingly, it seems better to think of this book as a slowly paced introduction to the final act of the *Iliad*.

BOOK 20: GODS PROTECT THE TROJANS

The New Plan of Zeus, 1-155

Thus at the ships the Achaeans were arming for battle as were the Trojans out on the plain. We expect them to attack each other, but this will not happen immediately, for we switch to Zeus on Olympus. A day of battle typically begins with Zeus as the steward of war setting the guidelines (as at the beginning of Books 2, 8, and 11; compare our comments on the opening scene of Book 4), but this has been delayed to describe Achilles' reconciliation with Agamemnon.

The present scene on Olympus introduces the *aristeia* of Achilles, especially the part of it that deals with the battle between the gods. This battle, which will be broken off in the present book (Book 20) and resumed and concluded in the next one (Book 21), will form a ring composition around a series of encounters of Achilles and create with them a stretch of narrative that amounts to a long retardation.

The description of Achilles' encounters in this narrative, which include a preliminary, abortive one with Hector, has its own climactic structure. His first opponent will be Aeneas; his last opponent the Scamander River who will almost overwhelm him (the wounding of the hero in his *aristeia)*; and this last encounter will lead into the culminating event of the battle between the gods in which the pro-Achaean gods defeat the pro-Trojan ones.

The fall of Troy and the uselessness of words in opposing the implacable Achilles are two prominent themes in this section as in the whole poem. We have seen the theme of the fall of Troy especially in Book 5 where Diomedes (the great offensive fighter of the Achaeans in Part 1) with the help of Athena wounded and drove the pro-Trojan deities, Aphrodite and Ares, from the battlefield; now the battle between the gods, which looks back to these events in Book 5, will show the pro-Trojan gods abandoning the defense of Troy. Now the implacability of Achilles will seem a more severe and terrible thing than it was in Parts 1 and 2. When he was refusing the supplications to give up his wrath, he was pitiless like Hades according to Agamemnon, and deaf like the rocks and the sea according to Patroclus. Now his enemies will supplicate him for their lives, and he will refuse to hear them. Again the images used by Agamemnon and Patroclus will seem appropriate, but we shall feel, like a new element, Achilles' horrible cruelty. In Book 24, before he takes pity on Priam, he will be characterize by Apollo as a wild animal, a sheep-devouring lion.

When we switch to Olympus, Zeus is ordering Themis, the goddess of law, to call the gods to assembly. All come including the rivers, except for Oceanus who, being a part of the world, must stay in his place. We are reminded of how in the last book, when Achilles called the assembly, everyone came including the cooks. The inclusiveness, here as there, emphasizes the importance of the occasion, and the specifying of the rivers, like that of the cooks, apparently anticipates (an example of *prooikonomia* according to schol. T) a coming episode, here Achilles' encounter with the Scamander River (in the next book) as there the argument over when the army should eat.

Thus there are certain parallels between the two assemblies. Moreover, they are closely related events. Achilles' wrath (begun in the assembly in Book 1) has come to an end, and the old plan of Zeus (the subject of Zeus' conversation with the gods at the end of Book 1) has been fulfilled. Now there is Achilles' new anger of vengeance proclaimed in the assembly in the last book, and so it seems appropriate that there should also be a new plan of Zeus. Zeus' first plan was to support the wrath of Achilles; his present plan is to prevent Achilles from taking Troy on this day. Thus in both instances he delays, for the time of the action of the *Iliad*, the destruction of Troy, a city of which he is especially fond but which is destined—the poet's inherited story—to fall. Achilles will be permitted to slay Hector, without whom Troy cannot survive, but Troy will not fall within the action of the *Iliad*.

When the gods have assembled, Poseidon asks the "plan of Zeus" (15).

> Why now, O Lightener, have you called the gods to assembly?
> Is it because of your care for the Trojans and the Achaeans
> when they're about to do battle in fiery close combat?   (16-18)

Zeus answers:

> You, Earthshaker, already know the plan I've conceived,
> why I've assembled you. Yes, I care for the dying,
> but I'll remain on Olympus in a secluded vale,
> seated and enjoying my ease as I look on. You others
> go and be joined with them, the Trojans and the Achaeans,
> to give your aid to whichever side you choose.
> For if Achilles shall fight with no gods intervening,
> the Trojans won't check him, the swift son of Peleus, a minute.
> Since before this the mere sight of him set them to fleeing,

> now when he's terribly angry (*choetai*) because of his comrade
> I fear he'll sack Troy's walls before it is fated.   (20-30)

Zeus is countermanding his prohibition in Book 8. When he says he cares for the dying, he apparently has the Trojans mainly in mind (no Achaean will die in the coming battle); the gods should participate in the battle in order that Achilles may not take Troy on this day. This purpose has worried scholars since antiquity, for the addition of the gods to the battlefield should add to the advantage of Achilles, since the pro-Achaean gods are stronger than the pro-Trojans ones. But the poet's chief concern, as schol. bT point out, is to put us on notice that the gods are going to help the Trojans against Achilles. The pro-Trojan Apollo will inspire Aeneas to go against Achilles and will defend Hector from Achilles' attack; and the river of Troy, the Scamander, will oppose Achilles. Moreover, the pro-Achaean god Poseidon will intervene to save the Trojan Aeneas. Thus Zeus' programmatic speech prepares us not only for the battle of the gods but for their role in retarding the attack of Achilles.

And it opens hostilities: thus "he roused ceaseless war" (31). The gods come onto the battlefield—five (Hera, Athena, Poseidon, Hermes, Hephaestus) to the Achaean side, six (Ares, Apollo, Artemis, Leto, Scamander, Aphrodite) to the Trojan side. Before their arrival the Trojans were filled with fear at the sight of Achilles, but now they are possessed by the spirit of strife. Athena shouts from the Trojan side of the Achaean trench, and Ares from the citadel of Troy and from a hill near the Simois, the smaller river of Troy.

Thus the gods rouse the Achaeans and Trojans to battle. In lines 54-74 the imminent clash of the two armies (what we expected to happen before the scene on Olympus) is described in terms of the pro-Achaean and pro-Trojan gods advancing to attack each other. This is the great climactic battle of the *Iliad*, and so it is fitting that it should be described in terms of a conflict between the gods. Zeus thunders on high. Poseidon shakes the earth, causing Hades to fear that the realm of the dead may be opened. Poseidon opposes Apollo; Athena Ares; Hera Artemis; Hermes Leto; and finally Hephaestus, the god of fire, opposes the Scamander River.

But then the poet postpones their battle by having Apollo rouse Aeneas against Achilles. Appearing to him in the form of Hector's half brother Lycaon, he taunts him with having vainly boasted that he would fight Achilles. Aeneas replies that earlier (before the action of the *Iliad*) Achilles with the help of the gods had almost slain him and that only Zeus had saved him but that if the gods would give him an equal chance he would do better. To this Apollo-Lycaon says that Aeneas should pray to the gods for help, for his mother, Aphrodite, is a goddess whereas Achilles' mother is only a Nereid; nor should he let Achilles frighten him with empty words. Then he breathes strength (*menos*, 110) into Aeneas. Later Aeneas will show in his speech to Achilles that he has remembered Apollo's words about his ancestry and about the emptiness of words in battle.

When Hera sees what Apollo is doing, she calls an on-the-battlefield council of the pro-Achaean gods. Addressing Poseidon and Athena, she says that they must either force Aeneas to turn back or support Achilles.

> We've all come down from Olympus to share in this battle,
> to see that he suffer no harm at the hands of the Trojans
> today. Later he'll have to suffer whatever
> fate was spun for him at the hour of his birth.
> If Achilles is not made aware of our help,
> he'll be frightened when one of the gods encounters him.
> Men find a god's full appearance hard to endure.   (125-32)

Thus the pro-Achaean gods (the "all" of line 125) have as their main purpose the protection of Achilles—which does not run counter to Zeus' desire that Achilles not take Troy on this day. Hera's premonition that some god may openly oppose Achilles foreshadows his encounter with the Scamander.

Poseidon answers by urging caution. Let them leave the fighting to the humans. But if Ares or Apollo should hinder Achilles, they should immediately oppose the pro-Trojan gods. Such a conflict, Poseidon is confident, will end with the pro-Trojan gods swiftly retreating to Olympus. His words look forward to the battle of the gods in the next book, which will grow out of Scamander's attack on Achilles and in which the pro-Trojan gods will be defeated.

In response to Poseidon's speech the pro-Achaean gods led by him go to a wall which the Trojans had built earlier for the protection of Heracles; and the pro-Trojan gods take their seats around Apollo and Ares on the hill near the Simois River. Zeus is sitting in command on high (155). The battlefield has been left to the human participants, among whom is Aeneas inspired by Apollo to attack Achilles.

Achilles' Encounter with Aeneas, 156-352

Aeneas is the challenger, but Achilles springs forward like a ravening lion (164-73, simile type 2). He asks Aeneas whether he imagines that Priam, who has plenty of sons to honor, will reward him for winning. But he will probably lose; he should remember how earlier he had fled before him in a cowardly way. He would be wise to withdraw now and not act like a foolish person (*nepios*, 198) who realizes the truth by sad experience too late.

Aeneas replies in a speech made long (200-58) by his genealogy. Achilles should not try to frighten him as if he were a fool (*neputios*, 200). Each of them knows the other's parentage, and either his or Achilles' parents will bewail the loss of their son today since neither he nor Achilles will be frightened by foolish (*neputioi*, 211) words. Yet he himself can boast of a very illustrious genealogy (213-41). Zeus begot Dardanus, the father of Erichthonius, famous for his stable of horses, among whom were twelve fillies sired by the North Wind and capable of running over the tops of the waves and the ears of grain. Erichthonius begot Tros, the father of Ilus, Assaracus, and Ganymedes, who was caught up to heaven to be the cupbearer of Zeus. Ilus begot Laomedon, and Laomedon begot Tithonus and Priam. Assaracus begot Capys, and Capys begot Anchises, the father of Aeneas, as Priam is of Hector. The elaborations about the fillies of Erichthonius and about Ganymedes show the divine favor with which the Trojan royal line, descended from Zeus, is blessed.

Why has the poet included this genealogy? As we soon learn, the Trojan royal line is destined to survive in the descendants of Aeneas. Since ancient authorities tell us that this actually happened, scholars have suggested that the poet may have wanted to praise these descendants, who had been Hellenized and still lived in the region of Troy when the *Iliad* was composed (a view supported by Scheibner 1939.124 -34 but criticized by Willcock 1976.223). More certain is the fact that this account of the Trojan royal line fits in with the theme of the fall of Troy (only the family of Aeneas survived), and it looks forward to Aeneas' being saved by Poseidon, for it puts before us Zeus' love of Dardanus and his descendants and makes understandable his desire that they not die out altogether.

Aeneas ends his speech by saying that he and Achilles should not continue to stand there talking like fools (*neputioi*, 244); thus he reverts to the comparison with which, having taken his cue from Achilles, he began. Speeches, he says in a digressive and wordy way (244-58, perhaps meant to be humorous), are often digressive and wordy, like those of women quarreling in the street, and they should stop talking and get down to fighting. He speech, because of its genealogy, has rightly been compared with that of Glaucus to Diomedes in Book 5 and that of Asteropaeus to Achilles in the present narrative (in the next book). Does the reliance on their ancestry show a certain nervousness in these men before their stronger opponents? "If so, there is comedy here, which the hearers would be expected to appreciate" (Willcock 1984.280). This first in the series of Achilles' encounters with the enemy is, appropriately, very low key.

Then Aeneas thrusts his spear into Achilles' shield which Achilles holds away from himself in fear, not realizing that the gifts of the gods do not yield easily to mortals. The shield makes a noise as the spear goes through it to the third layer. Then Achilles hurls his spear against Aeneas' shield which Aeneas holds away from himself in fear. The shield makes a noise as the spear goes through it at the rim and strikes the earth. Aeneas is frightened and seized with anguish (*achos*, 282). Then Achilles attacks with his sword, shouting, and Aeneas picks up a large rock such as two men of later times could not raise.

> Aeneas would with this rock have struck his attacker
> on helmet or shield, that protection from grievous destruction,
> and the son of Peleus would with his sword have slain him,
> if Poseidon the Earthshaker had not been observant.   (289-91)

As Scheibner 1939.79-81 has noted, the parallels in the description of the encounter between Achilles and Aeneas show how almost evenly matched they are, but clearly Achilles has the advantage, as the above lines introducing the intervention of Poseidon show.

Addressing the pro-Achaean gods, Poseidon says that he feels anguish (*achos*, 293) over the imminent death of Aeneas who has, like a fool (*nepios*, 296), allowed Apollo, who will not help him, to persuade him to challenge Achilles. Aeneas (297-99) is not to be blamed (for the Trojan War), but feels anguish (*acheon*, 298) because of what others (especially Paris) have done; he has always been pious. Moreover, Zeus will be angry if they do not save him, for, though he no longer favors the family of Priam, he has determined that the Trojan royal line will survive in the descendants of Aeneas.

Hera answers that she and Athena are sworn to eternal enmity against the Trojans, but that Poseidon may save Aeneas. Accordingly, he pours a mist over Achilles' eyes and, retrieving Achilles' spear, lays it before his feet. Then, having carried Aeneas in the air to a place of safety behind the Trojan lines, he asks him which god has inspired him to fight against Achilles "who is stronger than you and dearer to the immortals" (334). He should beware lest he die before his time. Only after Achilles has met his fate may he fight with whomever he pleases. Aeneas' being saved by Poseidon reminds us of how he was saved by Aphrodite in Book 5; and it acts as an anticipatory doublet to how Hector will be saved by Apollo in the next section. Aeneas is the greatest fighter on the Trojan side after Hector.

Then Poseidon, going back to Achilles, scatters the mist, and Achilles exclaims at the miracle and the fact that Aeneas, after all, was also dear to the gods. His encounter with Aeneas has given him glory, for Aeneas has survived him only by a special dispensation of Zeus. Now he will exhort the Achaeans and attack the other Trojans.

Achilles Slaughters the Trojans, 353-503

Thus Achilles leaps into the ranks of the Trojans as he exhorts the Achaeans to follow him. He needs their help, for not even Athena or Ares could fight against so many. Similarly Hector exhorts the Trojans. Although Achilles is stronger than he is, the gods may not grant him the victory.

> And so I'll go meet him, even if his hands are like fire,
> even if his hands are like fire, his spirit like hot iron.   (371-72)

He is describing the pitiless strength of Achilles. These speeches of exhortation introduce Achilles' general slaughter of the Trojans, but especially its initial phase which ends with the encounter between him and Hector—an abortive encounter foreshadowing their final fight in Book 22.

As the two sides clash, Apollo comes to Hector and tells him not to challenge Achilles for fear of being slain. At first Hector obeys. In the meanwhile Achilles slays four Trojans. He splits Iphition's head in two and boasts over him. Then he stabs Demoleon, a son of Antenor, in the head; then Hippodamas in the back as he is trying to flee, who dies bellowing like a bull being slain (403-5, simile type 9). Then (the climactic kill) he attacks Polydorus, the full brother of Lycaon (whom Achilles will slay in the next book); Priam has forbidden Polydorus to participate in the fighting since he is his youngest and dearest son. Achilles strikes him in the back; the spear-point comes out at the navel, causing him to collapse with his bowls in his hands. The description is pathetic; and Hector is moved to take vengeance. Achilles, seeing him coming, says:

> Here is the man my soul most wants to encounter,
> the one who slew my dear honored comrade. Now we'll

no longer hide in the ranks avoiding each other.   (425-27)

They are both motivated by the spirit of vengeance.

After the above speech—apparently spoken to himself—Achilles, scowling, makes a one-line challenge to Hector.

Come on closer in order the sooner to die.   (429)

Hector responds that Achilles should not try to frighten him with words as if he were a fool (*neputios*, 431; we are reminded of Aeneas' similar response to Achilles.) The gods will determine the winner. So saying, he hurls his spear, but Athena blows it back so that it lands at his feet; and Achilles rushes to slay him. At this moment of imminent danger (compare how Poseidon saved Aeneas) Apollo intervenes and saves Hector in a protective cloud against which Achilles strikes with his spear four times in vain. Achilles is frustrated much as he was when Poseidon saved Aeneas. Apollo has protected Hector; next time with the help of the gods, he, Achilles will slay him. Now he will attack the other Trojans.

He rapidly slays ten men. The fifth, Tros, the son of Alastor, is significant in that he vainly supplicates Achilles to spare his life.

> Tros, the son of Alastor, fell at his knees
> and begged him to spare him, capture him, take him alive,
> not kill him but pity (*eleesas*) a man in his youth like himself.
> The fool (*nepios*), he didn't suspect he wouldn't persuade him,
> for this was no sweet-souled man, one gentle in thought,
> but one very vehement. Tros reached out for his knees,
> begging for mercy, but he thrust his sword through his liver,
> forcing it out, and from it there flowed black blood
> filling his lap, and darkness covered his eyes,
> his spirit departed.   (463-72)

This is a doublet of Lycaon's famous supplication of Achilles in the next book; and we are also reminded of Polydorus' death. Another similarity between Tros and both Polydorus and Lycaon is his youth. And though he, unlike them, is not a son of Priam, his name reminds us of the Tros in the Trojan royal line. He seems to stand for every Trojan.

Achilles' eighth victim is Deucalion, whom he strikes with his spear in the elbow, thus rendering his fighting arm useless. Then, as Deucalion looks death in the face, Achilles' pitiless sword strikes off his head and helmet. The marrow shoots from Deucalion's backbone as he lies dead on the ground. Finally, Achilles slays Rigmus and Areithous as they try to flee in their chariot.

The poet concludes with two similes, as if admitting his inability to describe Achilles' attack in merely factual terms. Achilles is like a devastating forestfire (490-93, simile type 3): wherever he rushes the ground is red with blood. And his team of horses are like two oxen threshing grain: they ride over corpses and shields, the axle is spattered with blood thrown up by their hoofs and the wheels of the chariot.

> The son of Peleus rushed on to win glory,
> splattering with gore his irresistible hands.   (502-3)

BOOK 21: THE BATTLE OF THE GODS AND ACHILLES' ROUTING
OF THE TROJANS

The Fighting at the River, 1-210

There is no break between this and the preceding book. The Trojans are fleeing before Achilles, but Hera pours a mist in front of them, so that half of them, being unable to see, are crowded into the Scamander River like locusts fleeing a fire (13-15, simile type 4: flight and pursuit). The river is filled with horses and men. Then Achilles, leaving his spear on the bank, leaps in with his sword and slays them, like a dolphin putting the other fish to flight (22-24, simile type 5: the victor and his victim). When he is finally exhausted with killing, he captures twelve young Trojans, dazed like fawns (29; compare the comparison of the fleeing Trojans to fawns at 22.1, another type 4 simile), to be sacrificed at the funeral of Patroclus (23.175-76). Thus he begins to fulfill the promise made at 18.336-37, and thus we are kept in mind of his motivating grief.

Then he encounters Lycaon fleeing from the river; he had captured him earlier (outside the action of the *Iliad*) and sold him to the son of Jason on Lemnos, but the king of Imbros, a friend of the Trojan royal family, had ransomed him. Now some god has put him in the way of Achilles who is going to kill him (45-49); we are left in no doubt about the outcome of this encounter. Lycaon is easy to recognize, for he has thrown away his arms and armor in order to escape from the river. Achilles reacts ironically as if he were seeing a miracle. The sea, he says, has not been able to keep Lycaon from Troy; now he, Achilles, will slay him and see whether the earth cannot do this. But as Achilles raises his spear to strike him, Lycaon runs forward and, ducking under the spear, which is thrust into the earth behind him, grips it in one hand while with the other he seizes Achilles' knees. He begs Achilles to pity (*eleeson*, 74) him as a suppliant, for they had broken bread together when Achilles had captured him earlier. Now his family would pay a much greater ransom for his return. Though he expects to meet with the same fate as his full brother Polydorus, he asks Achilles not to kill him; he is only the half brother of Hector who has slain his gentle and strong companion. Achilles replies:

Foolish one (*nepie*), don't offer or speak of ransom to me.
Earlier, before Patroclus met his doom,
I would be sparing, that was my inclination,
and many a Trojan I took alive and sold.
But now there's no one who'll escape death, not one

> of those whom the god thrusts into my hands before Troy,
> not one Trojan, especially no son of Priam.
> But you too die, my friend. And why lament it?
> Patroclus also has died, a far better man.
> And I—you see how tall and handsome I am,
> my father is noble, the mother who bore me a goddess—
> I soon must meet my fated doom of death.
> Some morning is destined to come, some evening or midday
> when one of the enemy will take my life from me in battle,
> hurling a spear from a distance or shooting an arrow.   (99-113)

Lycaon responds by stretching out both his arms. Achilles draws his sword and stabs him in the neck, causing him to fall bleeding face down on the ground. Then, taking him by the foot, he throws him back into the river, saying:

> Go and lie there with the fish, for they'll take care of you,
> licking the blood from your wounds. Your mother won't be there
> to stretch you out on a bier and bemoan you, but swirling
> Scamander will carry you into the sea's broad bosom.
> Many a fish will leap up through the waves at the shuddering
> darkness to feed on the glistening fat of Lycaon.
> May all of you perish until we've destroy sacred Troy,
> all of you fleeing as I come killing behind you.
> The lovely, silvery-swirling river won't help you,
> to whom for a long time you've sacrificed many a bull,
> into whose streams sent single-hoofed horses alive.
> In spite of all this devotion you'll perish, all of you,
> and pay for Patroclus' death and the death of the Achaeans
> whom you've slain by the swift ships during my absence.   (127-35)

Achilles' saying that the river of Troy will not help the Trojans (130) and his pitiless slaying of the enemy (147) anger Scamander, who decides to inspire Asteropaeus, a Paeonian, the grandson of the river Axius, with strength *(menos)* to oppose him; and so Asteropaeus, who is ambidextrous, advances against Achilles with a spear in each hand. After identifying himself and telling of his illustrious ancestry, he lets go with both spears before Achilles can hurl his. One strikes Achilles' shield to the gold layer; the other wounds him slightly, grazing his right forearm and drawing blood. Then Achilles, his spear having missed and stuck in the bank of the river, leaps upon Asteropaeus with his sword. Asteropaeus tries to draw Achilles' spear out of the earth or even to bend and break it, but Achilles stabs him in the stomach, causing his bowls to pour forth, and, leaping upon him and stripping him of his armor, boasts that the descendants of rivers are no match for the descendants of Zeus (like himself, the son of Peleus, the son of Aeacus, the son of Zeus). Not even Oceanus, from whom all rivers and springs descend, can vie with Zeus. Again his words are a challenge to Scamander. Then he draws his spear out of the bank and, leaving Asteropaeus to be carried away by the water for the eels and fish to feed on, proceeds to attack and slay other Paeonians, who are fleeing in dismay.

The Fight with the River, 211-382

He would have continued his onslaught if Scamander, being angered and taking human form, had not intervened and cried out for him not to slay the Trojans in his waters. Achilles answers:

> I'll do, divine Scamander, as you command,
> but shall not cease to slay the arrogant Trojans
> until I've driven them into their city and made trial
> of Hector to see whether I shall slay him or he me.   (222-26)

His goals—to drive the Trojans back into Troy and then slay Hector—are the poet's program for this day of battle.

So saying, Achilles begins driving the enemy out of the river. But Scamander calls on Apollo to remember Zeus' command (made at the beginning of the last book) to protect the Trojans on this day, and roaring like a bull throws out the corpses and hides the living men. Then he attacks Achilles, dashing against his shield and sweeping him off his feet. Achilles, by throwing down a large elm across the river, slows it up and gives himself time to escape onto the plain. But Scamander rushes after him. Achilles flees like an eagle (252-53, simile type 4), but the river, like water outrunning a man conducting it in an irrigation ditch (257-62, another type 4 simile), is faster, for gods are stronger than men. Whenever Achilles tries to make a stand, to see if some god will help him, Scamander overwhelms him. Finally, Achilles cries out for help.

> O Zeus Father, will no god have pity and save me
> from dying like this. Saved now, I'd die any death.

> I don't blame any of the gods descended from Ouranus,
> only my mother who told me lies to beguile me,
> saying that under the walls of the well-armored Trojans
> I was destined to die from Apollo's swift arrow.
> I wish that Hector had slain me, this country's best man:
> noble the slayer then, and noble the slain.
> But I was destined to die a shameful death,
> drowned in a mighty river, like a swineherd boy
> swept off while trying to cross a storm-swollen river.   (273-83)

The present scene of desperation, after the slight wounding of Achilles' arm by Asteropaeus, brings to a climax the theme of the wounding of the hero in his *aristeia*. In answer to his prayer Poseidon and Athena appear to him in human form and pledge him their help. They have come, Poseidon tells him, with the approval of Zeus. Soon the river will retire; then—again the program for this day of battle— he should continue his slaughter of the Trojans until he has crowded them into Troy but should return to the ships after slaying Hector (291-97).

When Poseidon and Athena have left, Achilles rushes over the plain, which is swamped and filled with floating corpses and armor. He has new strength (*menos*, 303), given him by Athena—a motif in the *aristeia* of the hero. But Scamander continues to attack, being even more angered at Achilles, and calls on his brother river, the smaller Simois, to help him: together they can prevent Achilles from destroying Troy. Scamander envisions Achilles being overwhelmed by water, under the sand, pebbles, and slime; the Achaeans will be unable to find his bones for burial. We are thus given an idea of the terrible death that Achilles has prayed to avoid.

Scamander leaps upon him and is on the point of overwhelming him, but Hera intervenes. She calls to Hephaestus to help her, in a speech which parallels Scamander's to Simois.

> Rise, lame god, my son. Weren't you the one
> against whom swirling Xanthus [Scamander's divine name] was matched in
>   battle?
> I shall go off and stir up out of the sea
> Zephyrus and bright Notus to blow a hard stormwind together
> which will consume the Trojans, both corpses and armor,
> by spreading the wildfire, and burn up the trees that grow

on the banks of Xanthus, and set him on fire himself.
Don't let him deter you either with soft words or curses.
Don't cease to attack, don't abate your strength until
you hear me shouting to check your weariless flame.   (331-41)

Hephaestus has been set to fight Scamander since 20.73-74. Now he carries out
Hera's instructions exactly (so Scheibner 1939.100). He consumes the Trojan
corpses on the plain (343-49), then turns against the river and the trees along its
bank (349-55), and finally attacks the river itself (365). We feel the gradual
inevitable buildup. Scamander, boiling with fire like fat in a cauldron, cries out for
Hephaestus to stop and promises no longer to try to defend the Trojans. But
Hephaestus refuses to yield, no doubt remembering Hera's injunction to wait for
her signal. Then Scamander tells Hera that if she will call off Hephaestus he will
solemnly swear not to protect Troy even when the Achaeans are destroying it with
fire (369-76). Hera complies, saying that it is not fitting for gods to fight over
mortals (379-80); and so Scamander is able again to flow as usual.

The Battle of the Gods, 383-513

The fight between Scamander and Hephaestus is the first encounter in the
battle of the gods, which forms a ring composition with the pairing of the gods
against each other at the beginning of Book 20 and brings to a climax the incidents
that retard Achilles' pursuit of Hector. These incidents have often foreshadowed
the fall of Troy; and the battle of the gods will show the pro-Trojan gods being
defeated (compare Book 5).

We begin with a general description (385-90) which reminds us of the gods
attacking each other at the beginning of 20. The earth roars and Zeus laughs with
joy at the spectacle. There is humor in the battle of the gods; it is sometimes
described as a burlesque of a human battle. We are probably intended to laugh at it,
as Zeus does. "Zeus appears to have a just appreciation of the whole combat as a
parody of serious fighting" (Leaf II.412). The life of the gods as gods is imagined
as carefree and full of delight, in stark contrast to the life of human beings.

There are two main narrative sequences, the first (391-433) beginning with
the single combat between Athena and Ares, the second (435-513) with the
confrontation between Poseidon and Apollo. The second, which is longer and
more complex, can be thought of as creating a climatic parallel with the first.

Ares attacks Athena, after reminding her of her assault on him in Book 5, but
he is unable to pierce her shield, the aegis. Then with a huge rock, the size of an

ancient boulder used to mark the boundary between two farms, she strikes him in the neck and knocks him over; he is stretched out on the ground an area of seven acres. Laughing, she boasts over him, saying he was a fool to oppose her and will pay just retribution to his mother Hera who has cursed him for deserting the Achaeans to support the Trojans. Then Aphrodite helps Ares to his feet, but Hera exhorts Athena to attack her. Athena strikes Aphrodite on the breast and knocks her down. Now both Aphrodite and Ares are on the ground, and Athena boasts again. The pro-Trojan Aphrodite and Ares have been defeated, as they were by Diomedes with the help of Athena in Book 5. This brings to an end the first narrative sequence.

Now Poseidon challenges Apollo to begin their fight. He upbraids him for supporting the Trojans, as Athena has just upbraided Ares. Apollo is acting like a fool (*neputi'*, 441), for Priam's father, Laomedon, had once cheated them of their pay and dismissed them with threats. Apollo answers that it is insane for gods to fight on behalf of pitiable mortals, who "like the leaves at one time flame into life and eat the fruit of the earth, at another time miserably die" (464-66); accordingly, he and Poseidon should leave the fighting to the mortals. His words show the wisdom, the safe-mindedness (*sophrosyne*) for which Apollo was famous; and we are reminded of what Scamander said when he was giving up his fight with Hephaestus (360) and of what Hera said when she ordered Hephaestus to stop (379-80). The indifference of the gods to human beings is the counterpart of their pity for them. Apollo adds as an excuse for not fighting Poseidon that it would be wrong to contend with his father's brother. Again the pro-Achaean god is the winner, though Apollo, unlike Aphrodite, Ares, and Atrtemis, is left with his dignity. When his sister Artemis sees what Apollo is doing, she upbraids him, calling him foolish (*neputie*, 474), as Poseidon has done. Apollo must not again boast in the palace of Zeus that he will fight with Poseidon. Then Hera addresses Artemis angrily. How do you dare to oppose me? (They were matched to fight each other at the beginning of Book 20.) She takes Artemis' bow and boxes her ears with it. Artemis flees, crying, like a dove fleeing from a hawk into a cleft in a rock (493-95, simile type 4), and leaves her bow and arrows behind on the ground (compare the discomfiture of Aphrodite in the earlier sequence). Then Hermes excuses himself from fighting Leto because she is a wife of Zeus; she can boast that she has beaten him. And so Leto gathers up the bow and arrows of her daughter and takes them off to Olympus, where Artemis, still crying, has arrived at the knees of Zeus. Zeus, laughing, asks what has happened. Which of the gods has hurt her? Your contentious wife, she tells him. This scene in heaven reminds us of the scenes on Olympus in Book 5 with which Diomedes' woundings of Aphrodite and Ares were brought to an end.

Achilles Routs the Trojans and Threatens Troy, 514-611

Meanwhile Apollo has gone to Troy in order that the Achaeans may not destroy it on this day (515-16)—an example of *prooikonomia*, as schol. T remark, for Apollo will do what he can to protect his city. As for the other gods, they have returned to Olympus, the pro-Trojan gods in anger, the pro-Achaean gods in glory. The battle between the gods has shown that Troy lacks effective long-term divine support.

Now Achilles' attack on the Trojans is compared to a fire destroying a city (522-25, simile type 3: the hero's attack); and Priam descends from the tower on the wall to urge the gate-guards to open the gate. As soon as the Trojans are safely within, they should shut it to keep out Achilles. The gate-guards obey, and Apollo leaps forth to protect the Trojans.

Then the Achaeans would have taken Troy if Apollo had not inspired Agenor to oppose Achilles. Agenor, in a soliloquy, asks himself whether to flee with the others or to head for Mount Ida alone; in either case Achilles seems likely to kill him. He decides to make a stand, for Achilles, though Zeus is now giving him victory, is mortal like himself. Agenor's spirit is compared to that of a fearless leopardess confronting a hunter and his dogs (573-78, simile type 7: resistance). He taunts Achilles.

> No doubt you thought in your heart, glorious Achilles,
> that you on this day would destroy the proud city of Troy.
> Fool (*neputi'*), you must still endure many sufferings over it,
> for we, its many defenders, are valiant men,
> the protectors of Troy, and here you will meet your fate
> no matter how terrible and bold a fighter you are.   (583-89)

This speech, as Scheibner 1939.110 has seen, seems more like a boast after victory than a challenge before combat. Agenor hurls his spear, which bounces off one of Achilles' shinguards. Then Achilles moves to respond, but Apollo intervenes by carrying off Agenor in a cloud of invisibility and tricking Achilles by taking the form of Agenor. While Achilles is chasing after him, the Trojans escape into Troy. This is the purpose of Apollo's trickery. Only Hector, as we learn at the beginning of the next book, remains outside.

Owen 1946.214 has asked why Apollo does not take the form of Agenor at once instead of inspiring him to face Achilles, and suggests that this "has something to do with the soliloquy of Agenor (552-570) as a kind of preparatory attuning of the ear to the soliloquy of Hector a few lines further on [in the next book]." Similarly Fenik 1978.80 has described the Agenor-Achilles scene as an "anticipatory doublet" of the Hector-Achilles encounter in the next book. Hector, like Agenor, will debate with himself what he should do and will decide to face Achilles; and his dying speech, like Agenor's taunt to Achilles before their combat, will predict the death of Achilles. But Achilles will slay Hector. That is the big difference between the two episodes. Apollo, who has saved Agenor, will desert Hector.

BOOK 22: THE DEATH OF HECTOR

The Stage Is Set, 1-130

Three speeches by Priam, Hecuba, and Hector at the beginning and three speeches by Priam, Hecuba, and Andromache at the end, "the third speech in each case being the most affecting," surround the central main action, the narrative of Hector's encounter with Achilles. Thus Willcock 1984.291 well describes the structure of this book.

It begins by summarizing and developing the situation at the end of the last book. The Trojans have fled like fawns (1, simile type 4) into the city, but a baleful fate keeps Hector outside; and Apollo, in a "mocking tone" (Edwards 1987.291), reveals himself to Achilles. Achilles makes a rude reply and, with the swiftness of a proud race horse (22-23, simile type 2), resumes his attack on the city.

Hector, his only opponent, is standing before the Scaean Gate, on the tower above which are Priam and Hecuba. Priam sees Achilles approaching like the bright and baleful star Sirius (26-31, simile type 1), and begs Hector to come inside.

> Hector, my child, I beg you, don't wait for this man
> alone by yourself or else you'll soon meet your end
> at Achilles' hands since he is much stronger than you,
> a hard-hearted man. I wish the gods liked him as much
> as I do; soon the dogs and vultures would eat him
> unburied, and I'd find relief from my terrible grief (*achos*).
> He has bereft me of many good sons.   (38-44)

Priam goes on to say that he does not now see Lycaon and Polydorus within the safety of Troy and that he will ransom them if they are captives but that if they are dead there will be only pain for him and Hecuba. Thus he foreshadows his ransoming of Hector's body. We of course know that Achilles has slain Lycaon at 21.34ff. and Polydorus at 20.407ff. Then Priam adds that the only thing that could bring such bereavement upon the rest of the Trojans is the death of Hector, and he begs him to come within the safety of the walls in order to save them. He ends by calling on Hector to pity (*eleeson*, 59) himself, who will be destroyed in his old age after he has witnessed the slaying of his sons and the carrying off of his daughters—one thinks of Cassandra and also Andromache; he himself will be slain and stripped naked by the enemy and left to be eaten by his own dogs, a pitiable sight.

> So spoke the old man as he pulled the white hair from his head,
> tearing it, but didn't persuade the spirit of Hector.   (77-78)

Then Hecuba, holding up her breast and begging Hector to pity (*eleeson*, 81) her, says that if he remains outside Achilles will kill him, and she and Andromache will not be able to mourn over him, but dogs at the ships will devour his body. (Note that Hecuba pleas for pity, just as Priam did; and compare Andromache's plea for pity on herself at the end of Book 6).

There follows a summary statement of the effect that the pleas of his parents have on Hector.

> Thus they in tears addressed their dear son, imploring him
> earnestly, but didn't persuade the spirit of Hector.   (90-91)

Line 91, which repeats the thought of line 78 about the futility of Priam's plea, rounds off these introductory speeches by emphasizing Hector's determination, before we turn to a consideration of his state of mind as Achilles approaches. Comparable will be the summary statements of effect that will follow the laments of Priam, Hecuba, and Andromache after the combat.

Hector is waiting for Achilles like a poisonous snake circling its hole (93-95, simile type 7: resistance); the snake's position corresponds to Hector's in front of the Scaean Gate (so Ameis-Hentze on 22.93). Then, propping his shield against the tower of the gate, he speaks a soliloquy revealing his inner turmoil. He is unable to go within the walls because Polydamas will reproach him for not obeying his advice (at 18.249ff.) In his blindness of mind he has destroyed his people, and it will be better to die at the hands of Achilles than to be taunted with this. He realizes that begging Achilles for mercy will do no good; one should not try to speak with him as a lovesick youth to a girl. This of course is true: it is useless to plea with Achilles. We are reminded of what Aeneas said in his challenge to him at 20.251-55: they should not continue to bandy words like women quarreling in the street.

Chase and Combat, 131-404

There are two phases in the narrative of Hector's encounter with Achilles: the chase (131-213) and the combat (214-404). The chase, which prepares us for

Hector's death and Athena's role in bringing it about, can be divided into two parallel parts (a climactic parallelism). The first consists of fifty-eight lines (131-187). When Hector sees Achilles advancing against him like Enyalius (an epithet of Ares, 132, simile type 2), brandishing his terrible spear, his armor blazing like a great fire or the rising sun (134-35, simile type 1), he flees—a shock to the audience, coming "as suddenly as fear overwhelmed Hector" (Edwards 1987.295). The preceding section has impressed upon us his determination to make a stand, but the terrifying sight of Achilles is too much for him. Achilles chases after him like a hawk, the swiftest of birds, swooping upon a dove (139-42, simile type 4: flight and pursuit). They pass the look-out spot and the fig tree, keeping to the path around the walls, and come to the springs, one hot, the other cold, which are described at some length. This is no ordinary footrace, for the prize is Hector's life. They run around the city three times, like race horses (162-64, another type 4 simile). The gods are looking on, and Zeus, seeing and pitying Hector (*ophthalmoisin horomai, emon d' olophuretai etor*, 169), wants to save him. We should compare 16.435-38 where he wanted to save Sarpedon.

There are clear parallels between the deaths of Sarpedon and Hector, and, even more, between the deaths of Patroclus and Hector. In Book 16 Zeus considered having Patroclus die in the battle over Sarpedon's body but decided to let this happen soon afterwards at the wall of Troy, and Patroclus' death of course has led to Hector's in the present book. Kirk 1976.209-17 (see our comments on Book 16) treats the death of Sarpedon as the first step in the buildup to the climax of Hector's death. Hector's death-scene is longer and more complex than Patroclus', as Patroclus' was than Sarpedon's.

Now Athena uses the same words to oppose Zeus as Hera did in the case of Sarpedon.

> O most awesome son of Cronus, what are you saying?
> Do you want to bring back from ill-omened death
> a man who is mortal, one long fated to die?
> Do it, but we other gods won't all be applauding.   (178-81=16.441-43)

Zeus answers by saying that he has not spoken in complete seriousness (*thumo prophroni*, 183-84; compare his use of the same expression to Athena at 8.39-40); that is, in spite of his grief over the death of Hector, he does not really intend to go against fate and save him (so Erbse 1986.288). Accordingly, she may do as she wishes, and so she darts down from Olympus.

The second, shorter (twenty-six lines, 188-213) but climactic part of the chase opens with Achilles pursuing Hector like a dog running after a fawn (189-92, simile type 4; compare, in the earlier part, the simile of the hawk attacking a dove). At the center of this second description is another type 4 simile describing the frustration of both men.

> As in a dream one fails in pursuing another,
> one is unable to catch up, the other to flee,
> so this one failed in pursuit, that one in escape.   (199-201)

Before this simile (with which we can compare the horse-racing simile in the first part) Achilles prevents Hector from getting near the walls where the onlooking Trojans could help him by hurling missiles from above; and after it he signals to the Achaeans not to interfere, thus making them onlookers too, for he wants the glory all to himself. That Hector is able to keep ahead of Achilles seems unbelievable, but Apollo is supporting him for the last time—until Zeus decides to abandon him.

> But when they came again to the springs for the fourth time,
> then Zeus Father took up and held out his golden scales,
> and put in the pans two fates of woe-bringing death,
> that of Achilles and that of horse-taming Hector,
> and balanced the pans, and the day of Hector sank
> and passed down to Hades, and Phoebus Apollo left him   (208-13)

This is probably the beginning of the fourth circuit (so Leaf II.445) and therefore takes place at the same time as the earlier scene on Olympus, which occurred at the completion of the third circuit.

This synchronization is further emphasized by the fact that Athena, who left Olympus at the end of the first part, now arrives on the battlefield and goes to Achilles (214-15). And thus the narrative of the combat begins. She tells him that Hector can no longer escape his death, no matter how abjectly Apollo may grovel before Zeus, and that he should relax while she persuades Hector to fight. Accordingly, Achilles stops running and rests on his spear; we will not worry about him during Athena's conversation with Hector.

Taking the form of Deiphobus, Hector's dearest brother, she tells him that she will help him against Achilles. Hector is overcome by Deiphobus' concern for him, and Deiphobus-Athena claims to be motivated by grief (*penthos*, 242), apparently over the likely death of Hector. This seems diabolical.

Thus Achilles and Hector advance against each other. Hector speaks first, saying that now he will make a stand, but asking Achilles to swear with him that the winner will return the body of the loser for proper burial. Achilles, scowling in anger, replies that there can be no agreement between them, no more than between lions and men or wolves and lambs; Hector must fight now, and Athena will immediately subdue him under his spear.

> Now you shall pay for all the sorrows over
> my comrades whom you rushed to slay with your spear.   (271-72)

So speaking, he lets go with his spear. Hector ducks and the spear flies over him and sticks in the earth, but Athena gives it back to Achilles, unnoticed by Hector. Hector replies that Achilles has spoken only to frighten him, and that now it is his turn to try to dodge. His blow bounces off the center of Achilles' shield (compare how, at the end of the last book, Agenor's spear bounced off Achilles' shinguard— a sign of the futility of opposing Achilles; this is another way in which the Agenor-Achilles encounter can be thought of as an anticipatory doublet of the present one). Hector is angered and completely frustrated. He calls on Deiphobus for another spear, but Deiphobus is not there. And so Hector realizes that "the gods are summoning me to death" (297=16.693, of Patroclus; the poet makes increasingly clear the parallels with the slaying of Patroclus). He draws his sword and swoops upon Achilles like an eagle upon a lamb or a rabbit (308-10, simile type 5: the victor and his victim). Achilles, in his Hephaestus-made armor, the point of his spear shining like Hesperus, the most beautiful star (317-18, simile type 1), rushes to meet him. Finding an opening in his armor between the neck and shoulder, where death is swiftest, he drives the point through but without cutting the windpipe— thus leaving Hector the ability still to speak; Hector, Patroclus and Sarpedon are the only heroes in the *Iliad* who make dying speeches.

Achilles boasts:

> Hector, I suppose you imagined that having slain Patroclus
> you would be safe and thought not of me in my absence,
> fool (*nepie*), for I his companion, a much better fighter,
> I was left there behind at the hollow ships
> and now have loosed your legs. The dogs and birds will
> tear you hideously; he will be properly buried.   (331-36)

Hector, as he dies, begs Achilles not to give his corpse to the dogs but to accept the ransom which his father and mother will give. But Achilles, scowling, answers that this will never happen.

> Not even if ten times or twenty times so much payment
> they bring and weigh out and promise to add more beside,
> not even if Dardanian Priam command that you
> yourself be weighed out in gold, will your queenly mother
> arrange your bier and bewail you, the child whom she bore,
> but the dogs and the birds will devour you completely.   (349 -54)

These words are "designedly similar" (Macleod 1982.20) to Achilles' rejection, at 9.379-87, of Agammemnon's offer of reconciliation; the rejections of these supplications are features of the climactic parallel between the wrath and the vengeance. Here the offer and refusal also again foreshadow the ransoming of Hector's body.

Hector says that he could see from Achilles' face that his request was not to be granted, and then predicts Achilles' death, as Patroclus had predicted his.

> Take heed lest I bring on you the wrath of the gods
> on that day when Paris and Phoebus Apollo
> destroy you at the Scaean Gate in spite of your valor.   (358-60)

So saying, he dies.

> When he had spoken thus, the end of death covered him,
> his soul fleeing his limbs went down to Hades,
> bemoaning his fate, leaving his manhood and youth.   (361-63)

The same lines were used of Patroclus (16.855-57); and the first was used to introduce the passage in which the soul of Sarpedon was described as leaving his body.

Achilles answers that he is ready to die whenever Zeus and the other gods decide it should happen. Then he extracts his spear and strips off Hector's armor. The other Achaeans are amazed at how large and handsome Hector is, and each of them stabs him. At first Achilles says that since the gods have allowed him to slay Hector they should attack the city to see if the Trojans will not abandon it, but his grief over Patroclus is more important to him than the glory of taking Troy. Now they must return to the ships with the body of Hector, singing a paean of victory.

> So he spoke, and devising unseemly deeds against Hector
> pierced the tendons of both his feet from behind,
> from heel to ankle, and to them attached strips of hide
> and bound them to his chariot, leaving the head to drag.
> Then taking the glorious armor and mounting the chariot
> he whipped up the horses to run. They eagerly flew,
> and dust arose from the dragging, Hector's black hair
> being spread on the ground, his head lying all in the dust,
> that head once so handsome. Now Zeus had allowed his enemies
> to treat him outrageously even in his own native land.   (395-404)

We should compare the passage at the end of Book 16 in which Achilles' helmet, undirtied so long as it covered his handsome head, was bloodied and rolled off into the dust when Apollo struck Patroclus; then "Zeus gave it to Hector to wear on his head since death was imminent for him" (799-800).

The Laments for Hector, 405-515

The scene shifts to the walls, and we are given a summary picture (405-11) of the grief of Hecuba and Priam. She throws off her headdress and shrieks, he wails pitiably; and throughout the city the people respond, the women shrieking, the men wailing. Then a concluding simile: it was as if Troy had fallen and was being consumed by fire (compare the simile at 21.520-25). The death of Hector means and symbolizes the fall of Troy.

Now the people are restraining Priam who, grief-stricken, is eager to go out of the gate. This scene looks forward to Book 24. He rolls in the dust and insists on being allowed to try to ransom Hector's body. He will ask Achilles, monstrous man that he is, to pity his old age, reminding him of his own old father. He grieves for Hector more than for any of his many sons whom Achilles has slain. How he wishes Hector had died in his arms, and he and Hecuba could have had their fill of weeping over him.

> Thus he spoke, weeping, and the citizens [the men] groaned in response;
> and Hecuba led the women in sobbing lament.   (430-31)

She asks why she should live, now that Hector is dead, who was the protector of Troy, to whom the Trojans looked as to a god.

> So she spoke weeping, but his wife [Andromache] knew nothing yet
> about Hector, for no true messenger had come to her
> to report that her husband was staying outside the gate,
> but she was weaving at the loom far back in their high house
> a garment twofold and purple and covered with patterns,
> and was commanding her lovely-haired maids at home
> to set on the fire a great tripod cauldron, that there
> might be warm water for Hector returning from battle,
> poor fool (*nepie*), not knowing that very far off from washings
> gray-eyed Athena had helped Achilles to slay him.
> But now she heard from the gate the shrieking and wailing,
> her knees were shaking, the shuttle fell from her hand.   (437-48)

Line 437 begins "Thus she [Hecuba] spoke weeping" and, in keeping with formular usage, might have been continued with "and the women moaned in response." But instead the poet shifts our attention to Andromache. He will not give us the expected line—the last line of this book—until after Andromache has made her lament.

At 6.497-502 Andromache returned home to her weaving and set her maids to lament for Hector. Now the poet takes us back to that pathetic scene, and also to the beginning of the present book, for we are informed (438-39) that no messenger has reported to Andromache that Hector has stayed outside the walls. Moreover, we remember how Priam's earlier speech put us in mind of the fate of Andromache and Astyanax, and how Hecuba in her earlier speech said that if Hector should be slain she and Andromache would be unable to give him proper burial. The poet has been building up to Andromache's learning of Hector's death, as he did to Achilles' learning of Patroclus'.

Now, having heard the shrieking of Hecuba, she suspects that Achilles has slain Hector and rushes like a maenad to the tower, just as she did at 6.407. She sees Hector, as we last saw him, being dragged to the ships, and faints, throwing off her elaborate headdress, whose parts are enumerated (to concentrate our attention on the moment); the headband was Aphrodite's present to her when Hector brought her home as his bride. The sisters of Hector and his brother's wives catch her. When she has regained consciousness, she loudly laments among the Trojan women.

Her long speech (477-514) has been compared with the one she made to Hector in Book 6 (see Lohmann 1970.99). She equates her fate with Hector's. He has died, she is left to hateful grief, a widow. Hector will not help their son, nor will their son help him (that is, rescue his body and avenge him). Even if their son survives the war, he will still have to bear suffering and hardship. No one likes an orphan.

> Now without any father there'll be great suffering
> for Astyanax [Lord of the City]—this is the name the Trojans gave him,
> for you alone protected their high walls and gate.
> But now by the beaked ships, far away from your parents
> dogs will devour you, wriggling worms will finish what's left
> of you lying there naked. Clothes you have in your palace,
> clothes finely woven and lovely, the handwork of women,
> but these I shall all burn up in the flaming fire—
> they're of no use to you, you won't be lying in them—
> a glory for the Trojans and the Trojan women to tell of.   (505-14)

Thus she ends by making us think of the burial of Hector. And then, finally, comes the formulaic line, the first part of which appeared at the end of Hecuba's lament.

> So she spoke weeping, and the women moaned in response.   (515)

Now we are ready to turn to something new.

The slaying of Hector is often said to be the climax of the *Iliad*. It is the event toward which the action has been moving since the death of Patroclus and for which the poet has been planning since the farewell scene between Hector and Andromache; and we have seen how it is treated as a climactic parallel to the slaying of Patroclus. Moreover, the single combat between Achilles and Hector is the last depiction of heroism in this heroic epic; and it is the high point in the *aristeia* of Achilles, as the slaying of the hero's main opponent is in any *aristeia*. Nevertheless, the unburied body of Hector leaves us with an unresolved problem and a feeling of dissatisfaction. An *aristeia* usually ends with a fight over the body in which the hero is denied possession of it, a motif, as Krischer 1971.28 has pointed out, which shows that the gods care for the dead, and for which in the case of Hector the ransoming of his body in Book 24 stands as a substitute. We have several times noted anticipations of the ransoming in the present book. Hector is a very sympathetic character who has met his death bravely, overpowered by the much stronger Achilles helped by Athena; and the poet's critical comment (395) on Achilles' mistreatment of Hector's body seems to show that he and his pro-Achaean audience felt that this was wrong. Achilles is going too far in his vengeance just as he went too far in his wrath. But Achilles, we can believe, is the poet's favorite character; he is certainly the central and most complex character in the *Iliad*. Thus his victory over Hector in the present book requires the even greater climax of the scene between him and Priam in Book 24 where he will show himself capable of a universal pity.

BOOK 23: THE FUNERAL OF PATROCLUS

Rites, 1-256

It seems likely that this book about the funeral of Patroclus is indebted to earlier poetry about the funeral of Achilles, but it is difficult to be certain because our knowledge of Achilles' funeral comes from later sources. The earliest and most important of these sources is the last book of the *Odyssey*, which probably reflects pre-Homeric poetry about Achilles' funeral while at the same time showing the influence of the present book of the *Iliad* (so Heubeck 1986.337-46). The scene in the *Odyssey* passage is in the Underworld; and the soul of Achilles (accompanied by the souls of Patroclus, Antilochus, and the big Ajax) and the soul of Agamemnon (accompanied by those who were murdered with him) are comparing their fates. Achilles pities Agamemnon for having been murdered by his wife and her lover at home, and for not having died at Troy and been buried with full honors by the Achaeans there (as Achilles had been). Agamemnon responds as follows (I give his long speech in full because of its importance for our discussion):

> Son of Peleus, godlike Achilles, blessed were you
> to die at Troy far off from Argos. Around you
> the best of the Trojans and Achaeans died fighting
> over your body, as you in the whirling dust lay
> a huge figure stretched out forgetful of chariot and horse.
> We fought for the whole day and never would have cease from battle
> if Zeus hadn't caused us to stop by sending a great storm.
> We brought you to the area of the ships from the turmoil of battle
> and put you upon a bier, your beautiful skin
> cleansed with warm water and ointment; around you the Danaans
> were shedding hot tears and cutting their hair in your honor.
> On hearing the news your mother and the divine sea-maidens
> came from the sea. We heard them crossing the water,
> their wailing immortal, and fear seized every Achaean.
> We would have leaped up and fled to the hollow ships
> if we had not been restrained by the wise and experienced
> Nestor, whose plans had proved best on earlier occasions.
> He, advising us wisely, spoke and addressed us:
> Stay, Argives, stay, sons of the Achaeans, don't flee;
> his mother with her sisters, the divine sea-maidens, has come here

out of the sea to be with him, her son who has died.
So saying, he kept us, the great-souled Achaeans, from fear.
The daughters of the old man of the sea, piteously wailing,
surrounded you and put divine clothing over your body.
And the Muses, all nine, responding with beautiful voices,
were singing the dirge; you wouldn't have seen one tearless
Achaean, so piercing-sweet was the song of the Muses.
For seventeen days and nights we were weeping for you,
the gods immortal and mortal men, and then,
on the eighteenth, we consigned you to fire, slaying around you
many well-fatted sheep and well-horned oxen.
You were burned in the clothes of the gods with much ointment
and sweet honey, and as you were burning many Achaean
heroes paraded in armor around your pyre
on foot and in chariot, creating a very great noise.
But when the fire had consumed you, the flame of Hephaestus,
at dawn, Achilles, we gathered your white bones up
in unmixed wine and ointment. Your mother produced
a golden amphora, the gift of Dionysus,
she said, and the work of far-famed Hephaestus.
In it, glorious Achilles, your white bones lie
and those of the dead Patroclus, the son of Menoetius;
separate are those of Antilochus, whom above all
your companions you honored after the dead Patroclus.
We, the strong army of Argive spearmen, heaped over you
a great and perfect funeral mound as your tomb
there on a jutting promontory of the broad Hellespont
so that men far out on the sea might behold it,
both those now living and those to be born in the future.
Your mother, who had got from the gods very beautiful prizes,
set them in our midst for the best Achaeans to win.
You yourself have gone to the funeral of many a man,
many a hero, when, a king having died,
the young men gird up their loins to vie for the prizes,
but if you'd seen those, the very beautiful prizes
the goddess silver-foot Thetis offered for you,
you'd have been most amazed; so much were you loved by the gods.

Thus your name is not lost, not even in death,
but always, Achilles, your good fame will be among all men.
For me there was no such sweetness on completing the war,
for on my return Zeus devised my grievous destruction
at the hands of Aegisthus with the help of my accursed wife.

patroklos

(*Odyssey* 24.36-97)

The part about Patroclus may well come from the present book of the *Iliad* in which Achilles gives instructions that he is to be buried in the same urn as Patroclus; but the part about Antilochus may show the influence of pre-Homeric poetry. We know, from later reports, that Antilochus played a key role in the events leading up to Achilles' death: while trying to protect his father Nestor, he was slain by Memnon; then Achilles slew Memnon in vengeance and, soon afterwards, was slain himself by Paris and Apollo. Some scholars believe (and I am inclined to agree) that the role of Patroclus in the *Iliad* has been modeled on that of Antilochus in pre-Homeric poetry. In each case Achilles is aroused to avenge the death of a dear friend. Moreover, Antilochus in the *Iliad* stands closely in the shadow of Patroclus. He is the one who brings Achilles news of Patroclus' death. In the games in the present book we shall see that Achilles is especially fond of him, as he was of Patroclus. Antilochus is a very likable, amusing young man.

Another point at which pre-Homeric poetry, as reflected in Agamemnon's speech, may have influenced the *Iliad* is the role of Thetis and her sister Nereids at Achilles' funeral. We have already seen this in the description in Book 18 of how they come out of the sea to mourn the death of Achilles while he is mourning over Patroclus. In the present book Thetis will begin the mourning over Patroclus. This seems odd, and Kakridis 1949.84 has plausibly suggested that it shows the influence of an earlier account of Achilles' funeral.

Some of the similarities between the present book and Agamemnon's speech in the *Odyssey* may be due simply to the fact that both are describing the funeral of a great man, for it was no doubt typical on such an occasion to perform certain ceremonies and have games at which wonderful prizes were given. But it seems hard to deny that pre-Homeric poetry about the funeral of Achilles has influenced the description of Patroclus' funeral. We shall find another possible influence in the passage on how Iris summons the winds to cause the pyre of Patroclus to burn.

At the beginning of Book 23, the Achaeans having arrived in camp, Achilles, while the others disperse to their huts, has the Myrmidons remain to do honor to Patroclus. He leads them in their chariots around the body (now lying outside the hut; contrast 19.211 where it was left inside) while Thetis stirs up the desire of lamentation among them. Achilles tells Patroclus that now, in anger (*cholotheis*, 23) over his slaying, he is fulfilling his promise to give the body of Hector to the dogs and to cut the throats of twelve Trojan youths. Then, "devising unseemly deeds" (24), he dishonors Hector's body by stretching it face down in the dust beside the bier of Patroclus. The Myrmidons take off their armor, unharness their horses, and sit down by the ship of Achilles; and he gives them a funeral meal, the preparations for which are described in detail.

But the Achaean leaders come and take Achilles to Agamemnon's hut to eat. On arriving, they try without success to persuade him to wash. He will not wash until he has performed the funeral of Patroclus—cut off his own hair, burned the body, and built up a funeral mound—for he will never have a second such grief (*achos*, 47). But now they—he includes himself—should "yield to this hateful need to eat" (48) and tomorrow Agamemnon should

> dispatch the men to bring in sufficient wood
> for burning the corpse, for sending it into the darkness,
> that weariless fire may consume it quickly, making it
> vanish, and then the army may get back to work.   (50-53)

This speech is programmatic for the events of the present book. The supper which Achilles is now willing to eat is the meal of reconciliation between himself and Agamemnon mentioned in Book 19 (so Edwards 1987.302); we are reminded of his earlier refusal to eat.

After the meal, he returns to the Myrmidons and lies down among them to sleep on the seashore. Their position around him is preparation (*prooikonomia*) for their answering his lament when he awakes from his dream of Patroclus. The soul of Patroclus, coming to him in his sleep, complains of neglect and begs that his body be buried immediately and that Achilles now for the last time give him his hand; soon Achilles too will die under the walls of Troy, and then their bones should be buried together. Achilles is eager to carry out these requests, and asks the soul of Patroclus to come near, but as he reaches out his arms it goes under the earth like smoke, gibbering. Achilles leaps up and claps his hands in amazement. Alas, he says, speaking to the Myrmidons, the dead do live on, but only as breath and image, for the soul of Patroclus, weeping and wailing, has stood over him during the night telling him what to do. They lament until dawn, when Agamemnon sends men and mules to bring in wood for the pyre.

There is a detailed description of the bringing in of the wood. They set it down in the place Achilles has appointed for the burial mound. Then Achilles commands the Myrmidons to put on their armor and harness their horses for the funeral procession. The chariots go first, followed by the men on foot; in their midst Patroclus' close companions are carrying his body, which they have covered with their shorn hair. Achilles is walking behind the bier, holding the head of Patroclus and grieving (*achnumenos*, 137). When they arrive where the others are gathered, the Myrmidons begin to pile up the wood.

Then Achilles, cutting a lock of his hair and looking across the sea to his homeland, addresses the Spercheius River, saying that his father had vowed this lock to the Spercheius along with many sacrificial victims on condition that Achilles should return from Troy. Now, since he is not going home, Achilles will give it to Patroclus. Thus he stirs them all to lament, and they would have continued to mourn until sunset if Achilles had not told Agamemnon to send the army away to take their evening meal. The Myrmidons, he says, and the leaders should stay to bury Patroclus. Accordingly, Agamemnon sees to the dismissal of the rest of the army.

The Myrmidons build a pyre a hundred feet square and place the corpse in the center. Then they slaughter many sheep and oxen, and Achilles covers the body with fat and puts the sacrificed victims around it as well as jars of honey and ointment, and slays four horses and two of Patroclus' nine house dogs. He also slays the twelve Trojan youths. "He devised bad deeds in his mind" (176). Does this show the moral disapproval of the poet? I think so, with Ameis-Hentze and Willcock 1984.300 against Leaf II.484 and de Jong 1987.138.

Then, setting fire to the pyre, Achilles shouts to Patroclus that he has fulfilled his promise to sacrifice the twelve Trojan youths, and that he is giving the body of Hector to the dogs to eat.

> Thus he spoke threatening, but the dogs didn't come to this meal,
> for the daughter of Zeus, Aphrodite, warded them off
> night and day, and by anointing the body with olive oil,
> rose-scented, she kept it, when dragged, from being torn.
> And Phoebus Apollo sent Hector the gift of a dark cloud
> out of the sky to the plain and covered completely
> the place where his corpse lay, that the strength of the sun might not wither
> the skin on his sinews and limbs before he was buried.   (184-91)

Just as the body of Patroclus was preserved by Thetis until Achilles slew Hector, so the body of Hector will be protected by the gods until it is ransomed by Priam.

But now Achilles is faced with the unexpected problem that the pyre does not catch fire. His solution is to pray for the aid of the winds Boreas and Zephyrus. Iris, the messenger goddess, takes his prayer to where the winds are feasting in the house of Zephyrus. She stands on the threshold, and they rise to greet her, each of them offering her a seat next to himself, but she refuses, saying (a false excuse) that she must return to a feast among the Aethiopians; then she reports the prayer of Achilles. On her departure Boreas and Zephyrus come over the water tumultuously and fall upon the pyre, causing it to burn.

This scene increases the grandeur of Patroclus' funeral, but it comes unexpectedly; and the role of Iris, which adds a note of charm, even humor, in contrast to the prevalent mood of mourning, is unmotivated. Perhaps Kakridis 1949.75-83 is right in supposing that an earlier description of Achilles' funeral has influenced the narrative. According to Quintus Smyrnaeus, *Posthomerica* 699ff. (though a much later source, it may reflect pre-Homeric poetry), Zeus sent Hermes to summon the winds for Achilles' funeral. Kakridis suggests that the winds were staying away because they were the sons of the Dawn (according to Hesiod, *Theogony* 378ff.) and so brothers of Memnon, whom Achilles had slain shortly before being slain himself. Thus the absence of the winds at Achilles' funeral and Hermes role in summoning them—both well motivated actions—may have been the model for the unmotivated absence of the winds at Patroclus' funeral and Iris' unmotivated role in summoning them.

The winds howl all night while Achilles pours libations of wine, sobbing like a father who has lost his son. At dawn, when the fire has burnt out, he lies down to sleep. Then, as at the beginning of the previous day, Agamemnon and the others arrive (233; apparently the whole army, which is present at 258). Their coming wakes Achilles. He orders Agamemnon and the leaders to quench the fire with wine, gather the bones of Patroclus into a golden bowl, bury it in the center of the pyre, and heap a small circular mound over it. (I follow the interpretation of Petropoulou 1988). Later (outside the action of the *Iliad*) they must disinter the bones of Patroclus and put them with those of Achilles in a golden urn (larger than the bowl), and bury it in the same place, making the mound much broader and higher. Thus Patroclus is buried.

Games, 257-897

The transition to the games is somewhat abrupt, but they were probably a part of Achilles' funeral in pre-Homeric poetry, as reflected in Agamemnon's speech in the *Odyssey*, and were at any rate an expected feature in the funeral of any great man. Willcock 1973 has pointed out that certain passages seem to foreshadow events that lie outside the action of the *Iliad* and so seem to be influenced by them: the wrestling match between Odysseus and the big Ajax seems to look forward to their later contest for the armor of Achilles (offered as a prize by Thetis after the other games at Achilles' funeral, according to Quintus Smyrnaeus, *Posthomerica* 5.1ff.), and Achilles' growing affection for Antilochus seems to show the poet's knowledge of how later Achilles was grieved at Antilochus' death and avenged him by slaying Memnon.

The games set a new tone, one of joy and laughter, and show us the Achaean leaders again for the last time as the characters we have come to know. For instance, Diomedes is a natural winner and the big Ajax always comes in second (so Willcock 1973.3-4). The description of the different contests—especially the chariot race—is very true to life. We are often given a feeling of suspense. This was true on the battlefield too, but there we knew whom we favored. Whom shall we favor now when all the contestants are Achaeans, our friends? To whom will the gods give the victory?

The first and most important contest—it is much longer than any of the others—is the two-horse chariot race. Achilles, who introduces each contest and names the prizes, says that he could win the chariot race, for his are the immortal horses Poseidon gave to Peleus as a wedding gift, but now they are mourning for their lost charioteer. Accordingly, the others should enter.

Eumelus (known to us elsewhere in the *Iliad* only from the Achaean Catalogue in Book 2 where he is listed as a leader of the contingent from Pherae and Iolcus, 711-15, and as having the best horses with the exception of Achilles', 763-77), Diomedes, Menelaus, Antilochus, and Meriones step forward. They are introduced in such a way as to prepare us for their performances. Eumelus is praised for his skill as a charioteer. Diomedes is driving the horses of Tros (captured at 5.432ff. from Aeneas, whom Apollo saved; Apollo will show his hostility to Diomedes in the present race). Menelaus is driving his own horse and Agamemnon's mare Aithe. The youthful Antilochus, on whom the poet concentrates our attention, is told in a lengthy speech by his father Nestor that he can win only by skill since his horses, which are Nestor's, are the slowest (an exaggeration in view of the poet's comment at 530 that Meriones' horses are slowest). Finally, the last contestant, Meriones, is said to have horses with beautiful manes, a description which will not be belied by their poor performance.

Nestor, in his instructions to Antilochus, tells him that he must try to gain the advantage at the turning post. This has bothered scholars because, as it turns out, Antilochus actually gains the advantage in the home stretch. But, as Roisman 1988.119-20 has pointed out, the poet thus shows his inventiveness. Nestor's speech, by putting before us what usually happens, contributes to our delight in what happens unexpectedly; the element of the unexpected helps to create the feeling of reality about this race.

When the contestants have mounted their chariots, Achilles tosses their lots in a helmet to see in which order they should line up. Antilochus gets the best position (the inside track), Eumelus the next best, then Menelaus, Meriones, and finally Diomedes. Thus, all other things being equal, Antilochus should come in first and Diomedes last, but, as Willcock 1973.4 remarks, Diomedes' natural superiority, which we have come to know in the *Iliad*, makes it "in truth unthinkable that he should not come first in the chariot race; and thus we are fully prepared for his win, and would be surprised and disturbed by any other result."

Then Achilles points out the turning post and has Phoenix sit by it to report how the chariots round it. Again we see the importance of the turning post in chariot races, though not, as it will turn out, in this one.

After a general picture of the beginning of the race (362-72), we reach the decisive moment in the home stretch. Eumelus' horses are out in front, but Diomedes' would have passed them if Apollo, showing his anger toward Diomedes, had not struck his whip from his hands. Then Athena gives Diomedes back his whip and causes Eumelus' chariot to wreck. Diomedes swerves and gets out in front, and Athena puts strength in his horses and gives him the glory (399-400); in other words, he will win first prize. We are left in no doubt about this as we turn to the others.

Antilochus is behind Menelaus. He tells his horses, in a humorous speech, that it will be shameful to be beaten by Aithe, a mare, and that Nestor will kill them if they lose from not trying; he will look for a place in which to pass. His horses pick up speed, and in a narrow place he swerves to pass Menelaus. Menelaus shouts that Antilochus is driving like a mad man, and that the Achaeans were wrong to call him discerning (*pepnusthai*, 440); he will have to swear to have won fairly. Then, addressing his horses (a parallel with Antilochus' much longer speech to his; this creates a sense of competition, as in speeches before a duel), Menelaus tells them not to let Antilochus' pair, who are older and more apt to tire, put them to shame. We are thus left in suspense as to how this conflict—one of several in this book—will be resolved as we switch to the spectators.

Idomeneus is the first to see the racers. He thinks that Diomedes is out in front, and that the mares of Eumelus are not yet in view, but he is not certain. At this the little Ajax calls him a babbler, saying that he has the poor eyesight of a middle aged man, and claiming that the mares of Eumelus are still out in front. This angers Idomeneus, who challenges the little Ajax to a wager with Agamemnon as witness. Thus these two would have come to strife if Achilles, the resolver of conflicts in this book, had not told them to stop it; they will know soon enough who will win.

Diomedes, as expected, comes in first. Then comes Antilochus, having by trickery (515) passed Menelaus. The poet adds that the mare Aithe was running so swiftly that if any more of the race had remained Menelaus would have been second. Meriones, his horses being the slowest and he being the worst charioteer, comes in a spear's throw behind Menelaus. Eumelus on foot, driving his horses in front and drawing his chariot behind, comes in last.

Achilles, pitying Eumelus and asserting that he is the best charioteer, will give him the second prize, a mare, but Antilochus angrily ("I shall be very angry with you if you do this," 543) says that the second prize is his and that Achilles should give Eumelus something else. Achilles smiles in amusement at Antilochus' reaction, for "he was his dear companion" (556), and gives Eumelus, as a special prize, the breastplate he had taken from Asteropaeus at 21.83. "As has often been said, this must be the first time that Achilles has smiled since the death of Patroclus" (Willcock 1973.1).

Then Menelaus stands up, grieved (*acheuon*, 566) in spirit and very angry (*kecholomenos*, 567). When a herald has given him the scepter and called for silence, he charges Antilochus with not living up to his reputation for discernment (*pepnumene*, 570), and ends by bidding him to swear a solemn oath that he has not wronged him willingly. Plutarch, in *How a Young Man Should Listen to Poetry* (Babbitt 1969.169), cites Menelaus' speech as a good example of how to rebuke a young man: remind him that men of good sense, among whom he has been counted, do not act as he has. In answer Antilochus—the poet describes him here as a man of discernment (*pepnumenos*, 586)—begs to be excused in view of his youth and offers to give Menelaus the mare, which he still thinks of as his own prize, and something else besides. At this Menelaus' heart is softened, and he forgives Antilochus and gives him the mare, which he says rightly belongs to himself, taking the third prize, a kettle, instead. The conciliatory spirit of

Antilochus has shown his good sense and self-control. He makes us think of Achilles, a young man who has had a great deal more trouble in controlling himself. The present incident reminds us of the disastrous altercation between Agamemnon and Achilles in Book 1.

When Meriones has taken the fourth prize, Achilles gives the fifth one, a bowl, which remains, to Nestor as a souvenir of the funeral, saying that Nestor might well be the winner in boxing, wrestling, spear-throwing, or the foot race, if he were not so old. Nestor, showing his gratitude in a lengthy speech (626-50), wishes he were young, as when he competed at the funeral games of Amarynceus where he won first prize in the just mentioned contests, which he lists, putting spear-throwing last. Only in the chariot race was he defeated by the sons of Actor, who had the advantage of being inseparable (Siamese) twins. He praises Achilles for doing the right thing and asks the gods to bless him.

Scholars have suggested that the five contests mentioned by Nestor were the only ones originally included in the games of Patroclus. This would make the fight in armor, the throwing of the discus, and the archery contest later additions. The order of the events in Nestor's list (and other evidence for early games; see Willis 1941.398-402) also seems to show that the chariot race was held last. Homer, however, has put it first. We can compare how in the two other major catalogues in the *Iliad*, the Catalogue of the Achaean Contingents and the Shield, the longest section is first.

Next comes the boxing. Epeius (mentioned only here in the *Iliad*; in *Odyssey* 11.523 we learn that he built the wooden horse) boasts that no one can beat him, but Euryalus (one of the leaders of the Argives, with Diomedes and Sthenelus), whose father had defeated all other contenders at the funeral games of Oedipus, takes up the challenge. Diomedes wants him to win very much (682), but Epeius knocks him off his feet with a blow that sends him into the air like a fish leaping out of the water.

Next is the wrestling. The big Ajax and Odysseus come to grips, their arms like the rafters of the roof of a high house (712-13; Krischer 1971.66 compares type 6 similes describing a situation of even battle). Achilles calls a halt after two falls in which Odysseus seems to have had a slight advantage, saying that they should divide the prizes equally, without however telling how this can be done.

Then comes the foot race, for which a beautiful mixing bowl, obtained by Patroclus in exchange for Lycaon, is first prize. The little Ajax, Odysseus, and Antilochus, the best racer among the younger men, step forward, and Achilles points out the turning post. The foot race repeats motifs from the chariot race. At first the little Ajax is the front runner, but Odysseus, whom the Achaeans want to win (766-67; an indication that he will win?), is close behind him. When they reach the return lap, Odysseus prays to Athena for help, and she gives him extra speed and causes the little Ajax to slip in some ox manure. Thus Odysseus wins first prize. The little Ajax, taking second prize, blames Athena, as he spits out manure, for tripping him up; and all the Achaeans laugh. Antilochus takes the last prize, a half bar of gold, saying with a smile that the older men have won, Odysseus being the oldest with a green old age; no one but Achilles could have beaten him. This praise (we are reminded of Nestor's praise of Achilles at the end of the chariot race) so pleases Achilles that he adds another half bar of gold to Antilochus' prize.

Next is the fight in armor, with the sword of Asteropaeus, slain by Achilles at 21.179-83, to go to the winner, winner and loser to share the armor of Sarpedon. Winning requires the serious wounding of one's opponent. The big Ajax and Diomedes step forward. When Diomedes seems about to deal Ajax a bad wound, the Achaeans call for the contest to end. Achilles gives the sword to Diomedes.

Next is the discus throwing, the discus, a ball of metal, to go to the winner. The two Lapiths Polypoetes and Leonteus, the big Ajax, and Epeius step forward. Epeius throws first, in such a way that all the Achaeans laugh; Leonteus throws second. Then the big Ajax surpasses these, but Polypoetes wins with a throw which is compared to that of a herdsman with the stick he hurls to control his cattle.

Next is the archery contest. The mast of a ship is set up and a dove tied to it at the top. The first prize is to go to the man who hits the dove, the second to him who, missing the dove, cuts the rope. Thus the poet (unrealistically) prepares us for an accident which (perhaps under the influence of an earlier description) he is planning to happen; he will have the first shooter miss the dove and, accidently, cut the rope, the second hit the dove in flight. Teucer and Meriones step forward, and Teucer is chosen by lot to have first shot. He is thus destined to win second prize—a fate that he corroborates by failing to pray to Apollo before he shoots. Accordingly, his shot cuts the rope, and the dove flies into the sky. Meriones immediately seizes the bow and, praying to Apollo, hits the dove. Meriones' winning first prize here can be considered a compensation in advance for his having to take second prize in the final contest.

This is the spear-throwing, for which he and Agamemnon volunteer. But Achilles says:

Agamemnon, we know how superior you are to all,

> how much stronger you are, how best at throwing the spear.
> So take this bowl as your prize to the hollow ships,
> and we shall bestow the spear on the hero Meriones,
> if this is agreeable to you. I do not insist.   (890-94)

Agamemnon does as Achilles asks and has the herald Talthybius carry off the bowl while Meriones takes the spear. Thus the games end on a note of reconciliation between Agamemnon and Achilles. Perhaps we are meant to remember how Talthybius was one of the two heralds sent in Book 1 to bring Briseis from Achilles. Meriones does not question Achilles' decision.

The games serve the important purpose of showing Achilles at peace with his fellow Achaeans. He smiles and is gracious. Nothing is left of the old wrath. A light-hearted spirit prevails. There are repeated occasions for laughter. Moreover, the games give a sense of closure for the *Iliad* as a whole. Now we see the main Achaean leaders once more again after their absence during Books 20, 21, and 22; and we are often reminded of earlier events, like the exploits of Diomedes in Book 5. But the *Iliad* is not over yet, for the body of Hector remains unburied, being preserved from harm like the body of Patroclus until it was buried.

BOOK 24: THE RANSOMING OF HECTOR'S BODY

Preparations, 1-467

At the funeral games for Patroclus in the last book Achilles was the gracious and often happy host, but now he returns to his grief and anger over Patroclus' death. How can we explain this change in mood? Hogan 1979.290 suggests "scenic parataxis" or that Achilles has been distracted only for a while by the social responsibility of the games. I prefer the former explanation. We should note that Books 23 and 24 begin in similar ways, with Achilles mourning over Patroclus and mistreating the body of Hector (so Nagler 1974. 171-71). Then in Book 23 there is the funeral of Patroclus, in Book 24 the ransoming (and funeral) of Hector. In reality these episodes may have been interwoven, but the poet has given them to us in paratactic order, thus emphasizing the latter, more suspenseful one, in which Achilles finally gives up his vengeance, as the culminating event of the *Iliad*. In Book 24 anger yields to reconciliation and an acceptance of the fact that life must go on. The spirit of pity prevails and the vengeance ends, as the wrath did in Book 18. Book 24 has a Thetis-Achilles scene comparable to those in Books 1 and 18, and creates with Book 1—both also take up twenty-two days and show old men coming to the Achaean camp to ransom their children—a final ring composition.

The games being over, the other men take their evening meal and lie down to sleep, but Achilles is mourning over Patroclus, remembering all the things they had done together.

> As he remembered these things he was weeping copiously,
> at one time trying to rest on his side, at another
> on his back, at another face down, and then standing up
> was wandering over the shore. The sight of the dawn
> shining on headland and sea never escaped him,
> but when he had harnessed his swift horses and chariot,
> he bound behind it Hector to drag him; three times
> he pulled him around the tomb of the dead Patroclus,
> then, having stopped at his hut, he left him there
> stretched out in the dust face down. But Apollo protected him,
> keeping all harm from his flesh, for he pitied the man,
> dead though he was; over him he put the golden
> aegis to prevent him, when dragged, from being torn.   (9-21)

Achilles continues to rage like this for eleven days (31). As we said in our comments on the description of him maintaining his wrath for eleven days in Book 1 (488-92), that passage is similar to this one (noticeable are the interative tenses in both places); and it seems likely that the poet is conscious of creating a contrast between how the wrath began (after eleven days during which Achilles maintains his wrath Thetis goes to Zeus who promises to support it) and how the vengeance ends (after eleven days during which Achilles mistreats the body of Hector the gods decide that he must give it up).

We naturally feel pity for Hector. Apollo, who pities (*eleairon*, 19) him, protects his body. Macleod 1982.187 compares 23.184-91, where both Aphrodite and Apollo are said to do this, and suggests that only Apollo is mentioned now because only he counts in the following narrative. Most of the gods, seeing Hector, pity (*eleaireskon eisoroontes*, 23) him and urge Hermes to steal the body, but Hera and Athena (who remember how Paris preferred Aphrodite to them; the Judgment of Paris, 28-30) and Poseidon oppose this course of action. Thus a conflict arises among the Olympians which is not resolved until the twelfth day after Hector's death (31) when Apollo reproaches the anti-Trojan gods.

> But, O gods, you wish to give help to baneful Achilles
> who lacks a balanced mind, whose thoughts in his heart
> are unbending; he's wild, fiercely disposed like a lion
> that yielding to terrible violence and an arrogant spirit
> invades the flocks of men to look for his meal.
> So Achilles has destroyed all pity (*eleon*); there's no shame in him—
> something that greatly hurts and greatly helps men.   (39-45)

Apollo goes on to say that the Fates have given humans the ability to endure the death of loved ones, and that Achilles should beware of the vengeance of the gods for mistreating the senseless earth in his anger.

Hera answers that Achilles and Hector should not be honored equally. Hector was born of mortal parents whereas Achilles' mother is a goddess whom she herself raised (perhaps an ad hoc invention; so Macleod 1982.195) and at whose wedding all the gods were present including Apollo.

Then Zeus tells Hera that Hector will not be given the same honor as Achilles, but that he was the dearest of all the Trojans to the gods, and especially to himself. (This looks like a balanced assessment of the two main characters in the *Iliad*.) They cannot steal the body without Achilles' knowing it, for Thetis is always at his side. One of the gods should summon Thetis, for he (Zeus) will tell her that Achilles must allow Priam to ransom Hector. As Macleod 1982.96-97 points out, that Thetis is always by Achilles' side is something of an exaggeration, but Zeus by "bringing in Thetis (as if she were unavoidable) shows his good will towards her and her son," as we remember he did in Book 1.

Iris goes with this summons swiftly, like the sinker on a fishing line, to the bottom of the sea, where she finds Thetis among her sisters bewailing Achilles' imminent death. Thetis agrees to come in spite of her grief (*ache'*, 92), and they speed up to heaven.

Athena gives Thetis her seat next to Zeus, and Hera gives her a gold goblet. Then Zeus apologizes for disturbing her in her grief, but he will honor Achilles by having him release Hector's body.

> Immediately go to the camp and give my command to your son.
> Tell him the gods are angry, tell him that I most
> of all am wroth because in his crazed mind he keeps
> Hector beside the beaked ships and will not release him,
> so that perhaps he may fear me and give Hector up.
> I'll also send Iris to great-souled Priam to tell him
> to go to the ships of the Achaeans to ransom his dear son
> by bringing gifts to Achilles to gladden his spirit.   (112-19)

Thus in this programmatic statement we learn that the action will be divided between Thetis' visit to Achilles and Iris' visit to Priam.

Thetis speeds to the hut of Achilles and finds him sobbing among his companions who have just made breakfast (we are thus prepared for him to eat). She asks him how long he will continue to grieve (*acheuon*, 128) and advises him to return to normal life, eating, sleeping, and making love; he has such a short time to live. Then she repeats Zeus' command that he release the body.

Achilles replies:

> Let whoever comes with the ransom carry the corpse off,
> if the Olympian himself so insistently commands it.   (139-40)

Achilles is changing his mind by yielding to Zeus' insistence. He always obeys the gods, as he did Athena in Book 1 saying that "thus it is better; the gods gladly listen to whoever obeys them" (1.217-18). Notice that Thetis has said nothing about

Priam's being the one to bring the ransom. Priam's entry will be "a profound surprise" (Macleod 1982.101).

Then we switch back to Olympus where Zeus sends Iris to Troy. The two really simultaneous actions are told consecutively and—Zeus now knows that Achilles has complied—as if they happened consecutively (Zielinski's law). Iris must command Priam to go to the Achaean camp to ransom Hector, alone except for an old herald to drive the mule wagon in which to carry the gifts and bring back the body. He should have no fear, for the gods will send Hermes to guide him, and Achilles will even protect him,

> for he's neither foolish nor thoughtless nor a willful wrongdoer,
> but will be very careful to spare a suppliant.   (157-58)

Zeus' praise of Achilles balances Apollo's earlier criticism of him.

Iris flies off to Priam, whom she finds lamenting (just as earlier she had found Thetis, and Thetis had found Achilles) among his sons in the courtyard. He is closely wrapped in his cloak (163; compare the grieving Achilles in Illustrations 1 and 3). Iris tells him not to fear, for she is the messenger of Zeus who pities (*eleairei*, 174) him. Then she repeats Zeus' words, including his praise of Achilles, and departs.

Priam commands his sons to prepare the mule wagon and descends into his storeroom. Hecuba fears that Achilles will kill him: Achilles is so savage, she could eat his liver. We are being made to fear for Priam. But he is willing to die if only he can embrace the body in lamentation. He chooses his most beautiful treasures, especially a precious Thracian cup (234-35); then, back in the courtyard, reviles his sons for not preparing the mule wagon. The assembling of the wagon, which will be driven by the herald Idaeus, is described in detail, for this is a great moment. And Priam's chariot is made ready. By traveling on this he will have greater dignity and, as noted by Macleod 1982.115, Hermes will be able to be his driver (an example of *prooikonomia*). Hecuba brings wine for a libation and asks Priam to pray for Zeus' bird on the right. Priam, asking Zeus to be merciful (*eleesei*, 301), prays for this omen and that Achilles will treat him with pity (*eleeinon*, 309). Zeus sends a giant eagle on the right, and the Trojans rejoice. Priam on the chariot is preceded by Idaeus on the wagon. His sons and sons-in-law, bewailing him as if he were going to his death, accompany him as far as the plain but then return to the city.

Zeus sees the old king and pities (*idon d'eleese*, 332) him. He orders Hermes to lead him to Achilles secretly. Hermes with gold sandals and wand (with which we can imagine him later putting the guards to sleep) speeds off to Troy, where he takes the form of a young Myrmidon prince whose beard is just beginning to grow. The encounter between Hermes and Priam will foreshadow that between Achilles and Priam: a young Myrmidon comforts the old Trojan king. Priam and Idaeus have reached the ford of the Scamander River (the dividing line between Trojan and Achaean territory), and night has come, when Idaeus sees Hermes. Should they flee on the chariot or beg for mercy? Priam is terribly frightened. But Hermes, taking him by the hand in reassurance (361), offers to be his protector: he thinks of him as his own father. Priam feels that this handsome, intelligent youth is a blessing sent by the gods. Then the young man asks him if he is abandoning Troy, since their best man, his son, is dead, and praises Hector as a great warrior, especially during the battle at the ships, which he, being one of Achilles' men, has witnessed. Though this is the twelfth day (413) since Hector's death, and though Achilles has dragged the body around the tomb of his friend every morning, the gods have kept it safe. Addressing Hermes as "son," Priam remarks on the benefit of worshiping the gods as Hector has done, and offers to give him a beautiful cup (the precious Thracian cup mentioned in 234-35, I think, though Macleod 1982.122 disagrees) in exchange for leading him to Achilles with the help of the gods (dramatic irony). Hermes answers that he cannot accept any gift secretly from Achilles, whom he fears, but that he will gladly act as Priam's guide.

So saying, he mounts the chariot and drives the horses. When they come to the trench and the wall, the guards are just finishing supper. Hermes puts them to sleep and leads his charges into the camp. Achilles' dwelling is described at length: a courtyard surrounded by a wall with a gate whose bolt only Achilles can open by himself; it takes three normal men to do it, but for a god this is easy. Then, within the courtyard, Hermes reveals himself to Priam and tells him to go and supplicate Achilles.

We can compare Odysseus' arrival at the palace of Alcinous in *Odyssey* 7. Priam and Odysseus are both suppliants helped by a divinity (Odysseus by Athena), and the dwellings they are about to enter are described in awe-inspiring detail. We are made to feel apprehensive about the safety of both. This is especially true of Priam; we fear that Achilles, though he has agreed to yield to Zeus' command, may harm him. As Redfield 1975.214 has said, "The dramatic tension of the last book is not in Achilles' consent but in Priam's journey to Achilles."

Priam and Achilles, 468-676

Hermes returns to Olympus, and Priam, leaving Idaeus with the horses and mules, enters the hut, where Achilles is sitting with Automedon and Alcimus, having just completed the evening meal; it bodes well for Priam that Achilles has followed Thetis' advice and eaten. A huge figure, Priam falls at Achilles' knees and kisses the hands that have killed so many of his sons. Achilles and his companions are struck with amazement, like the members of a household among whom a manslayer suppliant has suddenly appeared. Priam begs Achilles to remember his father, Peleus, and enumerates the many sons that he, Priam, has lost in battle, ending with Hector whose body he has come to ransom.

> For him I've come to the ships of the Achaeans,
> to gain his release from you with boundless ransom.
> Honor the gods, Achilles, and show me your pity (*eleeson*),
> remembering your father. I am more pitiable (*eleeinoteros*) than he.
> I've endured more than anyone ever, putting
> my mouth to the hand of the man who murdered my son.   (501-6)

This causes Achilles to weep for his father, and he gently pushes Priam away. They weep together, Priam remembering Hector, Achilles his father—and also Patroclus. Priam's appeal has broadened Achilles' grief.

As soon as he can collect himself, Achilles rises and raises the old man, thus accepting him as a suppliant (so Clapp, comparing *Odyssey* 7.162ff.). Pitying (*oikteiron*, 516) his gray head and beard, Achilles says:

> Poor one, truly your heart has endured many evils.
> How dared you to come to the ships of the Achaeans alone,
> into the sight of a man, even me, who has slain
> many good sons of yours. You've a heart made of iron.
> But now sit on this chair and, and though we are grieved (*achnumenoi*),
> let us allow our pains to rest in our hearts,
> for nothing's to be gained by continuing chill lamentation.
> Thus the gods have spun for mortal men
> to live in grief (*achnumenois*) while they themselves are carefree.   (518-27)

He goes on to speak of the two jars Zeus has in his storeroom, one of evils, the other of goods, from which he apportions to human beings at birth: to some, like Priam and Peleus, a mixture, so that they have both good and bad in their lives, but to others only from the jar of evils. Thus the young man Achilles, out of his own grief and feeling the universality of grief, consoles the old king. His speech has much in common with later consolations. He ends by telling Priam to sit and allow his grief to settle.

But Priam refuses while Hector lies uncared for, and this causes Achilles' anger to flare up. Scowling, he tells him (560-70) not to provoke him further; he had determined on his own to release Hector, for his mother has brought word from Zeus for him to do it, and he knows that Priam could not have come to the ships without divine aid. Priam should beware of arousing his pain, lest he kill him, suppliant though he is.

Priam sits in fear. Achilles leaps from the room "like a lion' (572)—we remember Apollo's earlier description (24). Automedon and Alcimus, following him, unharness the horses and mules, lead in Idaeus, and take the ransom from the wagon, leaving behind clothing for covering the body of Hector. Priam, who has not intended to stay, is being forced to accept Achilles' hospitality.

Then Achilles calls out maid-servants to wash and anoint the body, which he takes into a separate room

> in order that Priam might not see his son,
> lest being grieved (*achnumenei*) in heart he not check his anger (*cholos*)
> on seeing his son, and stir up the spirit of Achilles,
> who then might kill him and violate Zeus' command.   (583-86)

Plutarch, in *How a Young Man Should Listen to Poems* (Babbitt 1969.163), remarks that these words of Achilles (as well as those at 560-70) show his self-understanding: "For it is mark of a wondrous foresight for a man whose hold on his temper is uncertain, who is naturally rough and quick-tempered, not to be blind to his own weakness, but to exercise caution, and to be on his guard against possible grounds for anger, and to forestall them by reason long beforehand, so that he may not even inadvertently become involved in such emotions."

When the body has been prepared, Achilles puts it on a bier and, with his companions, lifts it onto the wagon. Then he cries out to Patroclus:

> Don't be angry with me, Patroclus, if even
> in Hades you hear that I've released noble Hector
> to his dear father, for the ransom he gave me was seemly,
> and I'll apportion to you your appropriate share.   (592-95)

Presumably he will burn Patroclus' share (so Willcock 1984.318)—but not at the
funeral of Patroclus according to the *Iliad*. (Did Homer know of another version in
which the ransoming of Hector preceded the funeral of Patroclus? Such a version
would solve the problem of Achilles' sudden change in mood from happy
amusement at the end of the last book to persistent anger and grief at the beginning
of the present one.) Thus the body is released, and Achilles is honored, as is
Patroclus, in accordance with Zeus' will.

Achilles, returning to Priam, sits opposite him and says:

> Your son is released to you, old man, as you asked.
> He lies on a bier, and in the light of the dawn
> you'll see him, taking him home. Now let us eat.   (599-601)

Priam will not see the body until the dawn of the next day when he is no longer in
the presence of Achilles. This means that he must not only eat but sleep in Achilles'
hut. Achilles goes on to give him the example of Niobe who, though she ate, was
able to grieve forever. This speech, like that on the jars of Zeus, is comparable to a
consolation, but it shows an acceptance, even a welcoming, of the fact that some
griefs never die: we may share in the joy of living without any fear of breaking
these griefs. Then Achilles slays a sheep and serves the meat while his companions
serve the bread. When they have finished eating, the two men sit for a while
admiring each other's godlike appearance. Surely we are meant to admire them
both.

Then Priam asks to be given a bed. He has not eaten nor slept since Hector's
death, but only mourned. Accordingly, Achilles has beds prepared in the portico
looking onto the courtyard. Priam must sleep here lest an Achaean visitor see him
and report his presence to Agamemnon. (And thus also—an example of
prooikonomia—Hermes can help Priam to leave without involving Achilles.)
Finally, at Priam's request, Achilles promises to keep the Achaeans from fighting
during the period of Hector's funeral.

> This shall be done, old Priam, as you command.
> I shall hold off the war for the time you request.   (669-70)

These are Achilles' last words in the *Iliad*. So saying, he takes Priam by the hand
as a sign of reassurance (671; the gesture used by Hermes at 361). Thus Priam and
Idaeus sleep in the portico while Achilles lies within beside Briseis.

The Funeral of Hector, 677-804

All the gods and men are asleep except Hermes who is pondering how to bring Priam from the ships. He appears to him as a dream-figure and frightens him with the thought that Agamemnon and the Achaeans may learn of his presence. (Compare 2.1-2, where only Zeus is awake, pondering how he can fulfill his promise to Thetis, and decides to send a dream to Agamemnon. Here we can imagine that Hermes is still acting for Zeus who commanded him to go to Priam in the first place, lines 330-33.) Priam awakes to find Hermes actually there, and rouses Idaeus. Hermes guides them swiftly through the Achaean camp without being seen. When they reach the ford of the Scamander River, and the day is dawning, he returns to Olympus. This makes a ring composition with his coming to Priam at the same place on the previous evening.

Now, the body being visible, Priam and Idaeus loudly lament. Cassandra, who has gone up to the citadel, is the first to see them. Lamenting, she cries out for all the Trojans to come and behold Hector, if ever they rejoiced to see him returning from battle. We remember how the Trojan women met Hector at the gate in Book 6. Now Hecuba and Andromache run to the wagon tearing their hair and wail as they hold his head. They all would have continued to weep until sunset if Priam had not commanded them to yield.

At home in response to dirges, apparently sung by professional singers, there is the wailing of the women, out of which arise the laments of Andromache, Hecuba, and Helen. (So Macleod 1982.148; we can compare the roles of the Muses and the Nereids at the funeral of Achilles as told in *Odyssey* 24.58-61, translated at the beginning of our comments on Book 23. There the Muses apparently sing the dirges, like the professional singers in the present passage.) Andromache foresees her captivity and the death of Astyanax. Hecuba says that Hector was her dearest son. She contrasts the mercy Achilles showed her other sons with how he has treated Hector. Nevertheless, Hector's body is fresh and unharmed, like that of a man slain by an arrow of Apollo (a beautiful way to die). We remember Hector's meetings with Hecuba and Andromache in Book 6 and their laments for him in Book 22. Helen's lament comes somewhat unexpectedly, but Hector also talked with her in Book 6. She praises him for always being gentle to her whereas most Trojans shuddered to behold her. The fact that she is a foreigner adds to the objectivity with which his goodness is viewed.

Then Priam commands that the funeral be prepared, saying that Achilles has promised to keep the Achaeans from fighting until the twelfth day from now.

Thus he spoke, and they harnessed the oxen and mules
to the wagons and gathered immediately in front of the city.
They took nine days to bring in plenty of wood,
but when the tenth dawn shining on mortals appeared,
then as they wept they carried brave Hector out
and put his corpse on the top of the pyre and lit it.
When dawn rosy-fingered had early arisen again,
the people around the pyre of glorious Hector
gathered and, having come together there,
first put out the fire with shining red wine
completly wherever it still was glowing; and then
his weeping brothers and comrades—the tears were pouring
down their cheeks—gathered his white bones up.
When they had wrapped the bones in soft purple cloth,
they took them up and lay them to rest in a gold urn.
And immediately they dug the grave, a hollow place
with huge stones closely fitted around it, and quickly
heaped the tomb-mound up. And guards were everywhere
posted against an attack of the well-greaved Achaeans.
Then, having heaped up the mound and gone away,
they gathered together and ate a glorious feast
there in the palace of Priam, the Zeus-nurtured king.
Such was the burial of Hector, tamer of horses.   (782-804)

The *Iliad* ends in mourning, as befits a tragedy, with this brief cataloguing of the events of Hector's funeral. There is no comment or elaboration. It is all very formulaic, ritualistic, elegant, like the ending of *Hamlet*. The war must go on, but a universal pity demands that the dead be given proper burial. We are reminded, by way of contrast, of the picture of the unburied dead described in the proem.

SUMMARY OF PART 3

Part 3 (Books 19-24) describes the *aristeia* of Achilles. When Achilles enters the fighting it is as if he were the only Achaean on the battlefield, he so dominates the action. In Book 19 he puts on his armor, which gleams brightly portending his victory. In Books 20 and 21 he drives the Trojans into the Scamander River, slaughtering them mercilessly, but then the river stops him and would have overwhelmed him (the wounding motif) if Hephaestus had not come to his aid. In Book 22, having driven all the Trojans except Hector back into Troy, he kills Hector in single combat. But there is no fight over the body, for no other Trojan has remained with Hector outside the walls of Troy. This motif is replaced by the ransoming of Hector's body in Book 24. So Krischer 1971.28, who points out that the fight over the body in an *aristeia* shows that the gods are concerned for the vanquished (as they are for the dead Hector) and that there is a limit beyond which the victor cannot go.

The description of Achilles' vengeance in Part 3 creates a climactic parallel with the description of his wrath in Parts 1 and 2. Thetis plays a reluctant role in both, bringing him new armor from Hephaestus in which he can execute his vengeance (Book 19), just as she won Zeus' support for his wrath (Book 1); and when things have gone too far, she is the one who urges him to return to normal, telling him that he must give up his mistreatment of Hector's body (Book 24), just as she acquiesced in his return to the action in order to fight on behalf of his own people (Book 18). The death of Hector in which the vengeance culminates (Book 22) shows clear parallels with the death of Patroclus in which the wrath culminates (Book 16), and the supplications of Achilles for mercy by Trojans are similar to the pleas of Achaeans for Achilles to return to battle. The ransom given by Priam in Book 24 is like the gifts offered in Book 9 and given in Book 19. As the wrath ends with Achilles showing pity for his own people, the vengeance ends with him showing pity for all people including his enemy.

Part 3 has a long retardation similar to those of Parts 1 and 2. In Part 1, when we expected a Trojan victory, we were given, in Books 3-7, a description of Achaean successes. In Part 2 the attack of the Trojans on the ships was unexpectedly interrupted by the Poseidon retardation in Books 13-14. In Part 3 the expected event, to which we have been looking forward since Book 18, is the encounter between Achilles and Hector, but Achilles and Hector do not fight until toward the end of Book 22, and the earlier narrative is replete with retarding episodes. The big difference between this and the earlier retardations is that the forward thrust of the narrative is never reversed. Achilles is never forced back but merely slowed down; the retarding events, which are interwoven with his *aristeia*, add to his glory.

In Book 19 there is the assembly of reconciliation with its long debate on whether the army should eat before fighting—a low-key description after the moment of high excitement in Book 18 when Achilles returned. At the end of Book 19 Achilles leads out the Achaeans. But then, at the beginning of Book 20, we switch to Olympus where Zeus, having fulfilled his promise to Thetis to support Achilles' wrath, lifts his prohibition made in Book 8 against the gods' taking part in the battle. Now they are to prevent the fall of Troy on this day—a purpose that highlights the awesome power of Achilles. And thus also the poet introduces the battle of the gods.

This battle, however, is broken off until later by a series of events beginning with the encounter between Aeneas and Achilles. This encounter is a slow episode with several long speeches before Aeneas is saved by Poseidon. The next episode foreshadows the expected event: Hector and Achilles are about to fight, but Apollo carries Hector to safety. Then Achilles slaughters the Trojans in general (a motif in the *aristeia*) until he is opposed by the Scamander and saved by Hephaestus. The encounter of these two divinities brings the other pairs of gods, who in Book 20 were similarly set to fight each other, into action. Thus the battle of the gods creates a ring composition around the retarding narrative in Books 20 and 21.

The pro-Trojan gods are forced to flee, and Achilles drives all the Trojans except Hector back into Troy. This brings us to Book 22 where we move relentlessly but still slowly to the slaying of Hector. There are the speeches of Priam and Hecuba begging him to come within the walls of Troy and then Hector's debate with himself whether to face Achilles or run, and finally the long chase until Athena, after taking counsel with Zeus, tricks Hector into making a stand.

The narrative of Achilles' vengeance in Books 20-22 is framed by episodes in Books 19 and 23 (ring composition) showing his reconciliation with Agamemnon and his reintegration into the community of the Achaeans. In the Achaean assembly in Book 19 Agamemnon publicly admits his fault, returns Briseis, and gives the gifts he promised in Book 19. But there is no meal of reconciliation, for Achilles refuses to eat before he has slain Hector. Not until Book 23, at the end of this day of battle, with Hector dead and Patroclus avenged, is the reconciliation complete. Achilles goes to Agamemnon's hut for this meal and, in the funeral games for Patroclus in Book 23, where we see the Achaean leaders again for the first time since Book 19, acts very graciously toward Agamemnon.

The theme of the inevitable fall of Troy is especially prominent in Part 3. In Part 2 it was not emphasized so much because there the narrative was mainly concerned with describing the defeat of the Achaeans. In Part 1, however, it was expressed by Diomedes' defeat of the pro-Trojan gods Aphrodite and Ares in Book 5, and also frequently in terms of a "not yet": Troy was not yet destined to fall. Similarly, in Part 3, in the battle of the gods, which looks back to Book 5, the pro-Achaean gods defeat the pro-Trojan ones, and there is the concern of Zeus that Troy may fall prematurely on the day of Achilles' *aristeia*. Moreover, Poseidon's rescue of Aeneas looks forward to the fall of Troy: the royal family of Troy is destined to survive in the descendants of Aeneas. And the Scamander, when he begs Hephaestus to have mercy on him, promises in the future not to try to prevent the fall of Troy; the city is abandoned by its sacred river. Also, of course, the death of Hector is closely connected with the fall of Troy. He was its mainstay and protector, and the laments over his body foresee the destruction of his city.

Another theme that comes to a climax in Part 3 is that of the mutilation of the corpse. So Segal 1971.18, who points out that references to this theme are infrequent and scattered until the description of the slaying of Patroclus. At 16.336 Hector boasts over Patroclus that the dogs will devour him. At 17.39-40, during the fight over Patroclus' body, Euphorbus threatens Menelaus with decapitation, and at 17.125-27 Hector tries to gain possession of Patroclus' corpse in order to cut off the head and throw the body to the dogs to eat. At 18.157-77 Iris, in order to spur Achilles into action, tells him that Hector intends to fasten Patroclus' head on a pike. Thus Hector's threat to mutilate the corpse of Patroclus is the background for Achilles' mistreatment of his Trojan victims, and especially Hector, in Part 3. In Book 21, after he has slain Lycaon and Asteropaeus, Achilles throws their bodies into the water so that, as he gloatingly says, the fish and eels may eat them. Then, in Book 22, comes Achilles' boast over the dying Hector and his mistreatment of his corpse. When Hector begs for mercy for his body, Achilles answers (22.346-48) that he would like to cut up his flesh and eat it raw, and that no one will keep the dogs from his head. And now the threat of mutilation is actually carried out. The other Achaeans come up and each of them stabs the corpse with his spear, and Achilles pierces the ankles to tie the feet so that he can drag the body back to his hut behind his chariot. Then he sacrifices the twelve Trojan youths on the pyre of Patroclus, and drags the body of Hector around the tomb of Patroclus three times a day until it is finally ransomed in Book 24.

No Achaean warrior in the *Iliad* ever begs the enemy for mercy, but three Trojans do this in Part 3 (in Part 1, Book 6.45-65 Adrestus unsuccessfully supplicated Menelaus, and in Part 2, Book 11.122-47 the sons of Antimachus unsuccessfully supplicated Agamemnon). There is "a threefold rising sequence of Trojans supplicating Achilles in battle" (Thornton 1984.138-39) leading up to the final supplication of Priam's begging for Hector's body. First there is Tros at 20.463ff., then Lycaon at 21.64ff., and finally Hector at 22.338f. It is not until Book 24 that the supplication of Priam causes Achilles to show proper reverence for the body of his victims.

Achilles dominates Part 3 as a man dedicated to death. This dedication was already shown in Book 18 where he told Thetis of his willingness to die immediately after slaying Hector. Now his death is predicted in Book 19 by his horse Xanthus as he is going out to battle and in Book 22 by the dying Hector. In Book 23 the funeral of Patroclus looks forward to that of Achilles: when Achilles has died his bones will be buried together with those of Patroclus in the same urn. Finally, in Book 24 Thetis says that he should give up his constant mourning over Patroclus and return to normal living because so little time still remains to him to live. Achilles, a man controlled by grief, often speaks as if he were already dead; his words take on an ominous quality. This is especially evident in his replies to Lycaon and Hector as he kills them. In Book 24 this voice is modulated to express a universal pity for the human condition as the young man speaks to the old king consoling words of wisdom.

Pity for the Trojans appears in the *Iliad* especially in those stretches of the narrative where the Achaeans are being victorious, as in Book 6 where we were given a very sympathetic picture of Hector in Troy. In Book 8 and in Part 2, however, when the Achaeans were being defeated, our sympathies were elicited mainly for them. Finally, in Part 3, where the Achaeans are completely victorious, there is a crescendo of pity for the Trojans. As Achilles relentlessly mows down his opponents, it is difficult not to sympathize with them. One thinks of Polydorus, Tros, and Lycaon, and especially Hector. Book 22 cries out with pity for Hector in scene after scene. And in Book 24 our hearts are with the old king Priam as he dares to go into the enemy camp at night to try to ransom his son's body.

We can imagine that the ancient Greek audience must have lost patience with Achilles in Part 3 (as they did for a different reason in Part 2) when he carried his vengeance too far by mutilating and mistreating Hector's body. Surely Apollo expresses the reaction Homer expected his audience to have when he says at the beginning of Book 24 that Achilles is behaving in a non-human way, like a lion, without pity. Dead bodies should be properly buried.

The *Iliad* ends in a spirit of reconciliation, in contrast to how it began in a spirit of conflict. Book 24 reminds us of Book 1 in several ways: the number of days it covers, its Thetis-Achilles scene, and the fact that a revered old foreigner comes to the Achaean camp to ransom his child. But Priam succeeds where Chryses failed. Zeus has decided that Achilles will be given the glory of releasing Hector's body, and so Achilles accepts the plea of Priam. He treats him gruffly, for his grief and anger are very near the surface, but also tenderly, seeing in Priam his own father. We are given a picture of the two great enemies looking at each other in admiration after a meal of guest-friendship. And then Priam, with the permission of Achilles, takes Hector's body back to Troy and has it given proper burial. The *Iliad* begins with the horrible prospect of the dead bodies of Achaeans lying unburied as food for dogs and carrion birds, but ends with lamentation and burial in honor of a noble Trojan.

BIBLIOGRAPHY

The following abbreviations are used:

AJP	*American Journal of Philology*
CQ	*Classical Quarterly*
G&R	*Greece and Rome*
HSCP	*Harvard Studies in Classical Philology*
TAPA	*Transactions and Proceedings of the American Philological Association*

Ameis, K. F., and Hentze, C. 1905-32 I 2-II 4. *Homers Ilias*. Leipzig.

Andersen, O. 1978. *Die Diomedesgestalt in der Ilias*, Symbolae Osloenses. Suppl. 25. Oslo.

Arend,W. 1933. *Die typischen Scenen bei Homer*. Berlin.

Arieti, J. A. "Achilles' Alienation in *Iliad* 9." *Classical Journal* 82.1-27.

Armstrong, J. I. 1958. "The Arming Motif in the Iliad." *AJP* 74: 137-48.

Babbitt, F. C. 1969. *Plutarch's Moralia* I (Loeb Classical Library). Cambridge, Mass.

Bannert, H. 1981 "Phoinix' Jugend und der Zorn des Meleagros. Zur Komposition des neunten Buches der Ilias." *Wiener Studien* 15: 69-94.

Barth, H.-L. 1989. "Achill und das Schicksal des Patroklos." *Hermes* 117: 1-24.

Basset, S. 1922. "The Three Threads of the Plot of the *Iliad*." *TAPA* 53: 52-62.

_____ 1928. *The Poetry of Homer*. Berkeley.

Beye, C. R. 1966. *The "Iliad," the "Odyssey," and the Epic Tradition*. Garden City, N.Y.

Broccia, G. 1962. *Struttura e Spirito del Libro VI dell' Iliade*. Sapri.

Burkert, W. 1955. *Zum altgriechischen Mitleidsbegriff*. Erlangen.

Clapp, E. B. 1899. *Homer's Iliad Books XIX-XXIV*. Boston.

Clark, M. E. and Coulson, W. D. E. 1978. "Memnon and Sarpedon." *Museum Helveticum* 35: 65-73.

Claus, D. 1975. "*Aidos* in the Language of Achilles." *TAPA* 105: 13-28.

Collins, L. 1987. "The Wrath of Paris. Ethical Vocabulary and Ethical Type in the *Iliad*." *AJP* 108: 220-32.

Combellack, F. 1984. "A Homeric Metaphor." *AJP* 105: 247-57.

Davison, J. A. 1965. "Thucydides, Homer and the 'Achaean Wall'." *Greek, Roman and Byzantine Studies* 6: 5-28.

de Jong, I. J. F. 1985. "Fokalisation und die homerischen Gleichnisse."
Mnemosyne 38: 257-70.

Dodds, E. R. 1951. *The Greeks and the Irrational.* Berkeley/Los Angeles.

Donlan, W. 1989. "The Unequal Exchange Between Glaucus and Diomedes in
Light of the Homeric Gift-Economy." *Phoenix* 43: 1-15.

Duckworth, G. E. 1931. "*Proananphonosis* in the Scholia to Homer." *AJP* 52:
320-38.

_____ 1933. *Foreshadowing and Suspense in the Epics of Homer,
Apollonius, and Vergil.* Princeton.

Edwards, M. W. 1980. "Convention and Individuality in Iliad 1." *HSCP* 84: 1-28.

_____ 1987. *Homer, Poet of the Iliad.* Baltimore/London.

_____ 1991. *The Iliad: A Commentary, Vol. v: books 17-20.* Cambridge

Eichholz, D. E. 1953. "The Propitiation of Achilles." *AJP* 74: 137-48.

Erbse, H. 1961. "Betrachtungen über das 5. Buch der Ilias." *Rheinisches Museum*
104:156-89.

_____ 1969-88. *Scholia Graeca in Homeri Iliadem.* 7 vols. Berlin.

_____ 1986. *Untersuchungen Zur Funktion der Götter im homerischen Epos.*
Berlin/New York.

Eustathius 1825-26. *Commentarii ad Homeri Odysseam Pertinentes.* Leipzig.

_____ 1971-87. *Commentarii ad Homeri Iliadem Pertinentes*, ed. M. van der
Valk. Leiden.

Fenik, B. C. 1964. *Iliad X and the Rhesus: The Myth.* Collection Latomus 173.
Bruxelles-Birchem.

_____ 1968. *Typical Battle Scenes in the Iliad*, Hermes Einzelschriften 21.
Wiesbaden.

_____, ed. 1978. *Homer, Tradition and Invention.* Leiden.

_____ 1986. *Homer and the Nibelungenlied.* Cambridge, Mass./London.

Fittschen, K. 1973. *Der Schild des Achilleus.* Archaeologica Homerica II N, Teil
1. Göttingen.

Fränkel, H. 1921. *Die homerischen Gleichnisse.* Göttingen.

_____ 1931. "Die Zeitauffassung in der archaischen griechischen Literatur."
Zeitschrift für Ästhetik und allgemeine Kunstwissenschaft. Beilagenheft 25: 97-
18; reprinted 1960 in *Wege und Formen frühgriechischen Denkens.* Munich.

Frazer, R. M. 1985. "The Crisis of Leadership among the Greeks and Poseidon's
Intervention in Iliad 14." *Hermes* 113: 1-9.

_____ 1989. "The Return of Achilleus as a Climactic Parallel to Patroklos'
Entering Battle." *Hermes* 117: 381-90.

Griffin, J. 1980. *Homer on Life and Death*. Oxford.

Hainsworth, B. 1966. "Joining Battle in Homer." *G&R* 13: 158-66.

_____ 1969. *Homer*. Greece and Rome, New Surveys in the Classics No. 3. Oxford.

_____ 1972. Rev. Lohmann 1970. *Journal of Hellenic Studies* 92: 187-88.

_____ 1988. *A Commentary on Homer's Odyssey*, vol. 1, edd. A. Heubeck, S. West, J. B. Hainsworth. Oxford.

Hogan, J. C.1979. *A Guide to the "Iliad"*. Garden City, N.Y.

Heubeck, A. 1983. *Omero Odissea*, Vol III, Libri IX-XII. Milan.

_____ 1986. *Omero Odissea*, Vol. VI, Libri XXI-XXIV. Milan.

Howald, 1951. "Sarpedon." *Museum Helveticum* 18: 11-18.

Janko, R. 1992. *The Iliad: A Commentary, Vol. iv: books 13-16*. Cambridge.

Jebb, R. C. 1886. *Homer: An Introduction to the Iliad and the Odyssey*. Boston, Mass.

Johansen, K. F. 1967. *The Iliad in Early Grek Art*. Copenhagen.

_____ 1987. *Narrators and Focalizers: The Presentation of the Story in the Iliad*. Amsterdam.

Kakridis, J. T. 1949. *Homeric Researches*. Lund.

_____ 1956. "Homer, ein Philhellene," *Wiener Studien* 69: 26-32; reprinted with revisions as "*Aei philellen ho poietes?*" in *Homer Revisited* 1971:54-67.

_____1971. *Homer Revisited*. Lund.

King, K. C. 1987. *Achilles: Paradigms of the War Hero from Homer to the Middle Ages*. Berkeley.

Kirk, G. S. 1962. *The Songs of Homer*. Cambridge.

_____ 1976. *Homer and the Oral Tradition*. Cambridge.

_____ 1985. *The Iliad:: A Commentary, Vol. i; books 1-4*. Cambridge.

_____ 1990. *The Iliad: A Commentary, Vol. ii: books 5-8*. Cambridge.

Klingner, F. 1940. "Über die Dolonie." *Hermes* 75: 337-68.

Koehnken. 1975. "Die Rolle des Phoinix und die Duale im IX der Ilias." *Glotta* 53: 25-36.

Krischer, T. 1971. *Formale Konventionen der homerischen Epik*. Munich.

Latacz, J. 1977. *Kampfparänese, Kampfdarstellung und Kampfwirchlichkeit in der Ilias, bei Kallinos und Tyrtaios*. Zetemata 46. Munich.

Lattimore, R. 1951. *The "Iliad" of Homer* (trans.). Chicago.

Leaf, W. 1902 I-II. *The Iliad*. London.

Lesky. A. 1961. *Göttliche und menschliche Motivation im homerischen Epos*. Heidelberg.

_____ 1966. *A History of Greek Literature* (trans. of *Geschichte der griechischen Literatur*, 2nd ed. 1963). London.

Lohmann, D. 1970. *Die Kompositionen der Reden in der Ilias*. Berlin.

Lord, A. B. 1960. *The Singer of Tales*. Cambridge, Mass.

Macleod, C. W. 1982. *Homer: Iliad Book XXIV*. Cambridge.

Martin, R. P. 1989. *The Language of Heroes: Speech and Performance in the "Iliad"*. Ithaca, N.Y.

Michel, C. 1971. *Erläuterungen zum N der Ilias*. Heidelberg.

Monro, D. B. 1884 I; 1888 II. *Homer, Iliad*. Oxford.

Moulton, C. 1977. *Similes in the Homeric Poems*. Hypomnemata 49. Göttingen.

Mueller, M. 1984. *The Iliad*. London.

Nagler, M. N. 1974. *Spontaneity and Tradition: A Study in the Oral Art of Homer*. Berkeley and Los Angeles.

Nagy, G. 1979. *The Best of the Achaeans: Concepts of the Hero in Archaic Greek Poetry*. Baltimore and London.

Neschke, A. B. 1985. "*Boulephoros aner*—Zur Bedeutung der sogenannten Diapeira im 2. Buch des Ilias (B, 1-483)." *Antike und Abendland* 2: 25-34.

Notopoulos, J. A. 1964. "Studies in Early Greek Oral Poetry." *HSCP* 68: 1-77.

Owen, E. T. 1946. *The Story of the Iliad*. Toronto.

Palmer, L. R. 1963. *The Interpretation of Mycenaean Greek Texts*. Oxford.

Parry, A. 1956. "The Language of Achilles." *TAPA* 87:1-7.

_____ 1966. "Have We Homer's Iliad?" *Yale Classical Studies* 20:177-216.

Parry, M. 1971. *The Making of Homeric Verse: The Collected Papers of Milman Parry*. ed. A. Parry. Oxford.

Pedrick, V. 1982. "Supplication in the *Iliad* and the *Odyssey*." *TAPA* 12: 125-40.

_____ 1983. "The Paradigmatic Nature of Nestor's Speech in *Iliad* 11." *APA* 113: 55-68.

Petropoulou, A. 1988. "The Interment of Patroklos (*Iliad* 23.252-57)." *AJP* 109: 482-95.

Philipp, H. 1984. "Die Kosmographie Homers." *Mitteilungen des deutschen archäologischen Instituts, Athenische Abteilung* 99: 1-4.

Pope, A. 1967 VII-VIII. *The Iliad of Homer*. The Poems of Alexander Pope (Twickenham Edition). ed. M. Mack et al. London/New Haven.

Reeve, M. D. 1973. "The Language of Achilles." *CQ* 23 : 193-95.

Redfield, J. 1975. *Nature and Culture in the Iliad*. Chicago.

Reinhardt, K.1961. *Die Ilias und ihr Dichter*. Göttingen.

Richardson, N. J. 1980. "Literary Criticism in the Exegetical Scholia to the *Iliad*: a Sketch." *CQ* 30: 265-87.

Roisman, H. 1988. "Nestor's Advice and Antilochus' Tactics." *Phoenix* 42: 114-20.

Rothe, C. 1910. *Die Ilias als Dichtung*. Paderborn.

Rutherford, R. B. 1982. "Tragic Form and Feeling in the *Iliad*." *Journal of Hellenic Studies* 102: 145-60.

Schadewaldt, W. 1938. *Iliasstudien*. Leipzig; reprinted third ed. 1966, Darmstadt.

_____1959. *Von Homers Welt und Werk3*.Stuttgart; fourth ed. Stuttgart 1965.

Scheibner, G. 1939. *Der Aufbau des 20 und 21 Buches der Iliad*. Leipzig.

Schein, S. 1984. *The Mortal Hero: an Introduction to Homer's Iliad*. Berkeley/Los Angeles.

Schofield, M. 1986. "*Euboulia* in the *Iliad*." *CQ* 36: 6-31.

Schol.=Scholia. See Erbse, H. 1969-88 above.

Scodel, R. "The Autobiography of Phoenix: Iliad 9.444-95," *AJP* 103: 128-36.

_____ 1989. "The Word of Achilles." *Classical Philology* 91-99.

Scott. W. C. 1974. *The Oral Nature of the Homeric Simile*. Leiden.

Segal. C. 1968. "The Embassy and the Duals in Iliad 9.182-98." *G&R* 9: 101-14.

_____ 1971. *The Theme of the Mutilation of the Corpse in the Iliad*. Leiden.

Sheppard, J. T. 1922. *The Pattern of the Iliad*. London.

Taplin, O. 1980. "The Shield of Achilles within the *Iliad*." *G&R* 27: 1-21.

_____ 1992. *Homeric Soundings: The Shaping of the "Iliad"*. Osford.

Thalmann, W. G. 1984. *Conventions of Form and Thought in Early Greek Epic Poetry*. Baltimore.

Thompson, S. 1955-58. *Motif-Index of Folk Literature*. Bloomington.

Thornton, A. 1984. *Homer's Iliad: its Composition and the Motif of Supplication*. Hypomnemata 81. Göttingen.

Traill, D. A. 1989. "Gold Armor for Bronze and Homer's Use of Compensatory Time." *Classical Philology* 84: 301-5.

Tsagarakis, O. 1982. *Form and Content in Homer*. Wiesbaden.

van der Valk, M. 1953. "Homer's Nationalistic Attitude." *L'Antiquité Classique* 22: 5-26.

_____ 1982. "Zu Einigen Kompositionsfragen der Ilias." *Mnemosyne* 35: 136-38.

Von der Mühll, P. 1952. *Kritisches Hypomnema zur Ilias*. Basel.

Wade-Gery, H. T. 1952. *The Poet of the Iliad*. Cambridge.

West, M. L. 1980. "Homeric and Hesiodic Poetry." In *Ancient Greek Literature*. ed. K. Dover. Oxford.

Whitman, C. H. 1958. *Homer and the Heroic Tradition*. Cambridge, Mass.

_____ and Scodel, R. 1981. "Sequence and Simultaneity in *Iliad* 13, 14, and 15." *HSCP* 85: 1-15.

Wilamowitz, U. von. 1920; reprinted 1966. *Die Ilias und Homer*. Berlin/Zurich/Dublin.

Willcock, M. M. 1964. "Mythological Paradeigma in the *Iliad*." *CQ* 58: 141-54.

_____ 1970. "Some Aspects of the Gods in the *Iliad*." *Bulletin of the Institute of Classical Studies*, University of London 17: 1-10.

_____ 1973. "The Funeral Games of Patroclus." *Bulletin of the Institute of Classical Studies*, University of London 20: 1-11.

_____ 1976. *A Companion to the Iliad*. Chicago/London.

_____ 1977. "Ad Hoc Invention in the *Iliad*." *HSCP* l81: 41-53.

_____ 1978 I;1984 II *The Iliad of Homer*. London.

Willis, W. H. 1941. "Athletic Contests in the Epic." *TAPA* 72: 392-417.

Winter, F. J. 1956. *Die Kampfszenen in den Gesängen 13,14, 15 der Ilias*. Frankfurt am Main.

Wyatt, W. F. 1985. "The Embassy and the Duals in *Iliad* 19." *AJP* 106: 399-408.

Zielinski, T. 1901. *Die Behandlung gleichzeitiger Ereignisse im antiken Epos*. Philologus Suppl. 8. Leipzig.

INDEX

Achilles, 11-13; friendship toward Achaeans, 31, 207, 220; kindness before wrath, 77, 99, 219, 257; his vengeance against Hector a climactic parallel to his wrath, 2-3, 13, 19, 29-30, 34-36, 45-46, 99-100, 201-4, 206, 211, 232, 250, 259

Achos (grief): Achilles' two different kinds of, 13; and vengeance in battle, 13, 45, 121, 139, 154, 170, 174-76, 179, 185, 197, 201-3, 208, 217, 219

Ad hoc inventions, 64, 69, 79,162, 250

Agamemnon: easily discouraged, 57, 97, 121, 148-49; protective of Menelaus, 57,106-7

Ameis-Hentze, 39, 86, 228, 241

Aner boulephoros (man of good counsel), 32-38, 42-43,50, 100, 119, 124-25, 185, 187

Arend, W., 2

Aristarchus, 41

Armstrong, J. I., 166

Barth, H.-L., 183

Bassett, S., 29

Burkert, W., 19, 92

Catalogues, 6-8, 16-19, 68, 74, 79, 144-45, 246

Clapp, E. B., 254

Climaxes, 53, 58,60, 73, 137, 150, 170, 179, 190-91, 194, 197, 210, 235, 236

Climactic kills, 120-21, 139, 143, 154, 168, 212, 216

Cimactic parallels, 3-4, 12-13, 28, 58, 60-61, 63, 65, 88, 93, 123, 126, 150, 164, 166, 169, 183-84, 186-87, 194-95, 207, 223, 229-32, 236, 259; *see* Achilles

Collins, L., 42,75

Combellack, F., 209

Comments of poet, 4, 16, 14, 38, 44, 52, 68, 71, 73, 78, 108, 113, 124, 130-32, 142, 165, 167, 171, 173, 176-79, 188, 207, 217, 233-34, 236, 240-41, 243-45

Davison, J. A., 10

De Jong, I. J. F., 15, 241

Donlan, W., 73, 83

Duckworth, G. E., 4, 5

Edwards, M. W., 2, 3, 30, 34, 36, 48, 49, 50, 51, 54, 58, 97, 137, 166, 171, 176, 182, 191, 203, 206, 208, 227, 229, 240

Erbse, H., 63, 88, 229

Eustathius, 11, 101

Fall of Troy, 38, 52, 56-60, 69, 75, 77, 79, 85, 113, 187-89, 196, 210-14, 223, 232-34, 261

Fenik, B., 110, 123, 174, 180, 182, 226

Foreshadowing, 3, 4, 8, 13, 48, 63 81, 95, 115, 160, 165, 193, 202, 209, 213, 216, 223, 228, 233, 235, 243, 253, 262; *see* Suspense

Fränkel, H., 7

Frazer, R. M., 183

General views: followed by detailed descriptions, 16, 58, 74, 91, 141, 170; *see* Catalogues

Griffin, J. 14, 20, 73

Hainsworth, B., 4, 130

Hector: foolishly optimistic, 78, 80, 90, 94, 108, 112, 122, 128, 132-34, 145, 163, 173, 178, 195; instrument of Zeus, 119, 122, 129, 161, 195

Hesiod, 41, 242

Heubeck, A., 81, 237

Hogan, J. C., 249

271